First and Second Peter, James, and Jude

INTERPRETATION
A Bible Commentary for Teaching and Preaching

INTERPRETATION

A BIBLE COMMENTARY FOR TEACHING AND PREACHING

PHEME PERKINS

First and Second Peter, James, and Jude

A Bible Commentary for Teaching and Preaching

John Knox Press
LOUISVILLE

Library of Congress Cataloging-in-Publication Data

Perkins, Pheme.
First and Second Peter, James, and Jude / Pheme Perkins.
p. cm. — (Interpretation, a Bible commentary for teaching and preaching)
Includes bibliographical references.
ISBN 0-8042-3145-1 (alk. paper)
1. Bible. N.T. Peter—Commentaries. 2. Bible. N.T. James—Commentaries. 3. Bible. N.T. Jude—Commentaries. I. Title. II. Series.
BS2777.P47 1995
227′.907—dc20 94-38274

This book is printed on acid-free paper that meets the American National Standards Institute Z39.48 standard. ∞
96 97 98 99 00 01 02 03 04—10 9 8 7 6 5 4 3 2
Printed in the United States of America
John Knox Press
Louisville, Kentucky

SERIES PREFACE

This series of commentaries offers an interpretation of the books of the Bible. It is designed to meet the need of students, teachers, ministers, and priests for a contemporary expository commentary. These volumes will not replace the historical critical commentary or homiletical aids to preaching. The purpose of this series is rather to provide a third kind of resource, a commentary which presents the integrated result of historical and theological work with the biblical text.

An interpretation in the full sense of the term involves a text, an interpreter, and someone for whom the interpretation is made. Here, the text is what stands written in the Bible in its full identity as literature from the time of "the prophets and apostles," the literature which is read to inform, inspire, and guide the life of faith. The interpreters are scholars who seek to create an interpretation which is both faithful to the text and useful to the church. The series is written for those who teach, preach, and study the Bible in the community of faith.

The comment generally takes the form of expository essays. It is planned and written in the light of the needs and questions which arise in the use of the Bible as Holy Scripture. The insights and results of contemporary scholarly research are used for the sake of the exposition. The commentators write as exegetes and theologians. The task which they undertake is both to deal with what the texts say and to discern their meaning for faith and life. The exposition is the unified work of one interpreter.

The text on which the comment is based is the Revised Standard Version of the Bible and, since its appearance, the New Revised Standard Version. The general availability of these translations makes the printing of a text in the commentary unnecessary. The commentators have also had other current versions in view as they worked and refer to their readings where it is helpful. The text is divided into sections appropriate to the particular book; comment deals with passages as a whole, rather than proceeding word by word, or verse by verse.

Writers have planned their volumes in light of the requirements set by the exposition of the book assigned to them. Biblical books differ in character, content, and arrangement. They also differ in the way they have been and are used in the liturgy, thought, and devotion of the church. The distinctiveness and use of particular books have been taken into account in decisions about the approach, emphasis, and use of space in the commentaries. The goal has been to allow writers to develop the format which provides for the best presentation of their interpretation.

The result, writers and editors hope, is a commentary which both explains and applies, an interpretation which deals with both the meaning and the significance of biblical texts. Each commentary reflects, of course, the writer's own approach and perception of the church and world. It could and should not be otherwise. Every interpretation of any kind is individual in that sense; it is one reading of the text. But all who work at the interpretation of Scripture in the church need the help and stimulation of a colleague's reading and understanding of the text. If these volumes serve and encourage interpretation in that way, their preparation and publication will realize their purpose.

The Editors

CONTENTS

JAMES

JUDE

SECOND PETER

INTRODUCTION

First Peter, James, Jude, 2 Peter, and 1–3 John belong to a group of writings traditionally referred to as the "catholic epistles." The designation appears in the church historian Eusebius (c.300 C.E.). He concludes the account of the life of James, the brother of the Lord, with the comment:

> Such is the story of James, to whom is attributed the first of the "general" epistles. Admittedly its authenticity is doubted since few early writers refer to it, any more than to Jude's, which is also one of the seven called general. But the fact remains that these two, like the others, have been regularly used in very many churches. (*History of the Church* 2.23.25)

This comment combines two understandings of the designation "catholic" or "general," a writing addressed to the church at large rather than to a specific community, and a writing that is widely used in the church. Eusebius recognizes that in the case of James and Jude the term "catholic" might appear inappropriate in both senses. When Eusebius discusses the books that Origen (d. c.254 C.E.) considered canonical, he notes that 2 Peter was probably not by Peter (*History* 6.25.9). With the exception of 1 Peter and 1 John, the catholic epistles belonged to the disputed "edges" of the canon along with Hebrews and Revelation until the end of the fourth century.

The question of their apostolic character emerges again in the Reformation. The Sorbonne censured Erasmus for not refuting ancient doubts about Hebrews, 2–3 John, Revelation, Jude, and 2 Peter in his edition of the Greek New Testament. Luther considered Hebrews, James, Jude, and Revelation to be less true and certain than the other writings in the New Testament. Until 1539, the Tyndale editions of the New Testament separated the four doubtful works (Hebrews, James, Jude, and Revelation) from the rest of the New Testament. Although these writings belong to the canon of all Christians today, many people feel that they are "second class" or, in the case of Hebrews and Revelation, too convoluted and obscure for the average believer. A glance at the *Revised Common Lectionary* shows that Eusebius would have a hard time finding that

1 Peter, James, Jude, or 2 Peter are "regularly used in very many churches." Eight readings from 1 Peter are used: one on Holy Saturday (omitted in many parishes), one in Lent of Year B, and six during the Easter season of Year A. James appears five times during Ordinary Time of Year B and once during Advent of Year A. Second Peter appears twice, once as a reading for the Transfiguration in Year A and once during Advent of Year B. Jude is not used at all. Since many Christians plan their personal Bible study around the lectionary cycle, it is not surprising that these epistles are practically unknown.

If "catholic" and "canonical" describe those expressions of the apostolic faith that form the belief of Christians at large, then these writings are marginal indeed. As one parishioner told me, "Well, you write the book, and I'll read it and see if there's anything there." Modern scholarly work on these writings has attempted to meet the challenge of understanding their significance by revisiting issues of authorship, composition, and church setting.

Authorship

Conservative scholars have argued for the apostolic authorship of 1 Peter, James, and Jude. Second Peter has clearly used a section of Jude and differs so markedly from 1 Peter that a similar case cannot be made for its author. However, some scholars attempt to push what most consider an early second-century work back to the last decades of the first century (see Bauckham). Other scholars concur with the position taken in this commentary that the evidence for apostolic authorship remains thin for James, Jude, and 2 Peter. We have already seen that these writings were not widely recognized in the first two centuries, an awkward fact if they were known to be by prominent apostles. Legendary traditions and apocryphal writings attributed to both James and Peter abound in this period, so the neglect cannot be due to lack of interest. The extensive vocabularies of unusual words and familiarity with conventions of Hellenistic rhetorical style also make it unlikely that these works were written by their announced authors. First Peter might have been dictated by the apostle, as those who support his authorship argue. However, Pauline traditions play a strong role in the composition of the work. The author's self-designation as "fellow-elder" (1 Peter 5:1) and the direction of the work to churches in Asia Minor that were not otherwise associated with a Petrine mission makes the argument for Petrine authorship weak (see Perkins; Pesch).

The most interesting question about the authors of these letters does not lie in debates over whether they were written by those to whom they were attributed. It lies in the fact that some first-century Christians looked to them as examples of true, apostolic faith. Most modern scholars agree that these epistles were more than merely general compilations of traditional material. Each letter appears to be directed toward specific issues facing Christian communities. The apostolic pseudonym brings the authority of a revered tradition to bear on the difficulties of the present. Just as the four-Gospel canon reminds Christians that a true understanding of Jesus requires four different perspectives, so a tradition of apostolic letters that includes the catholic epistles reminds them that Paul was not the only apostle. By the time 2 Peter was written, a collection of Pauline letters had come to enjoy scriptural authority in the churches. Its author must counter appeals to those writings by his opponents (2 Peter 3:15–16). At the same time, 2 Peter has also used material from Jude. In this instance, the concurrence of another apostolic tradition provides the foundation for the faith that 2 Peter defends.

First Peter, James, and Jude do not raise issues of apostolic authority directly. Even if James 2:14–26 on faith and works is directed against a sloganeering Paulinism, the author's formulation of faith is independent of the theological agenda of Paul's letters (see Dibelius and Greeven, 178–79). James and Peter play leading roles in the Jerusalem meeting that determined the place of Gentiles in the new Christian community according to Acts 15. There the "apostles and elders" send a letter to the Gentiles in Antioch, Syria, and Cilicia (Acts 15:23–29). None of the issues in that dispute appear in James or 1 Peter. However, the depiction of the apostles Peter and James in Acts supports the claim that both were concerned for the ongoing welfare of Gentile Christians. Both 1 Peter and James are striking applications of Jewish traditions to the instruction of Christians who are certainly Gentiles in 1 Peter and probably so in James. Jude demonstrates the strength of a Jewish Christian tradition for some sectors of the earliest communities. Its author simply describes himself as "a servant of Jesus Christ and brother of James" (1:1).

Setting

We can leave the details of the setting in the individual letters to the commentary. These letters highlight the Jewish character of early Christianity. Dibelius suggests that proselytes in Hellenistic Judaism provide the clue to how the recipients of these letters perceived their Jewish heritage:

> But in Diaspora Judaism where proselytes and "God-fearers" obeyed the message of ethical monotheism, one could have Jewish convictions without being a Jew. (Dibelius and Greeven, 176–77)

Studies of the relationships between Jews and Gentiles in the ancient world have suggested that the boundaries between Jew and Gentile were more complex than the expression "have Jewish convictions without being a Jew" might suggest (see Conzelmann; Feldman). Analysis of these letters should provide a perspective that differs from the focus provided by the conflicts in the Pauline letters.

The Jewish Christian perspective of these letters should play an important role in churches today. The Holocaust taught Christians the terrible consequences of forgetting their Jewish roots. Even so, many people rarely read the Old Testament. They are surprised by the suggestion that the Greek translation of the Old Testament, the Septuagint, won sympathizers and adherents to Judaism in antiquity (Feldman, 313). For many, the Old Testament is merely background music played while one waits for the feature film to start. It does not touch the core of their faith. These letters challenge us to reflect on the Jewishness of Christian faith.

Issues concerning the relationship between Christians and the larger society also play a prominent role in 1 Peter, James, and 2 Peter. Just as Jews were resident aliens and outsiders in the Diaspora cities, so are the Christians of Asia Minor addressed in 1 Peter. Merely being identified as "Christian" isolates a person from his or her non-Christian associates. For James, the tensions are played out in the conflict between the faithful endurance of the righteous "little ones" and the arrogance of the wealthy and powerful. Christians must keep their hearts focused on the wisdom of God. Second Peter faces the challenge of Christian teachers who claim that Christ's coming in judgment is no more than a fancy myth. At least part of their argument was predicated on what could be called the "scientific atheism" of the first century, namely, Epicurean philosophy (see Neyrey 1980).

For all four authors Christianity is a minority group whose commitment to an exclusive monotheism inhibits complete assimilation into the larger pagan environment. Christians face irrational hostility because they have broken some of the "cultural ties that bind" when they adopted their new faith (1 Peter 4:1–6). Many Christians today feel that an era of easy accommodation between Christianity and culture is ending because a secular pluralism has no place for religious convictions, practices, and celebrations in public life. Shortly before Christmas, several parents were distressed when their children were told to fill in Winter Solstice along with Hanukkah and Christmas on calendars at school. Should we permit the schools to teach our children that Jewish and Christian religious feasts are "just like" the ancient pagan ones? James draws on traditions of Jewish wisdom literature as well as the commands to love one's neighbor and to care for the poor to challenge established views of wealth, power, and prestige. Again, many Christians today find themselves caught in a lifestyle that has exalted things over persons. Our local clergy association received an angry reply from the school superintendent when an Easter letter to the residents of the town questioned the wisdom of letting athletic events and teenagers' jobs cut into time for worship and for family on Sundays.

Finally, the tensions between the methodological atheism of science and technology and the religious perception of human persons and their world constantly surface. Christians recognize that biblical authors describe the world in categories appropriate to their own age. The materialistic fatalism faced by 2 Peter stemmed from Epicurean atomism, not modern science. Yet, the problem of how knowledge gleaned from a scientific perspective that only recognizes religion as a human phenomenon, a form of human behavior, shapes our understanding of faith remains an issue for believers. Several high schoolers in our confirmation class reported conflicts with their biology teacher. The issue was not evolution but "the soul" or "mind." They were required to learn that all human thought, feeling, and activity was completely controlled by "brain states." The "soul," she insisted, was merely a leftover from the prescientific view of the world. Naturally, Christians cannot accept this view as the "whole truth" about reality without surrendering the apostolic faith.

Despite the evident tensions with the larger society, these early Christian authors remain confident that it is possible for Christians to live in that world. Their options for response are certainly restrained by the social and economic position of Christians within first-century society. Today we would not expect believers to remain subservient to abusive employers or husbands. The household code of 1 Peter 2:18—3:6 must be understood within its own social context (see Balch 1981). Christians today are not merely participants in a social and political world whose structures they are unable to influence. For Christians who are among the "privileged" the voices from the margin reflected in these letters might serve as a call to responsibility for our suffering brothers and sisters. Instead of hearing the words "accept the authority of your masters with all deference, not only those who are kind and gentle but also those who are harsh" (1 Peter 2:18, NRSV) as a call to passivity, Christians should hear in them the voice of the poor and afflicted. James 2:15–16 reminds readers that those who see a suffering brother and sister and do nothing to help gain nothing from professing to be Christians. This example indicates the challenge that some sections of these letters pose for teaching and preaching today. We are not only seeking to understand what the individual writers were saying to the churches of the first century but also trying to hear their voices as a challenge in our own situation.

Ancient Letters

All four epistles begin as letters (1 Peter 1:1–2; James 1:1; Jude 1—2; 2 Peter 1:1–2). The greeting of ancient letters typically includes the following elements:

a. designation of the sender or senders
b. designation of the recipients
c. a phrase such as "greeting" or some other form such as the "grace and peace" of Pauline letters (cf. 1 Cor. 1:1–3; Philemon 1—3)

Letters from officials may expand the designation of the sender with a phrase indicating the individual's position (see White). Paul's letters regularly expand on his apostolic status. They also add qualifying adjectives and phrases to the name of the recipients and a formula to the "grace and peace" wish that describes the source as "God, our Father, and the Lord, Jesus Christ" (e.g., Philemon 3). Of the four, James is furthest from the expansive greeting common in the Pauline letter tradition. First Peter and Jude/2 Peter share a common greeting formula, as shown in Table 1 (using RSV).

A "health wish," frequently in the form of a prayer for the well-being of the recipients, usually followed the greeting in an ancient letter. All the Pauline letters except Galatians have expanded this formulaic phrase into a thanksgiving (Phil. 1:3–11) or blessing (2 Cor. 1:3–7). Another series of formulaic phrases was used to mark the transition to the body of the letter. These may indicate that information is to be given, "I want you to know that . . . ," or that a request is to be made of the recipients, "I am astounded . . ." (credulity or dissatisfaction) or "You would do well to . . ." (see White, 200–208). Pauline transitional formulae fit the conventional forms (e.g., 2 Cor. 1:8; Gal. 1:6; Phil. 1:12). First Peter includes an extended blessing (1:3–9 [10–12]) and transition to the body of the letter with an imperative (v. 13). Jude begins directly with a transition to the body of the letter that indicates the author's determination to write (v. 3). James and 2 Peter depart from this literary model.

Ancient letters concluded with a farewell greeting, which often included greetings to others associated with the author or added greetings to individuals associated with the addressees, as well as a reference to travel plans or some final instruction. Sometimes a health wish or blessing concluded the letter. The Pauline letters follow this pattern with a wish for God's grace to be with the recipients (1 Cor. 16:19–24; 2 Cor. 13:11–14; Gal. 6:18; Phil. 4:21–23; Philemon 23—25). First Peter 5:12–14 provides a similar conclusion. It is formally a letter in the general tradition of Christian letter writing (see T. Martin, 41–79). The other examples lack final greetings. Those who argue that James and Jude are actual letters from James and Jude respectively can account for the lack of a conclusion by noting the lack of specific addresses in the initial greeting. The writings are not directed toward specific churches. Elements in the conclusion of James, Jude, and 2 Peter might be designed to remind readers of the letter genre. Second Peter has reminded readers of Paul's letters (3:15–16) and concludes with a wish for grace and a doxology (v. 18). Jude concludes with a benediction (vv. 24–25). As in the other categories, James diverges further from the

Table 1
The Letter Opening

	1 Peter	*James*	*Jude*	*2 Peter*
Sender(s)	Peter,	James,	Jude,	Simeon Peter,
Expansion	an apostle of Jesus Christ,	a servant of God and of the Lord Jesus Christ,	a servant of Jesus Christ and brother of James,	a servant and apostle of Jesus Christ,
Recipients	To the exiles of the Dispersion in Pontus, Galatia, Cappadocia, Asia, and Bithynia,	To the twelve tribes in the Dispersion:	To those who are called,	To those who have obtained a faith of equal standing with ours
Expansion	chosen and destined by God the Father and sanctified by the Spirit for obedience to Jesus Christ and for sprinkling with His blood:		beloved in God the Father and kept for Jesus Christ:	in the righteousness of our God and Savior Jesus Christ:
Greeting	May grace and peace be multiplied to you	Greeting	May mercy, peace, and love be multiplied to you	May grace and peace be multiplied to you
Expansion				in the knowledge of God and of Jesus our Lord

Christian letter patterns evident in the Pauline epistles. The exhortation concludes with instructions to win back the erring brother (James 5:19–20). This conclusion resembles the ending of 1 John (5:16–21), which is not a letter but a discourse to which an epistolary introduction has been added (see Dibelius and Greeven, 2–3).

As this brief survey of their use of the letter form indicates, 2 Peter has recast material from Jude but has no direct relationship to 1 Peter beyond the apparent reference to the earlier letter in 3:1–2. Although Jude invokes the fictive author's relationship to James in the letter opening, it has no formal relationship to the epistle of James. In fact, Jude is somewhat closer to the formal conventions of the Christian letter tradition than is James. Since 2 Peter has used Jude, we will follow the lead of other recent commentators and discuss it after Jude rather than after 1 Peter.

THE BOOK OF

First Peter

Introduction

Authorship

First Peter 1:1 designates the author as the apostle Peter. This identification was not questioned in antiquity (see Eusebius, *History of the Church* 4.14.9). Some modern scholars continue to accept that view since the letter is close to the form of Christian letters found in Paul and it does not refer to the martyrdom of the apostle under Nero (Dalton; Michaels). The case against direct Petrine authorship seems to be the more plausible. Paul's letters show that Peter was commonly referred to by the Aramaic form of his nickname, "Cephas" (so 1 Cor. 1:12; 9:5; Gal. 1:18; 2:9, 11; also John 1:42). Michaels explains the peculiarity of Peter using a Greek form of his name by linking the Greek form "Peter" with the commission as apostle to the circumcised (as in Gal. 2:7–8). However, Paul had no qualms about using the Aramaic form in writing to the Corinthians. With the exception of John 1:42, the evangelists never use the Aramaic form. Therefore this form of the name is more likely the usage of a later author. Elements in the composition of 1 Peter also differ from what one would expect from the apostle himself. Biblical citations refer to the Greek Old Testament. First Peter also employs techniques of composition and ethical exhortation characteristic of Greek-speaking traditions. Further, the picture of Christian communities projected by the letter suggests that outsiders have established prejudices against anyone who belongs to the Christian group. The author presents himself as "fellow elder," not apostle (1 Peter 5:1).

Although the composition as a whole fits the genre of an early Christian letter, it lacks the personal references to relationships between the author and recipients (or persons known to them) that one finds in personal letters (see Brox, Elliott 1981, Goppelt, Perkins).

Lack of details about Peter's death does not provide a clue as to when 1 Peter was written (against Dalton). Luke, who must have known that Paul and Peter had been martyred in Rome, does not provide information about the death of either in Acts. Our first direct indication of Peter's martyrdom appears in the letter from Clement of Rome (c.96 C.E.) to the Corinthians:

> Let us set before our eyes the good apostles: Peter, who because of unrighteous jealousy suffered not one or two but many trials, and having thus given his testimony went to the glorious place which was his due. (*1 Clement* 5.3–4)

First Peter locates the sender and his associates in "Babylon" (5:13). Evidence for the identification of "Babylon" with Rome comes from Revelation (14:8; 18:2). It constitutes our only New Testament evidence for the place of Peter's death. The letter may presume that its readers know that the apostle lost his life in Rome and so became an example of the suffering endurance being urged upon its readers.

First Peter follows the contemporary letter closing form by referring to others who are associated with the author in sending the letter (5:12–13): Silvanus, who is identified as the person who wrote the letter, and a certain Mark referred to as "my son." Both Silvanus (= Silas) and Mark were associated with Paul's missionary efforts. Silvanus worked with Paul and Timothy in the mission to Corinth (2 Cor. 1:19) and Thessalonica (1 Thess. 1:1; 2 Thess. 1:1; further references to Silvanus and the Greek mission appear in Acts 16:19, 25, 29; 17:4, 10, 14, 15; 18:5). Mark is one of those referred to in the final greeting of Philemon (v. 24; also Col. 4:10). Both Silvanus and Mark appear in Acts 15. Acts 15:36–40 asserts that Mark had left the Pauline mission to work with Barnabas after the Jerusalem Council. However, the Pauline letters presume that Mark continued to be part of the Pauline effort (2 Tim. 4:11). Their presence in Rome might have been due to Paul's imprisonment there. Acts 12:12 asserts that Mark's mother held meetings of Christians in her Jerusalem home. Mark had met Peter there prior to his activities in the Gentile mission. This detail might be reflected in the epithet, "my son," that we find in 1 Peter 5:13. Later tradition held that the Gospel of Mark embodied reflections that Peter had given Mark prior to his death (Eusebius, *History of the Church* 2.15; 3.39.13–17). Eusebius attributes this tradition to Papias. In both cases, he notes that Papias referred to the fact that Mark was mentioned in 1 Peter.

These notices suggest the possibility that 1 Peter was sent from a group of missionaries who had arrived in Rome with Paul or Peter. Their activities in the Gentile churches of the Pauline mission gave them experience with the difficulties faced by these churches. Elliott (1980) describes this circle as a "Petrine group." The letter does not create a fictional image of Peter as author by including details about the apostle. The reference to "Peter" as sender strengthens the letter's claim to apostolic teaching. Its purpose is to commend the content of the letter as fundamental to Christian faith (see Pesch, 150–51).

Addressees

The addressees are referred to as "exiles" (Gr. *parepidēmoi*) of the Diaspora (NRSV: "Dispersion"). Exegetes often read "exile" solely as a metaphor for the Christian's separation from Christ in this world (cf. Paul's reference to the Christian's "commonwealth in heaven" in Phil. 3:20). However, scholars interested in the social setting of early Christianity now look to these references as clues to the actual situation of the addressees. Elliott's studies of 1 Peter have emphasized the importance of the various terms for exile, resident alien, and household (Elliott 1981). The Greek word *parepidēmos* refers to persons who are aliens temporarily resident in another place. They are said to be members of the Diaspora in Pontus, Galatia, Cappadocia, Asia, and Bithynia. The term "diaspora" refers to Jews living among the Gentiles. The Old Testament sees the Diaspora as a continuation of Israel's exile from its true home. When God gathers the dispersed exiles together, the Gentiles will recognize the truth of Israel's God (cf. Isa. 49:6; 2 Macc. 1:27). Other texts use the term "diaspora" in the geographical sense of the place where such exiles live (Judith 5:19; *T. Asher* 7:3).

Since Jews usually could not become citizens in the cities they inhabited, living in the Diaspora always implied some form of alien status. *Testament of Asher* 7:2 provides a blunt statement of the pain such an existence could cause:

> You will be scattered to the four corners of the earth; in the dispersion you shall be regarded as worthless, like useless water, until such time as the Most High visits the earth.

Aliens could always be forced out of the cities in which they were living. The Jewish community in Rome had faced expulsion on several occasions. Some examples are directly associated with proselytizing activity (see Feldman, 47). Under Tiberius, 4,000 descendants of freedmen were shipped to Sardinia and the rest ordered to leave Italy unless they renounced Jewish rites (Tacitus, *Annals* 2.85.4). According to Suetonius, those of military age were singled out to be banished to an unhealthy region (Suetonius, *Tiberius* 36). The same author reports that Jews were expelled because of disturbances over a certain "Chrestus" under the emperor Claudius (c.48 C.E.; Suetonius, *Claudius* 25.4). Acts 18:2 notes this expulsion as the reason Aquila and Priscilla emigrated from Italy to Corinth where Paul met them. Presumably proselytizing by Christians led to the disturbances mentioned by Suetonius.

Civil strife between Jews and non-Jews in Alexandria and other eastern cities erupted during the reigns of Caligula and Claudius (see Feldman, 113–17; White, 125–37). After receiving embassies from both Jews and the Greek citizens of Alexandria, Claudius reaffirmed the right of the Jewish community to their ancestral practices. However, he warned both sides against further hostilities:

> I have stored up within me an immutable hostility against those who renewed the conflict. Simply stated, if you do not lay to rest this destructive and obstinate hostility against one another, I shall be forced to show what a benevolent ruler can become when turned to [inflict] a justified wrath. (White, 136)

Nor is the Jewish community to receive new immigrants from other regions:

> Nor are they to bring in or to admit Jews who are sailing down from Syria or Egypt, by means of which I will be forced to conceive an even more serious suspicion. Otherwise, I will take vengeance on them in every respect, just as though they were a plague infecting the whole inhabited world. (White, 136)

Claudius's letter also cut off once and for all any demands for Alexandrian citizenship. Jews cannot be admitted to the "gymnasium" and athletic contests, which are the prerogative of male citizens. Instead, the emperor tells them:

> Rather, they must enjoy the advantages that derive from their own status, and, indeed, they have a plentiful abundance of good things in an alien city. (White, 136)

Citizenship in Alexandria made persons eligible for military service and eventual Roman citizenship. Roman citizens and Greek citizens of the city were also exempt from the poll tax assessed against other inhabitants. A fragmentary petition survives in which an Alexandrian Jew whose father was a citizen protests the fact that he has suddenly been required to pay the tax. The petitioner's education and participation in the rites accorded other citizen males should have ensured his rights as a citizen, the petitioner claims. Presumably, his status has been downgraded because his mother was not a citizen. In any case, he speaks of himself as now "in danger of being deprived of my own homeland . . ." (White, 128). Presumably the petitioner would not be forced out of Alexandria by this new determination of his legal status. However, his loss of the privilege of citizenship makes him an alien in what he had regarded as his own city.

These examples provide concrete evidence for the social and political tensions massed behind the terms used for the letter's addressees, "exiles of the Dispersion." At the conclusion of the letter, readers are reminded that Peter himself is a temporary alien in a hostile city. Though the initial designation refers to foreigners who are only temporary residents, later references speak of those who have "resident alien" status as well (Gr. *paroikos;* 1:17; 2:11). Although the opening of the letter would suggest that the addressees are Jews living in the Roman provinces of Asia Minor, the rest of the letter indicates that its recipients are converts from paganism (cf. 1:14; 2:10; 4:3–4). They face hostility from friends, associates, and relatives.

The five provinces listed in the letter opening cover the Roman divisions of Asia Minor north of the Taurus mountains. However, the list does not reflect Roman administrative divisions, since Bithynia and Pontus had been a single province since 64 B.C.E. The address does not refer to particular cities, churches, or individuals as was the case with the Pauline letters. First Peter appears to be a general letter directed to Christians living in the rural interior of Asia Minor, not the populous cities of the coast (Elliott 1981, 59–63).

Though the recipients are Gentile converts, 1 Peter consistently refers to them as heirs to the promises of Israel. These references contain no indications of disputes between Christians and Jews over the Christian claims to be God's chosen people (see Michaels, xlix–l). Feldman's discussion of Judaism in Asia Minor during this period sheds some light on this situation (Feldman, 69–74). Strong ties existed between Jewish communities in the coastal regions of Asia Minor, but inscriptions from the inland cities of the region show that the Greek-speaking population was in the minority. Fewer Jewish cult objects and menorahs have been found in this part of Asia Minor. The Jewish population may have been much smaller and less attached to the traditional symbols of Jewish identity. Feldman notes that Jewish inscriptions from Asia Minor are unlike those from elsewhere in the Diaspora. They lack the conventional pious sentiments that refer to love of the Torah, Jerusalem, or longing for the rebuilding of the Temple. Nor does one find depictions of the ark where the Torah scrolls were kept (Feldman, 72–73).

Feldman concludes that while the number of Christians in Asia Minor during the first two centuries was much smaller than that of Jews, the peculiarities of Jewish life in Asia Minor facilitated conversion to Christianity:

> This difference between the Jewish communities of the coast and those of the interior may also perhaps account for the different responses to the message of Christianity. The relative lack of contact between the Jews of Asia Minor and the fountainhead in the Land of Israel may explain why Christianity seems to have made relatively great progress in Asia Minor, presumably among Jews, by the beginning of the second century. (Feldman, 73)

First Peter suggests that the success of the Christian mission lay in its ability to use the communal symbolism of its Jewish heritage to create communal solidarity among persons who were otherwise without a clearly defined social identity. Feldman's description of the relative isolation of Jews in inland Asia Minor sharpens our picture of life in the region.

Occasion

The danger that persistent, local harassment and persecution might weaken the faith of Christians in Asia Minor led to the dispatch of 1 Peter (1:6–7). There is no evidence that imperial policy dictated the persecution of Christians or outlawed their religious practices. When Pliny, governor of Bithynia (c.117), wrote the emperor Trajan concerning the Christians, he indicates that he has no precedent to guide him in evaluating such cases. Charges are being pressed by local citizens. Trajan has been unable to find any evidence that Christians are disruptive or dangerous to the state. Nevertheless, those whose accusers are willing to bring charges personally will be forced to recant or be punished (Pliny, *Letters* 10.96 and 10.97 [= Trajan's reply]). Charges filed anonymously would be thrown out by the governor.

This correspondence indicates that the situation that called forth 1 Peter had continued to exist. Hostility did not destroy the growing movement. Nor did the experience provoke the rhetoric of apocalyptic condemnation that we find in Revelation, where divine vengeance will unseat the "whore of Babylon" (= Rome; Revelation 17—18). Pliny's reference to the growth of Christianity in the region suggests that opposition to conversion fueled the hostility. Similar objections from the pagan population provoked various expressions of anti-Jewish sentiments in antiquity (Feldman, 119, 298–300). Augustine cites the first-century philosopher Seneca on the spread of Jewish sympathizers, "The vanquished have given laws to the victors" (Augustine, *City of God* 6.1; Feldman, 299). Until ordered to commit suicide (62 C.E.), Seneca was an adviser to Nero. His comment represents the reaction of Roman intellectuals to Jewish sympathizers within their own circles at the time Peter and Paul were executed.

First Peter does not explain why others are hostile to the Christians (2:12; 3:16; 4:4, 14–16). The mere "name" is sufficient to invoke persecution (4:14). Withdrawal from some earlier associations is provided as a rationale in 1 Peter 4:1–4. Separation from an earlier way of life made it possible for converts to join the new household of the church (1:22; 2:5). Christians are not isolated in their suffering, since they now belong to a family that exists throughout the world (2:17; 5:9; Elliott 1981, 75–76). A letter from Petrine circles in Rome would reinforce that message. The relative isolation of communities in this section of Asia Minor would make receipt of such a message a significant event in the life of those communities.

Theological Themes

Discussions of the social context of the recipients of 1 Peter have highlighted the social importance of the letter. Elliott has pointed out that Christians might have responded to the hostility of outsiders by intensifying their isolation from nonbelievers (Elliott 1981, 83). Instead, 1 Peter insists that their good behavior and ready account of their belief might win others to salvation (2:12; 3:15). Our modern familiarity with sociological categories and political calculations concerning the effectiveness of institutional responses to various crises could produce a one-sided reading of 1 Peter. Its appeal is not grounded in social or political prudence. There is no program for the transformation of social structures (Elliott 1981, 78). First Peter's argument is theological. A sustained vision of the transformation effected by conversion (sanctification, rebirth, purification; 1:2–22) reminds readers that they can no longer return to life as lived before they became Christians. A governing image of the value of suffering grounded in the saving death of Christ provides the basis for explaining how Christians should respond to their own experiences of harassment (2:21–24). A certain hope that God's judgment will vindicate the righteous sufferer and condemn the oppressor allows believers to rejoice in their sufferings (1:4–9).

God

Monotheism was one of the features for which Judaism was admired in the ancient world. The brief formula that Paul uses in 1 Thess. 1:9–10 speaks of conversion to the true God and anticipation of Christ's coming as evidence for the conversion of the Thessalonians. Piety toward God was considered the suitable response to knowledge of God. Philo of Alexandria (d. c.50 C.E.) spoke of the Jewish synagogues as schools of virtue in which God is worshiped:

> For what are our places of prayer throughout the cities but schools of prudence and courage and temperance and justice and also of piety, holiness and every virtue by which duties to God and men are discerned and rightly performed. (Philo, *Life of Moses* 2.39.216)

First Peter's descriptions of God are consistently related to Christ (Michaels, lxviii). Though God predestined the Gentiles for salvation (1:2), they would not come to know God prior to the death and resurrection of Christ (1:10–12). Therefore, God is primarily known as "Father of our Lord Jesus Christ" (1:3). God's Spirit sanctifies the community of the elect that is built on Christ (1:2). God's power can be relied on to defend the faithful (1:5; 5:7, 10). It was effective in raising Christ from the dead (1:21). First Peter calls on its readers to be confident that the same God will bring them to glory at the judgment (1:21). They are God's possession as his household (4:17). The general orientation of Christian piety consists in doing the will of God (2:15, 20; 4:2). Non-Christians whose immorality violates the will of God will be called to account in the judgment (4:5, 17). First Peter does not treat judgment as divine retribution for evils inflicted on the righteous. Believers are not encouraged to look on God as one who destroys their enemies. Rather, divine judgment condemns those who do what is against God's will.

Jesus Christ

The suffering and death of Jesus as the key to the salvation of the unrighteous forms the center of 1 Peter's understanding of suffering. Imagery from Isaiah 53 supports the affirmation that Christ's suffering has rescued a sinful humanity. His death as the unblemished lamb ransomed the Gentiles from their sinful past (1:17; 2:24). As suffering servant, Christ did not respond to the insults against him but trusted the justice of God (2:21–24; cf. Isa. 53:4–12; Achtemeier). Christians can imitate the example that the story of Christ's passion sets before them. Roman Christians may have had a particular affection for the suffering servant as an example. *First Clement* cites Isa. 53:1–12 as an example of the humility required of those who would be leaders in the Christian community (*1 Clem.* 16.1–10; cf. 1 Peter 5:1). However, only the suffering of the "unblemished lamb" can take away the condemnation that the sins of unrighteous humans deserve. Christians who imitate Jesus' example are acting according to the holiness that his death made possible for them. Only Jesus' wounds can heal others (2:24) and bring the unrighteous to God (3:18).

Just as the suffering of Jesus provides an example for Christians to follow, so the heavenly exaltation and glory of Jesus reminds them of the hope they have for the future (5:13–14). The present life of believers is as much a testimony to the exaltation of the risen Christ as it is to his death (1:3). Christ is the living foundation of the new community to which Christians belong (2:4–5) as well as its true shepherd (2:25; 5:4). He is also the "Lord" to whom Christians owe reverence (3:15). His exaltation forms the basis of the clean conscience that Christians have before God (3:21–22).

A few passages point to the preexistence of Christ. The correspondence between the suffering of Jesus and the prophetic testimony of Isaiah is guaranteed by the "spirit of Christ" operating within the Old Testament prophets (1:11; Achtemeier, 184–86). Christ was already destined to bring salvation prior to creation, even though he was not revealed until the "last days" (1:20). In the "last days" after his death, Christ preaches to the spirits—apparently the angelic powers responsible for sin at the time of Noah (3:20). These passages do not add up to a clearly articulated picture of the preexistence of Christ. The dominant image in the letter is that of the crucified and exalted Lord.

Christian Life

We have seen that Hellenistic Judaism emphasized the link between piety toward the true God and the life of virtue. This piety should demonstrate the superiority of a Jewish way of life to outsiders. The apologetic argument for Christianity follows the same pattern in 1 Peter. Christians should "do good" so that their lives demonstrate the truth of their claims (2:11–12). Conversion to Christianity involves a moral rebirth that frees persons from the domination by the passions that was characteristic of their pre-Christian life (1:14–15; 4:2). The language of moral conversion and healing of the soul was common in philosophic exhortation of the time (Malherbe 1987). Jewish moralists associate the vices of those who are ignorant of wisdom with idolatry. Similarly, 1 Peter assumes that his readers engaged in various evils prior to their conversion (4:3–4). Even though the apologetic argument that a "good life" demonstrates the truth of one's religion presumes that non-Christians know and admire virtue, the question of "pagan virtue" is never seriously entertained in 1 Peter. The possibilities of salvation and virtue are coextensive with membership in the Christian community.

A major section of 1 Peter contains conventional forms of exhortation. Christians are to be willing subjects to those institutions which order human society, including the Roman emperor. God has created these institutions to promote human well-being (2:13–17; cf. Rom. 13:1–7). The comment "For it is God's will that by doing right you should put to silence the ignorance of foolish men" (2:15) suggests that charges of being a danger to civic order were a common experience. For persons who were temporary and resident aliens, suspicions could have serious consequences. This section is followed by another traditional form of moral exhortation, a catalogue of "household duties" (2:18—3:7; cf. Eph. 5:22—6:9; Col. 3:18—4:1). Such codes defined the proper obligations and behavior of various members of the household. Unlike the examples in Colossians and Ephesians, 1 Peter emphasizes the conduct of slaves and women. Reciprocal relationships are not described. No word is addressed to masters and only a brief word is addressed to husbands (3:7). The exhortation also omits children and parents. These alterations adapt the code to the situation of the addressees. Slaves and wives of non-Christian husbands are both vulnerable to the will of others. As we have already seen, the advice to suffer the abuse of unjust masters or to be quietly submissive to one's husband creates pastoral problems if it is applied literally to suffering Christians today. In both cases, the vices that slaves and women respectively are to avoid reflect common stereotypes of the servile but disobedient slave and the demanding, luxury-loving wife. Christians should not act like characters who appear in the local comedies.

The suffering Christ as moral example provides the major departure from conventional moral exhortation. Christians renounce the verbal retaliation by which they might have responded to the abuse heaped on them (2:22–23; 3:9–11, 16). Though 1 Peter does not directly commend love of enemies (Michaels, lxxiv), renouncing all retaliatory speech in imitation of Christ surely constitutes a significant challenge.

The references to conversion, which remind readers that life is no longer what it was, also imply new obligations to members of the Christian community. Internal relationships do not appear to constitute a major problem in 1 Peter. Occasional injunctions provide us with some insights into the life of these churches. The holiness of the community as a whole is a function of the fidelity of its members (1:14–17). Love for fellow Christians is a sign of holiness (1:22; 2:17; 3:8). Prayer, mutual love, hospitality, mutual exhortation, inspired prophecy, and other forms of service describe the internal life of the community (4:7–11). The concluding exhortations remind the "elders" charged with the supervision of the community that they should follow the example of Peter and of Christ himself in caring for the flock of God (5:1–4). Humility applies to the relationships between all Christians, regardless of their status or age (5:5) because it was exemplified by Christ himself.

Holiness in 1 Peter is constituted by the Christian life of wholehearted obedience to the will of God. It promises believers a share in Christ's glory that is yet to be revealed. The letter concludes with an apocalyptic explanation of the struggle that Christians face. The "devil" seeks to destroy God's work (5:8). Though 1 Peter does not employ the full scenario of an apocalyptic battle with evil, the topos of a conflict between God and the devil introduces a new dimension to understanding what is at stake in Christian life. There are nonhuman powers in the world that seek to undo the goodness that reflects God's will. Christians can resist such powers, but they cannot put them out of business. This passage from 1 Peter 5:8–9 has been part of the Office of Compline, or Night Prayer, among Catholics for centuries. After the day's struggles have been reviewed, all things are surrendered to God's care. Even in that gesture, Christians are reminded that their individual lives belong to a larger context in which struggle and suffering have not yet been vanquished.

OUTLINE OF FIRST PETER

The Holy People of God	1:1—2:10
Greeting	1:1–2
Blessing: Born to a New Hope	1:3–9
Revealed in the Prophets	1:10–12
You Are Called to Holiness	1:13–25
You Are the New People of God	2:1–10
Living in a Non-Christian World	2:11—3:12
Good Conduct as Testimony to God	2:11–12
Respect for Human Authorities	2:13–17
Household Code	2:18—3:7
Slaves, Obey Masters	2:18–20
Follow the Example of Christ	2:21–25
Wives, Defer to Husbands	3:1–4

Follow the Example of Sarah	3:5–6
Husbands, Honor Wives	3:7
Relationships with Others	3:8–12
Do Not Fear Suffering	3:13—4:19
The Righteous Accept Unmerited Suffering	3:13–17
Christ's Suffering Made the Unrighteous Holy	3:18–22
Suffering Is Preferable to Past Immorality	4:1–6
Relationships within the Community	4:7–11
Rejoice in the Time of Trial	4:12–19
Shepherding the Flock of God	5:1–14
Humility Governs All Relationships	5:1–7
Elders, Be Examples	5:1–4
Defer to Those Who Shepherd the Flock	5:5
Show Humility to Each Person	5:6–7
Resist the Devil and God Will Reward Your Suffering	5:8–11
Final Greeting	5:12–14

The Holy People of God

1 PETER 1:1—2:10

The opening section of 1 Peter highlights the transformation its readers have experienced when they became Christians and points forward to the glory that will be the outcome of their faith (1:3–9). The expression "we have been born anew to a living hope" (1:3) sums up the outlook of the entire letter. Older commentaries on 1 Peter often spoke of this opening section as a "baptismal homily." Some even went so far as to detect the stages of a baptismal liturgy in the letter as a whole (see the summary in T. Martin, 17–37). However, references to conversion do not establish the situation addressed by the letter. For the readers, the moment of conversion and baptism lies in the past. They are now members of the holy people of God (2:9–10). Similarly, the full experience of salvation lies in the future, "set your hope fully on the grace that is coming to you at the revelation of Jesus Christ" (1:13).

The letter exhorts readers to live out the holiness that they received in baptism in the present. It does this by reminding them of their life before they became Christians, of their conversion and initiation into the Christian fellowship, and of the future that awaits them. First Peter establishes the framework for interpreting the present experience of its readers. Since the liturgical images used to describe Christian initiation and the topics of ethical exhortation are formed of conventional expressions, this method does not provide a detailed account of the actual experience of individuals. When we ask Christians today to plot their life journey and their faith journey along parallel time lines, the expressions are much more personal than formal. But the technique used by 1 Peter can help Christians today to evaluate their journey of faith. It is easier to experience the call to holiness in the present when we remember the call to holiness by which we became Christians and the holiness we hope to share in the future.

Table 2 (using RSV) lists the attributes of each of the four aspects of life as they are described in this section of 1 Peter. The focus of the imagery in this section is on the present experience of the addressees as members of a Christian community. The descriptions of those who are not Christians contrasts the letter's recipients who were destined to become part of the holy people of God (1:2) from others who will remain disobedient to the Word (2:8). The descriptive lists refer all vices to the past. They belong to what was put aside when the recipients were reborn through the Word.

Exhortations to rejoicing, hope, obedience, and the like are aimed at ensuring that believers are worthy of the salvation or imperishable inheritance that awaits them. This section of 1 Peter only contains brief hints of the main threat to that hope: the concrete trials that Christians face in their daily lives. Readers are told to rejoice in such trials, since only trials can demonstrate the genuineness of Christian faith (1:6–7). If we take the references to being "exiles" or "visiting residents" (1:1, 17) as indications of the actual, social situation of the addressees, then the references to becoming a "spiritual house" (2:4) and passing from the state of being "no people" to being "God's people" (2:10) take on additional significance. When referred to their heavenly inheritance (1:4), the "exile" in which Christians live

Table 2
Stages of Christian Life

Pre-Christian	*Christian Initiation*	*Christian Present*	*Future Hope*
destined by God (1:2)	sanctified by Spirit (1:2, 22)	obedience (1:2, 14, 22)	imperishable inheritance, kept in heaven (1:4)
desires; ignorance (1:14)	redeemed by Christ's blood (1:2, 18)	living hope (1:3, 13, 21)	salvation to be revealed (1:5, 9, 13)
followed ancestral traditions/ futile (1:18)	accepted good news preached to you (1:12, 25)	guarded through faith by God's power (1:5)	glory; honor (1:7)
vice list: malice, guile, insincerity, slander (2:1)	born anew through imperishable word (1:23; 2:2)	rejoice in trials; proving faith genuine (1:6–7)	God's judgment (1:17)
disobedient stumble over Christ/stone (2:8)	tasted kindness of the Lord (2:3, 10)	love, believe in Jesus whom you have not seen (1:8)	
"no people" (2:10)	accepted Christ as living stone (2:4)	rejoice (1:8)	
no experience of God's mercy (2:10)	became people of God (2:9–10)	virtue list: gird up minds; be sober; hope (1:13)	
in darkness (2:9)	called into light (2:9)	be holy (1:15)	
		exiles/ temporary residents (1:1, 17)	
		confidence in God who raised Jesus (1:21)	
		love one another (1:22)	

Pre-Christian	*Christian Initiation*	*Christian Present*	*Future Hope*
		seek spiritual food (2:2)	
		built into spiritual house (2:5)	
		offer spiritual sacrifices (2:5)	
		chosen race/ royal priesthood/ God's people (2:9–10)	
		declare God's wonderful deeds (2:9)	

continues to be a pressing reality of life (1:17). In that respect conversion did not change the socioeconomic situation of the addressees.

When read in the context of the transition from the futility of their pre-Christian past to a present reality as "living stones" in God's house, however, believers already live in a place that they can call "home." Later in the letter we learn that some members of these churches are household slaves (2:18). First Peter 1:18–19 tells believers that they have been redeemed from the futility of their traditional ways by the blood of Christ, not by gold or silver. Slaves who knew that they could purchase their freedom for an agreed sum or that they could always be sold to another must have found this image a striking affirmation of their new identity in the Christian community. Similarly, the imagery of being built as living stones into a structure founded on Christ must have had particular significance for visiting aliens living in Asia Minor. This geographical area did not include large cities or busy seaports with frequent communications to other ports. Someone living here might know very little about what is happening "at home." As archaeological evidence has suggested, the Jewish communities in this region did not have strong links with Jerusalem.

Believers have entered into a community that fills these holes in their lives. The slaves are probably exiles as well. As we saw in the introduction, much of the Jewish community in

Rome was descended from persons who had been brought to Rome as slaves. The imagery in 1 Peter assures Christian slaves that Jesus has paid their ransom price. It tells those who are visiting foreigners that they already belong to a "household" even though the inheritance that members of this new family receive is in heaven. Today Christians and churches are often comfortable members of the social and political scene. Those churches face the challenge of adding the new "living stones" that come from different ethnic, racial, or socioeconomic circumstances.

1 Peter 1:1–2
Greeting

As we have seen in the general introduction, the opening follows the established pattern for the ancient letter. Each of the elements in the address has been expanded with an epithet or expression that indicates the Christian character of the sender and addressees. Even though it is not likely that Peter, himself, wrote the letter, he is designated as its author. Neither Peter nor those mentioned in the final greetings appear to have direct knowledge of churches in the provinces to which they are writing. Information about conditions there had probably been brought to Rome by others. Even though there are no historical traditions that link Peter with this area, he was known to Gentile converts in this region, as Paul's references to him in Galatians indicate. The simple phrase "apostle of Jesus Christ" indicates to the recipients that this letter carries the authority of one of Jesus' most famous disciples. For those who have accepted faith in a Jesus also far removed from their experience (1:8), such a letter would have been an extraordinary event.

We have also seen that the terms used to refer to the recipients in 1:1 speak of exiles, aliens temporarily resident in the Roman provinces of northern Asia Minor. The term "diaspora" (NRSV: "Dispersion") refers to Jews living outside the land of Israel. Jews in exile suffered the hardships of being alien residents. Peter, Silvanus, and Mark were also familiar with the circumstances of such exiles. We soon learn that the addressees are Gentile converts (1:18; 4:3–4). Michaels has suggested that the social stigma attached to Jews was transferred to those who became Christians (Michaels, 6). However, the evidence we have for the Jewish Diaspora in this region suggests that it was unlike that in the larger, cultural centers. The strong Jewish imagery in 1 Peter addresses the plight of the readers by affirming their membership in the worldwide Christian fellowship. Thus, it is a vehicle for overcoming the alienation that was part of their everyday lives. There is no evidence that Christianity's Jewish origins were the cause of the harassment that the addressees suffered.

Anyone who has ever lived in a traditional, premodern society will be struck by the asymmetry between the brief epithet attached to Peter's name and the extended statement about the addressees in verse 2. Ordinary conventions of honorific speech attach effusive epithets or words of praise to the more honored party in a relationship. When Paul writes to the Roman church, which he did not found, he follows his own name and apostolic status with several verses recapitulating the early creed and affirming his role as apostle to all the Gentiles including those at Rome (Rom. 1:1–6). The designation of the community is considerably shorter, "to all God's beloved in Rome, who are called to be saints" (Rom. 1:7). Epithets in the greetings of private letters typically indicate differences in status between the parties. Imperial letters are most expansive. Here is the greeting from the letter of Tiberius that included the instructions concerning Alexandrian Jews:

> Tiberius Claudius Caesar Augustus Germanicus the Emperor, Pontifex Maximus, holder of the tribunician power, consul designate, to the city of the Alexandrians, greeting. (White, 133)

Anyone who did not know that "Peter, apostle of Jesus Christ" was one of the most important of Jesus' disciples might think that the sender is inferior to those addressed.

The tension between "apostle" and "exile," the first a term of authority by virtue of the individual for whom the apostle acts; the second a clear indication of inferior status, makes verse 2 even more of a surprise. The "exiles" of the Diaspora are given more honor than Peter. Jesus Christ appears in both verses suggesting that he is the basis for the relationship between sender and recipients. The trinitarian structure of the formula in verse 2 has expanded the more common Pauline references to the Father and Jesus Christ by including the Spirit. The emperor indicates his status both in his lengthy name and in a list of offices. First Peter indicates the dignity of those to whom the letter is addressed by associating their very existence with the Father, Spirit, and Jesus Christ. The terms for the divine activities in this formula are taken from the Old Testament. Israel is the elect people of God (Exod. 19:6; Isa. 43:20–21). The people were sprinkled with blood at the covenant sacrifice (Exod. 24:3–8). However, the sacrifice that cleanses the new people of God occurred on the cross. It ratifies their obedience to Jesus Christ, rather than to the law as in Exodus.

The greeting concludes with a common early Christian phrase, "grace and peace." The asymmetry in the formulae heightens the significance that Peter attaches to the new life of the addressees. As the elect people of God, they are as great or greater than the apostle himself. Thus the greeting of 1 Peter poses an interesting challenge to Christians today. Rather than use titles and other status indicators as our society normally does, we should use those special images of status with God to exalt the foreigners, the visitors, and the other marginal persons in our midst. Speak to others in a way that shows awareness of the worth those persons have in God's eyes. A young person working in a homeless shelter came into the office one day. She was very disturbed because some seminarians working at the shelter indicated by their words and actions that they considered the women who came to the shelter worthless. She herself had once been scared of the women in the shelter. Now that she knew many of their stories, she considered these women "people like anyone else." One way to begin to change the situation would be to require the volunteers to speak to the women in the same way, with the same tone of voice, body language, and the rest that they use when addressing people they meet outside the shelter. Further reflections on speech occur later in the letter as 1 Peter indicates how Christians should respond to hostile or abusive speech directed at them (1 Peter 3:9–11).

1 Peter 1:3–9
Blessing: Born to a New Hope

An extended thanksgiving or blessing section typically followed the greeting in the Pauline letter (2 Cor. 1:3; Eph. 1:3). Conventional letters had a shorter prayer or wish for the health of the recipient. Verse 3 states the basis for praising God: Christians have been reborn to a new hope through Jesus Christ. Verse 9 summarizes the letter's message to its recipients, a secure faith will bring them salvation. The grammatical structure of verses 3–12 is difficult because the passage consists of a long string of clauses that depend on God as the subject. English translations break the long sentence up into several shorter ones. The most recent Greek editions of the New Testament conclude the opening sentence at the end of verse 9. Some interpreters include verses 10–12 in the construction of the sentence (see T. Martin, 52–68). However, verses 10–12 are better understood as a digression attached to the initial blessing formula. The grammatical subject changes from God's activity to the Spirit of Christ working through the prophets.

Another grammatical peculiarity of the sentence lies in the shift from the first person plural in verse 3, "God and Father of *our* Lord Jesus Christ," "having given *us* new birth" to the second person plural in verse 4 and following. Some ancient scribes apparently felt this difficulty and read "our souls" in verse 9 instead of "your souls." This grammatical shift creates a distance between the author and the audience being instructed. It also supports the suggestion of some interpreters (see Dalton) that the reference to what the prophets foresaw in verses 10–12 was intended to refer to the inclusion of Gentiles in the people of God.

Although the blessing does not appear to be an early Christian hymn as some earlier commentators thought, most of the phrases are formulaic descriptions of salvation (cf. Titus 3:5; Heb. 7:19). However, the author has introduced a note of tension into the rejoicing, reference to the trials that will test the faith of Christians (vv. 6–7). First Peter instructs readers to rejoice in such times because a faith that comes through the "testing" is proven to be genuine. Further, such trials are part of the divine order of things. The translation of verse 6, "you have had to suffer" (NRSV), masks the Greek phrase "it being necessary," a phrase that suggests that God requires such testing. Wisdom of Solomon 3:5–6 understands the suffering of the righteous, who now enjoy peace with God (vv. 1–2) as a form of divine testing:

> Having been disciplined a little, they will receive great good, because God tested them and found them worthy of himself; like gold in the furnace he tried them, and like a sacrificial burnt offering he accepted them. (NRSV)

Since Christians will be told to take Christ as their model in suffering, the model of the suffering righteous is central to the account of suffering given in the letter.

In this section, the reference to suffering is imbedded in the image of God as the Father who has established a new, imperishable inheritance for his children. Verse 3 does not refer to the death of Christ, mentioned in the greeting (v. 2), but to his resurrection. Christians can see the resurrection of Christ as evidence for the imperishable, secure inheritance that awaits them in heaven (v. 4). They are also reminded that God's power will protect them until they attain this inheritance (v. 5). The final petition of the Lord's Prayer makes a similar point. "Lead us not into temptation (Gr. *peirasmos*)" uses the same word that is translated "trials" in 1 Peter 1:6. It reminds us that no Christian seeks the "testing" of his or her faith. Nor does God set up such trials as an obstacle course or entrance exam. But Christians have known from the beginning that no genuine faith will exist without them. Just as the book of Wisdom spoke of the "wicked" who sought to kill the righteous person for no other reason than their own dislike of having such persons around (Wisd. Sol. 2:12–20) so all those who seek God's righteousness suffer (Matt. 5:10). "But deliver us from evil (or 'the Evil One')" points to the other side of the process, confident prayer that God will deliver Christians from such trials. As we have seen, the conclusion of 1 Peter will turn from the evils themselves to the Evil One (the devil) who is responsible for their existence.

Commentators have frequently argued over the extent to which 1 Peter treats salvation in apocalyptic categories. In this passage it refers to "salvation ready to be revealed in the last time" (v. 5) and "praise, glory and honor at the revelation of

Jesus Christ" (v. 7). For the present, Christians believe in a Jesus whom they do not see (v. 8). From this perspective, the imperishable, heavenly inheritance that constitutes the "living hope" of Christians is attained at Christ's second coming. First Peter does not envisage the "inheritance" as something that each individual Christian attains upon his or her death. Wisdom of Solomon 3:1–6 has an individualized eschatology that presumes that the righteous pass from suffering into peace and eternal life with God (also see Wisd. Sol. 4:20—5:16). However, apocalyptic imagery points toward the restoration of the community of the righteous and the destruction of evil. We have already seen that 1 Peter does not revel in anticipating the condemnation of persecutors as apocalyptic visions do.

Although the reference to a mode of salvation that is yet to come is fairly clear, the question of whether 1 Peter thinks that Christians are now living in those "last days" is more difficult to answer. Verse 6 begins with the prepositional phrase "in this" (Gr. *en hōi*), which may refer to the previous noun "in the last time" or to the sentence that follows, as in the NRSV translation and in recent editions of the Greek text that conclude verse 5 with a period. In that case, the relationship between the present period of trials and the final coming of salvation remains unspecified. If "in which" refers to the previous phrase, "in the last time," the sentence might imply that 1 Peter understands suffering Christians to be living in the "last days" (Michaels, 27–28). If the present infinitive, "rejoice," is understood as a future, then the phrase could mean no more than that Christians will rejoice when the last days come because their faith has been proved genuine by their present trials. First Peter 4:13 assures readers that just as their sufferings are a share in the sufferings of Christ, so they will also rejoice when his glory is revealed. Resistance to the attacks of the devil (1 Peter 5:9) forms part of the image of a community of the righteous that withstands the trials of the end time (so T. Martin, 65).

If 1 Peter sees its own age as the "end time," then the suffering of the righteous community signals the approach of the revelation of Christ, which means salvation for the faithful. Rather than see such trials as a threat to the community of the faithful, they are a sign of election and unity with Christ. Consequently, 1 Peter calls on readers to rejoice in the sufferings that they experience (Elliott 1981, 142–43). However, this apocalyptic perspective creates a dilemma for modern readers who do not feel that the return of Christ is imminent. Is there any sense in which they might be said to "rejoice" in a faith tested by suffering? As we read through 1 Peter, we discover that the trials to which it refers are those that are in some sense related to a person's individual Christian confession. They are inflicted by persons who fit the category of "the wicked" in Wisd. Sol. 3:1–6. Testimony to the truth of the gospel stirs up anger, taunting, skepticism, and the like, the aim of which is to demonstrate that the righteous are not in fact what they appear to be. The distinctive behavior of believers under trial witnesses to the power and truth of the gospel. Other forms of suffering such as natural disasters or catastrophic illnesses are not in view.

The danger at hand is that such trials will shake the faith of Christians, especially through the consistent prodding of friends and associates. First Peter presumes that Christians are interacting with persons who do not share their faith much of the time. It is easy for believers to feel that something must be wrong with their witness to the faith when family and friends do not come to share that faith. Grandparents often speak with frustration over the lack of religion among their grandchildren. Why isn't Christianity more effective? people often ask. One parishioner decided to lay the blame at the feet of the risen Jesus. He should have appeared to Pilate, Caiaphas, and other leaders and that would have accomplished more to make Christianity effective! Of course, if that were really the point, then Jesus' suffering as the righteous one would not make sense. Jesus did not choose to overwhelm his enemies with power. Persuasion, love, and faith are very different realities. They leave the pathway for rejection or merely civilized disregard wide open. So "rejoice," 1 Peter says. Trials show that individuals and their churches are succeeding in placing the challenge of the gospel before the world.

The eschatological perspective of 1 Peter provides a corrective to the tendency to evaluate the performance of Christians in the present. Sometimes the Christian message is "sold" with the promise that accepting Jesus as Savior will lead to personal peace and prosperity in this life. First Peter insists that such promises are false. All that counts is the "faith proved by trials." Its worth cannot be evaluated in the present. The value of testimony to the Lord will only be known when he returns in glory (v. 7). However, this warning about future judgment should not shake Christian confidence in salvation. As we have seen, most of this section of the letter stresses the present experience of salvation in Christian life. Christians have already experienced the mercy of God as they turned from ancestral traditions to the Lord.

1 Peter 1:10–12
Revealed in the Prophets

Verse 10 picks up the term "salvation" from verses 5 and 9 in order to establish the principle that this salvation was the object of Old Testament prophecy. The idea that the prophets did not speak about their own times but about those events that would initiate the "last days" commonly appears in apocalyptic texts. The term "time" (Gr. *kairos*) in verse 11 is also picked up from verse 5. Once again, the passage consists of a long series of dependent clauses that modern translators and editors of the Greek text have divided into two sentences by placing a full stop at the end of verse 11 and converting the relative pronoun "to whom" of verse 12 into the indirect object of the verb "it was revealed." The prophets are said to have investigated two facts: (a) the salvation [= grace] experienced by Christians (v. 10); and (b) the time of the sufferings of Christ and the glories to follow that suffering (v. 11). The Spirit of Christ made the facts of his suffering and glory clear to the prophets. Verse 12 indicates that the prophets knew that the things now preached as the gospel to believers did not refer to their times but to the future. Their inquiries also have shown them things even the angels desired to know.

Scholars today generally agree that the "prophets" referred to must be the Old Testament prophets, not Christian prophets. The idea that ancient prophets received a revelation whose meaning could not be understood until the "last days" appears in apocalyptic writings. Daniel 9:1–19 describes the prophet looking back into the prophecies of Jeremiah in order to determine the time that must elapse between the exile and restoration. Daniel's own words are to remain sealed until the end time (Dan. 12:5–13). The prophet will not see God's deliverance during his lifetime but will be resurrected at the end (v. 13). Second Esdras 4:51–52 has the prophet ask whether he will be alive during the end time about which he has spoken. The angel says he can give only a partial answer to the prophet's questions, but he cannot respond to the question about Ezra's own life (see Stone, 101–5). Mark 13:32 points to a similar ignorance of the timing of the end. Even the Son does not know the hour that the Father has determined.

This topos explains the final comment in verse 12, "into which angels long to look." Jesus' death and glory are the events of the "last days" that angels did not know. The affirmation that the readers know things unknown to the angels points to the certainty of Christian salvation. Essene commentaries on the prophets found at Qumran presume that the Old Testament prophets spoke of their community as the eschatological gathering of the righteous in the last days. According to the author of their commentary on Habakkuk (1QpHab) God revealed to the prophet what would happen in the last days but not the time. The community's founder was able to explain all the secrets contained in the prophets to his followers:

> and God told Habakkuk to write down that which would happen to the final generation, but He did not make known to him when time would come to an end. And as for that which He said, *"That he who reads may read it speedily"* (Hab. 2:2): interpreted this concerns the Teacher of Righteousness, to whom God made known all the mysteries of the words of His servants the Prophets. (1QpHab 7:1–2; Vermes, 286)

The question of "time" as key to the prophetic quest appears in verse 11a. The Greek expression *"tina ē poion kairon"* should be rendered as though both pronouns referred to time, "which or what sort of time" (Michaels, 41), not as though the Greek *tina* referred to a person, leading to the NRSV: "about the person or time." As in the Qumran example, then, the prophets asked either about the time or about the particulars of the endtime events.

The Qumran commentary on Habakkuk suggests that the community's founder had special insight into the hidden meaning of the prophets. First Peter 1:12 attributes similar inspiration to those who preached the gospel to the readers. They were not merely the agents of a human institution but evangelized along with the Holy Spirit (v. 12), which the readers have experienced as the source of their sanctification (v. 2).

This passage contains an unusual affirmation about Christ, he is active in the prophets (Achtemeier, 186; Goppelt, 107). This expression suggests a Christology that attributes preexistence to Christ. It also distinguishes 1 Peter's account of prophetic inspiration from the Jewish tradition. In 1 Peter the one about whom the prophets speak has inspired what they say about him. First Peter insists that all the events of salvation were predestined by God, including the election of believers (1:2, 17). The prophetic testimony is less concerned with the community than with the suffering and exaltation of Jesus that made its existence possible (v. 11). Readers will learn the details of that prophetic testimony when Christ is presented as the suffering servant of Isaiah (2:21–25; Achtemeier).

The difficulty that this section of 1 Peter poses for Christians today lies in its appropriation of the Old Testament. The letter never suggests that there is another community of Jewish readers for whom the prophets do not describe Jesus. Attempts to detect some theology of two covenant communities in 1 Peter fail to acknowledge the author's description of a single community of faith (Michaels, xlix–l). Liturgical use of prophetic texts during the Advent/Christmas and Lent/Easter seasons often conveys a similarly naive understanding of the relationship between the prophets and Christianity. Even after several weeks of Bible study on Isaiah during Advent, several parishioners commented that it was "just amazing that he could predict everything about Jesus."

No doubt persons who had grown up as members of the Qumran sect might say the same about the prophets and their origins. But in the world today, Christians need to be more self-conscious than 1 Peter about the difference between reading the prophets as witnesses to their own time, as commentators on the Jewish Torah, and reading them as witnesses to Christ. We cannot suppose, as 1 Peter argues, that God had only the Christian community of faith in mind throughout the Old Testament. We might prefer to begin from the other end. Jesus himself and those who formulated the gospel about him already understood their times by reflecting on the prophets, psalms, and the like. This understanding was incorporated into the preaching of the early community and into the narratives about the events of salvation. Christians cannot understand the traditions that have been handed down to them without knowing the Old Testament texts that formed and informed the New Testament. But the story of Jesus does not form the sole framework for understanding the faith of the Old Testament.

First Peter 1:11 appears to narrow Christian reading of the Old Testament to what can be said to point to Christ. If we say instead that the God who is the source of our salvation revealed many dimensions of faith in the experiences of Israel, then Christians may learn about God in the prophets and other writings of the Old Testament without assuming that everything points directly to Christ. Christians can acknowledge the possibility that the Jewish community can be obedient to the word of the Lord in the law and the prophets without being obedient to the word of the gospel.

1 Peter 1:13–25
You Are Called to Holiness

"Therefore" plus the imperative "hope in the grace being brought to you" (v. 13) marks the transition to the body of the letter (T. Martin, 70–71). Two participles prior to the command have the force of imperatives as well, "gird up [the loins of] your mind" (NRSV: "prepare your minds for action") and "sober up". They summon the reader to pay attention to what follows. The tone of the letter shifts from the descriptions of salvation in the opening section to direct exhortation. Christians must live with the holiness of those who have been reborn. Though the image of "girding up loins" suggests the Exodus command (Exod. 12: 11), 1 Peter does not use the Exodus metaphors of wilderness, wandering, or journey. Instead, 1 Peter focuses on the imagery of exile (v. 17).

The blessing section introduced the image of God as Father who will give his children an imperishable inheritance (1:3–5). The familial imagery returns in verses 14–16. The addressees are reminded to be "obedient children" and model their behavior on their divine Father by substituting holiness for the passions characteristic of their pre-Christian lives. Since 1 Peter refers to the former lives of its readers as "ignorance" and later speaks of the "folly of your ancestral way of life" (v. 18), the readers are clearly Gentiles who did not know God (cf. Acts 17:23, 30). First Peter returns to the association between believers as "children" and "obedience" in the exhortation to Christian wives (3:6). The command to be holy as God is holy has been taken from Lev. 19:2. Christians are more familiar with the variant that Matt. 5:48 uses in summarizing the sayings on love of enemies, "You, therefore, must be perfect as your heavenly Father is perfect." First Peter applies the injunction generally to "all your conduct" (v. 15). This exhortation does not have particular moral virtues in mind. There is no evidence that 1 Peter has detailed information about the churches to which it is addressed.

Many Christians find the injunction to "be holy as God is holy" objectionable. After all, we are fragile human beings in need of God's forgiveness, not saints. Matthew's version, which uses the word "perfection," is even more offensive to those who have grown up with a sense of being unable to fulfill the expectations of a demanding parent. When asked why they felt so angry that such statements were in the Bible, a group of adult parishioners quickly identified the tensions they could not resolve in their lives: (a) mothers who have to work, struggling to meet all the claims on their time; (b) fathers whose careers have been sidetracked in the economic downturn; (c) parents whose adult children are in various sorts of difficulty, and the like. Life is just too tough to have God requiring perfection, they insisted. No doubt 1 Peter's audience could come up with a list of hardships to justify such a conclusion. The letter seeks to encourage them not to slide away from the new life they had adopted as Christians. In today's terms, when the list of obligations and demands on our time seems impossible to manage, God is often the first to go.

The image of God as impartial judge (v. 17) that 1 Peter uses to underline the importance of a concern for holiness during their time of exile also creates difficulty for many Christians today. First Peter tells readers to "conduct yourselves with fear." For most of its readers that injunction would not seem as harsh as it does to twentieth century Americans. "Fear" or "reverence" was the way in which one related to more powerful superiors in an hierarchical society. Martin cites a section of the first-century Stoic Musonius Rufus that exemplifies the obedience of a son toward his father:

> As a student of philosphy he will certainly be most eager to treat his father with the greatest possible consideration and will be most well-behaved and gentle in his relations with his father. He will never be contentious or self willed, nor hasty or prone to anger; furthermore, he will control his tongue and his appetite whether for food or for sexual temptations, and he will stand fast in the face of danger and hardships. (Musonius Rufus 16, 17; T. Martin, 170)

The privilege of calling God "Father" only came to the letter's readers with their conversion. They must be reminded of its responsibilities. First Peter 2:18 turns to another group in the ancient patriarchal household, slaves. They must obey their masters with "fear" or "reverence." Since God is impartial, those who call on him as "Father" should not expect special exemptions for their conduct.

This emphasis on obedience does not wipe out the mercy that readers have experienced in their call to become Christians. As 2 Esd. 7:52–70 observes, without the compassion that God shows his creatures, only a few would survive divine judgment (Goppelt, 120). The inheritance that Christians expect because they belong to this new household is far greater than anything they might lose by obedience to the will of God.

Verses 18–21 remind Christians of the price paid for their redemption. This complex sentence has combined an allusion to Isaiah 52:3 LXX, "sold for nothing, redeemed without silver" (v. 18), and hymnic or creedal phrases (vv. 20–21; Michaels, 53). The center of the passage highlights the ransom paid by Christ as unblemished lamb. First Timothy 2:5–6 contains a hymnic phrase that refers to Christ's giving himself as "ransom." Since many resident foreigners came to live in other cities because they had been taken there as slaves, the reference to "ransoming" may have connected the readers' experience with the biblical imagery of Exodus (Exod. 6:6; 15:13). Though they have been ransomed, the letter's readers remain in exile and subject to the constraints of obedience. However, readers have been "freed" from another form of slavery, that of their ancestral way of life. The hold of ancestral customs and religious cults may have been weaker for the slaves and alien residents of the cities in Asia Minor. For ancient society, the idea that ancestral laws could be set aside would seem "ironic." Jews in the Diaspora maintained their identity by insisting on the right to practice ancestral traditions. To other aliens in the region, Jewish refusal to assimilate and even the "hatred of humanity" for which they were known in intellectual circles (Feldman, 42–47) may have indicated an ancestral tradition that was more vital than their own. Christ's death makes it possible for others to enter that tradition. The author does not distinguish Christian and Jewish versions of the "holy people of God." He invites readers to replace their ancestral ways with the holy customs of Israel (Spicq, 67).

The final verses of this section (vv. 22–25) pick up the imagery of purity and obedience along with the contrast between what is transient and the security of God's promise. At the same time, attention shifts from the Christian and outsiders to the community of believers. The command that governs their relationships does not echo the reverent obedience of the patriarchal household but the egalitarian love between brothers. The command to "love one another" (v. 22) appears in numerous variants in the New Testament as a characteristic mark of the Christian community (e.g., Rom. 12:10; 1 Thess. 4:9; Heb. 13:1; 1 John 3:11, 14; 4:11–12, 20–21). In the Qumran rule, "love the sons of light" carries with it an overtone of firm adherence to sectarian boundaries (1QS 1:9–11; 3:4–9; 4:20f.), an emphasis that is evident in 1 John as well. Since nothing in the context suggests a threat to the loyalty of its addressees, there is no reason to assume that the exhortation carried such implications.

First Peter shifts its metaphors for "new birth" from the family to seed (v. 23). Mutual love becomes evidence that members of the Christian community have not been born of "perishable seed but of imperishable." God's word is the agent of this birth. Old Testament images of the enduring word of God (Ps. 33:9) and its fruitfulness (Isa. 55:10–11) underlie the image. First Peter 1:24–25a cites Isa. 40:6–8 LXX to establish the contrast between God's word and what comes into being through merely natural processes. It then reminds the audience of their own encounter with that word, the preaching that was responsible for their faith (v. 25b; cf. 1:12).

The metaphors of the concluding section are easier to apply to a contemporary context than those in the earlier verses. Sincere mutual love between members of the community fits into our metaphors of familial relationships. Reverent deference in speech, desires, and actions to the will of a family patriarch does not. Acknowledgment that our faith was born and nourished when others spoke God's word to us is a common

Christian experience. Being purchased from slavery at the cost of someone's blood, whether human or animal, is not. We can understand the correlation between the unfamiliar metaphors and the lives of 1 Peter's recipients. Effective preaching of the word of God must always speak in a way that permits God to transform the lives of those who receive it. The key to new life in 1 Peter lies with the Christian community that acknowledges God as Father. The philosophical tradition extols obedience regardless of the character of one's father. First Peter's readers know a great deal about the "Father" whom they are encouraged to revere. God's mercy has made them heirs of an imperishable reward that cannot be lost unless Christians turn away from the traditions of God's household.

The demand for holiness is not embodied in an extended series of rules. It begins with God's gracious reaching out to bring human beings into relationship with himself. In this way, 1 Peter continues the structure of the covenant faith of Israel that is oriented toward Jesus. Human obedience follows upon God's merciful concern to liberate those in slavery. It would be irrational to be disobedient and ungrateful in the face of such a gift. Preachers can find modern examples of family relationships that are more suitable to our society. We are much more outraged when young persons from loving families reject all the opportunities they have been given and engage in behavior that harms themselves and others than we are when the offenders have had no opportunities. For 1 Peter, God has reached out to those who had no reason to expect anything from him. How could they be anything but grateful and obedient?

1 Peter 2:1–10
You Are the New People of God

The previous section introduced the importance of relationships within the community. First Peter uses Old Testament images to depict the church in this section. These metaphors will once again remind his readers to rejoice in the unexpected grace of God. Those who had no claim to being a people have become God's people (2:4–10). The social consequences of their new identity appear to be complex. The language of separation from ancestral traditions and the exhortation to be obedient children in the new household of God has led Elliott to suggest that the churches were a conversionist sect. Believers were encouraged to turn to one another and away from the world of their past associations (Elliott 1981; 1986). Balch, who focuses on the parallels to Greco-Roman ethics in the next section of the letter (2:11—3:12) insists that Christians are being encouraged to live within the larger society, not merely within the church (Balch 1981; 1986). The evidence from studies of Diaspora Judaism in Asia Minor suggests that both proposals represent the author's agenda. Christians cannot help but break some of their past ties. The distinctive character of their association is evidence enough to provoke hostility. First Peter must remind readers of how special that new community is. However, the socioeconomic situation of those addressed makes it impossible for them to be isolated from the larger society. Whatever the tensions, they will also have to live within its confines. If they accomplish that task well, others may be drawn to their way of life.

The motif of reborn children forms the center of another exhortation to a transformation in the believer's life (2:1–3). Since the community will be depicted in cultic metaphors, its holiness requires setting aside all evil. Verse 3 reiterates the letter's progressive picture of salvation. It begins with an experience of the goodness of God that continues to be a reality that structures Christian growth. The image of tasting the goodness of the Lord (v. 3) echoes Ps. 33:9 LXX. Verse 1 uses a conventional list of vices to characterize the past life that is put aside. Although such catalogues are usually conventional, the list of vices may be related to the concrete situation of the readers (Michaels). Such evils as deceit and slander characterize the sufferings that Christians will experience at the hands of others (2:12, 15; 3:16). Christ will teach them how to suffer without speaking out in deceit (2:22). When insulted by others, Christians must learn not to respond in kind (3:9). Although 1 Peter has not begun to address the particular sufferings of his readers directly, this advice already warns them against adopting the behavior of those who harass them.

The metaphor of milk being given to babes (v. 2) was commonly used for elementary teaching to be given those who were just beginning to convert from past evils to the new way of life prescribed by philosophy (used for Christianity in 1 Cor.

3:1–2; Heb. 5:12–13). "Milk" indicates the primary instruction required before real doctrine can be learned:

> First, then, it [= soul husbandry] makes it its aim to sow or plant nothing that has no produce, but all that is fitted for cultivation and fruit-bearing. . . . But who else could the man that is in each of us be save the mind whose job it is to reap the benefits derived from all that has been sown or planted? But seeing that for babes milk is food, but for grown men wheaten bread, there must also be milk-like nourishment for the soul, suited to the time of childhood, in the shape of the preliminary stages of school learning. (Philo, *On Husbandry* 8–9)

First Peter lacks the contrast between preliminary, childish food and adult nourishment. However, the adjectives attached to the term "milk," "pure, spiritual," indicate that the metaphor does refer to the true teaching necessary for growth as Christians. Perhaps the readers are to conclude that the exhortation contained in the letter constitutes such "pure milk." The reference to tasting the goodness of the Lord in verse 3 provides another referent for the image of babies drinking milk.

First Peter takes the term "Lord" from the psalm as a reference to Christ. Verse 4 shifts to the metaphor of a building constructed out of the "rejected" stone Christ and then the Christians as stones of the building. Unlike the saying about the rejected cornerstone (Mark 12:10; Acts 4:11), 1 Peter does not refer to the Jews. Those who rejected the stone are simply identified as "human beings." There is no indication that 1 Peter thinks of Jews as those who were responsible for the rejected stone. In the Pauline tradition, the image of building was associated with the church as body of Christ (Eph. 2:21; 4:12, 16). First Peter does not use the metaphor of the community as "body." The house can also be identified as a temple in which the faithful offer "spiritual sacrifices" to God (v. 5; cf. Rom. 12:1).

Some interpreters have suggested that "living stone" reflects a traditional use of the expression for stones that have not been cut (T. Martin, 175–76). However, 1 Peter has used the term "living" to modify other nouns: (a) the hope that reborn Christians now possess (1:3) and (b) God (1:23). Here, both Christ and believers are "living stones." The epithet marks the building that is built up as God's work, a spiritual and not a human reality. Romans 12:1 indicates that the language of spiritual sacrifices pleasing to God refers to the moral life of Christians. First Peter probably reflects conventional exhortation. Sirach 35:1–7 treats the virtues of a righteous life as equivalent to sacrifice:

> The one who returns a kindness offers choice flour, and one who gives alms sacrifices a thank offering. To keep from wickedness is pleasing to the Lord, and to forsake unrighteousness is an atonement. (Sir. 35:3–5)

First Peter departs slightly from this tradition by emphasizing God's agency in creating the new spiritual house in which these sacrifices are offered. The verb *oikodomeisthe* is a passive imperative, "let yourselves be built" (T. Martin, 181). The image suggests that the readers are the ideal temple that God was expected to establish in the end time.

The Community Rule found at Qumran describes that group as the holy dwelling for Aaron that has been established on the foundation stone of Isa. 28:16:

> It shall be an Everlasting Plantation, a House of Holiness for Israel, an Assembly of Supreme Holiness for Aaron. . . . It shall be that tried wall, that *precious corner-stone,* whose foundations shall neither rock nor sway in their place (Isa. 28:16). It shall be a Most Holy Dwelling for Aaron, with everlasting knowledge of the Covenant of justice and shall offer up sweet fragrance. It shall be a House of Perfection and Truth in Israel. (1QS 8:5–10; Vermes, 72f.)

This example indicates how the metaphors in 1 Peter were used by a sectarian Jewish community to describe its own destiny. But in 1 Peter these images do not carry with them the requirement that believers adhere to the precepts of the law. Instead, the metaphors that define God's holy people are extended to Gentiles. They would have been familiar with the necessity of ensuring that sacrifices were acceptable to the deities from their past observance of pagan religious cults.

Verses 6–10 support the exhortation with citations from the Old Testament: Isa. 28:6 (v. 6); Ps. 118:22 (v. 7); Isa. 8:14 (v. 8); and "elect people" Isa. 43:20 LXX; "royal priesthood" Exod. 19:6; Isa. 61:6; "holy nation" Exod. 19:6; "a people for possession to declare the great deeds" Isa. 43:21 LXX (v. 9). Verses 9b–10 echo two other prophetic passages: "darkness into light" Isa. 9:2 (v. 9b) and "once no people, now people of God" Hos. 2:23 (v. 10). The comments that punctuate the series of quotations remind readers of their own past and the new reality that separates them from others. The stone that the Lord has laid is precious to believers but a stumbling stone to those who do not believe (v. 7a). Unlike the readers, who obeyed the word that was preached to them, unbelievers were destined to reject it (v. 8b).

The imagery in this passage highlights the dignity of the community that is built on Christ, the "elect and precious cornerstone." By emphasizing God's mercy and election, readers can understand the hostility shown by outsiders as a sign that others have not been chosen to receive this precious gift. Instead of shaking the faith of the community, its experiences of rejection serve as reminders of what God has done for them. This passage also points out the obligation that follows from being God's people, "declare the wonderful deeds of him who called you out of darkness into light" (v. 9). The expression to "declare the wonderful deeds of God" can refer to singing God's praises in worship (Ps. 118). But another dimension of "declaring the deeds of God" becomes evident when the letter addresses the situation of its readers. Their lives and words will have to be testimony to outsiders so that they too might glorify God (2:12).

Although the images in this section are familiar from the Old Testament, many Christians find them somewhat alien. A number of Americans do not consider identification with a particular church community central to their identity even though they describe themselves as practicing Christians when asked. God may be at work building up the church in some global sense, but they feel that local churches are human institutions. These "grand metaphors" do not seem to describe our day-to-day experience as Christians. Of course, the same may have been true for the addressees of this letter. After all, they did not even have separate buildings dedicated to worship. If they lived, whether as slaves, dependents, or wives, in a pagan household, they were surrounded by pagan religious art even at home. Temples and other shrines were everywhere. Christians had no art, no buildings, no sacred places. Everything took place within the assembled community of believers.

Our images of community have an important impact on our behavior and relationships with others. An ongoing conflict in our local church pits those who want silence before worship against those who greet friends, exchange news, and the like.

One group thinks of the church as a place where the mystery and awe of God ought to be respected, hence silence. The other group thinks of the church as a large, extended family. If people are happy to be together, they will express it in exchanging greetings. Many of the older widowed adults are particularly pleased when young people come over to say hello or even sit with them. While we try to build quiet time into the service, the noisier crowd prevails. People join our church because they feel that others are genuinely glad to see them walk in the door. The church as extended family has prevailed over the church as sacred space.

Living in a Non-Christian World

1 PETER 2:11—3:12

The expression "Beloved, I beseech you . . ." marks a transition within the body of an ancient letter. The two terms that follow, "aliens" and "exiles," echo earlier references to the status of the community (1:1, 17). As part of the Diaspora, Christians must live as aliens or visiting foreigners in a world of non-Christians. Some interpreters emphasize the use of such images as a metaphor for the fact that Christians cannot attain their heavenly inheritance (1:4). Others point out that the combination of terms, like "Diaspora," "visiting foreigner," and "resident alien," and the hints the letter contains about the social status of its addressees suggest that the reference is both metaphorical and descriptive. Throughout the sections of the letter that refer to how believers are to conduct themselves, the addressees are subordinate to or dependent on the opinion of outsiders. Peter, and other Jewish Christians in Rome, would have been in a similar position.

The question of suffering echoes throughout the letter from 2:11 to 4:19. Some commentators treat the whole section as a single unit. However, 1 Peter 2:11—3:12 incorporates the discussion of suffering into a traditional piece of exhortation, the household code, while 3:13—4:19 presents an independent development of the exhortation to rejoice in suffering. Therefore, we have divided the section into two units with 1 Peter 3:12 as a transitional verse that concludes this unit and opens the unit that follows.

The most difficult elements in this section of the letter for Christians today are the repeated exhortations to be obedient to superiors. Bitter experience has taught Christians that such advice often permits dictatorships to abuse the weak and the rich to oppress the poor, and makes the churches complicitous in social injustice. The offensiveness of such advice is much greater if the indications of social status are only being used metaphorically. If they tell us something about the social setting of the Christians to whom the letter is addressed, then the advice is merely "good sense." As we have seen, aliens and foreigners had no rights in their cities of residence. Such persons could easily be exiled again. First Peter never says that it is right for a master to beat his slaves irrationally, but that is a common fact of life. Rebellious behavior would not gain anything. Therefore, 1 Peter counsels taking Christ as one's model and submitting to such treatment. This exhortation is a way of gaining what dignity and honor the oppressed slave can from the situation. It does not claim that the situation itself is ideal.

1 Peter 2:11–12
Good Conduct as Testimony to God

The section begins with a general exhortation to renounce "passions of the flesh" that are waging war against the soul. This topic was commonly discussed by first-century moralists. They argued that those who were self-controlled and not subject to desires for material things are truly free. The Stoic moralists taught that a slave who possesses this independence from passion is superior to the master who is ruled by desire. The following selection from the Stoic Epictetus, who had once been a slave, illustrates this topic:

> He is free who lives as he wills, who is subject neither to compulsion, nor hindrance, nor force, whose choices are un-

> hampered, whose desires attain their end, whose aversions do not fall into what they would avoid. Who, then, wishes to live in error?—No one.—Who wishes to live deceived, impetuous, unjust, unrestrained, peevish, abject?—No one.—Therefore, there is no bad man who lives as he wills, and accordingly no bad man is free. And who wishes to live in grief, fear, envy, pity, desiring things and failing to get them, avoiding things and falling into them?—No one at all.—Do we find, then, any bad man free from grief or fear, not falling into what he would avoid, nor failing to achieve what he desires?—No one.—Then we find no bad man free, either. (Epictetus, *Discourses* 4.1.1–5; quoted in Malherbe 1986, 159)

As this passage indicates, conventional moral wisdom exalted persons who were not driven by passions. Consequently, Christians who could show that their religion had enabled them to achieve this status could use their conduct to make a claim for its truth. Much of the next two sections depends on the premise that Christian conduct must show outsiders the validity of Christian belief. There is no need to specify what the "good works" are in detail, since conventional lists of virtues and vices were generally agreed on in the culture.

First Peter does not specify the type of "bad things" being said about Christians either, though there is no doubt that general suspicions attached to foreign cults would be sufficient to generate hostility. In addition, anti-Jewish sentiments attached to their proselytizing and separation from the activities of other people. In the case of dependent family members or slaves, departure from the religious tradition of the household would also appear suspicious. Aliens were expected to mind their own business and avoid arousing envy (Cicero, *De Officiis* 1.125). They had to maintain the goodwill of local patrons in order to remain in the city.

1 Peter 2:13–17
Respect for Human Authorities

The first explicit description of the lifestyle expected of Christians picks up the meanings of being subject and being free found in Epictetus. Christians can be subject to human "institutions" (v. 13) and yet be exhorted to live as "free persons" (v. 16) since this freedom does not serve as an occasion for evil. We have seen that when strife broke out between Jews and the Greek-speaking citizenry of Alexandria, the dispute was resolved by decrees from the emperor Claudius. The exhortation to honor the emperor or the governor who represents him reflects Jewish experience in the Diaspora. The higher Roman authorities could be relied on to support limited Jewish privileges against the attempts of local authorities to terminate them. Members of the Herodian family, brought up in Rome, enjoyed strong personal relationships with various emperors (Feldman, 95–101).

This section also contains parallels to the advice about relationships to civil authorities in Rom. 13:1–7 (also 1 Tim. 2:1–3; Titus 3:1–3). First Peter and Romans may represent independent variants of a common Roman tradition, as shown in Table 3 (using RSV). Paul's version of this tradition in Rom. 13:1–7

Table 3
Pauline Parallels to 1 Peter 2:13–17

1 Peter	*Romans*
Be subject for the Lord's sake to every human institution, whether it be to the emperor as supreme, (2:13)	Let every person be subject to the governing authorities. For there is no authority except from God, . . . (13:1)
or to governors as sent by him to punish those who do wrong and to praise those who do right. (2:14)	. . . who resists the authorities resists what God has appointed, and those who resist will incur judgment. For rulers are not a terror to good conduct, but to bad. (13:2–3a)
For it is God's will that by doing right you should put to silence the ignorance of foolish men. (2:15)	Then do what is good, and you will receive his approval, for he is God's servant for your good. (13:3b–4a)
Live as free men, yet without using your freedom as a pretext for evil; but live as servants of God. (2:16)	[For you were called to freedom, brethren; only do not use your freedom as an opportunity for the flesh, but through love be servants of one another. (Gal. 5:13)]
Honor all men. Love the brotherhood. Fear God. Honor the emperor. (2:17)	love one another with brotherly affection; outdo one another in showing honor. (Rom. 12:10)

emphasizes the divine basis for the authority exercised by those in power much more directly than 1 Peter does. In fact, 1 Peter 2:13 read literally does not speak of "every human *institution*" (NRSV) but "every human creature/creation" (Gr. *ktisis*) or possibly, if a secular Greek meaning is employed, "foundation" (of a town or house). Some interpreters conclude that the expression should be translated "every human creature," that is, "every human being" (Michaels, 124). However, this translation makes an awkward transition into the directive to be subject to specific persons: the emperor or his representative. The expression may be intended to underline the human character of such imperial rule, rather than of those who exercise it. Translations like "institution" fail because 1 Peter clearly is not referring to what we consider an "institution."

We have seen that the injunction to "live as free men" (v. 16) belongs to a different pattern of exhortation, the command to overcome the passions (v. 11). The second half of the verse introduces a Christian modification of this form. Instead of contrasting Christian freedom with the slavery of others, freedom is qualified by reminding readers that they are to make use of freedom as "slaves of God." The household code will begin with advice to those who are slaves in the human sense as well. Many of the readers may have come to live as resident aliens in foreign cities because they or their ancestors had been taken there as slaves. Inscriptions from Asia Minor show that in some instances of manumission freedmen were designated slaves of the god or goddess in whose temple the preliminary registration to free the person had taken place. Slaves who managed the affairs of wealthy masters often enjoyed considerable power and status in society. Some inscriptions show that slaves built their own tombs and could have free persons as inferiors or dependents (D. Martin, xvii–xix). The slaves referred to in the household code appear to be more common household slaves. Either a relatively low-status free person or a common household slave might easily consider "slave of God" to be an advance in status. Other inscriptions erected by slaves and former slaves show that those who served an important person might identify themselves as "slaves of X" (D. Martin, 47). Earlier 1 Peter reminded its readers of their new dignity by speaking of them as children newly born into the household of God. Here they can enhance their status by living as slaves in the service of God.

As long as 1 Peter's readers are aliens, they must be careful not to provoke jealousy among the local citizens. The warnings to be subordinate to all governing authorities and to honor all people are directed toward the situation of aliens. As long as nothing in their conduct causes offense, Christians can expect assistance from Roman officials (T. Martin, 196–205). Contrary to those who think that the persecution referred to in 1 Peter should be identified with some official persecution (such as that by Nero and Domitian), this passage presumes a positive verdict by Roman officials (Michaels, 126). The household code that follows this section makes the requirements of "honoring all" more specific.

1 Peter 2:18—3:7
Household Code

This section follows a familiar pattern of exhortation described as a "household code" (Balch 1981). Variants of this form appear in Col. 3:18—4:1 and Eph. 5:21—6:9. The form lists duties of various members of the household. In some cases, ancient philosophers are speaking to those who govern the household:

> That department of philosophy which supplies precepts appropriate to the individual case, instead of framing them for mankind at large—which, for instance, advises how a husband should conduct himself towards his wife, or how a father should bring up his children, or how a master should rule his slaves—this department of philosophy, I say, is accepted by some as the only significant part. (Seneca, *Epistles* 94.1; Malherbe 1986, 127)

The Christian examples begin with the inferior members of the household: wife, children, slaves. Colossians and Ephesians contain reciprocal admonitions to the superior members of each group as well. Clearly 1 Peter does not reproduce the full pattern. The descending order, wives, children, slaves, has been reversed, and children omitted altogether.

This exhortation has been shaped by the concrete circumstances of the Christian churches in Asia Minor. Masters or heads of large households do not appear to have been part of the community. Husbands are addressed with the short form of exhortation typical of the genre (3:7). The points that 1 Peter highlights concern those who are dependent on pagan superiors: slaves and women (Michaels, 122). Each group is presented with an example to use in determining behavior in that situation. Slaves are to look to the suffering Christ (2:21–25); women, to Sarah, wife of the patriarch Abraham (3:5–6). Scholars have raised questions about the function of this advice. For some, it expresses the effort of Christians to accommodate their behavior to the standards of the larger society (Balch 1981). For others, the communal concern with holiness indicates a commitment to being different from the world. The household code points to areas in which Christians fall under suspicion. Good behavior toward outsiders (2:12, 14–15, 20; 3:6) and withdrawal from former relationships (4:4) describe the community's attitude toward society (Elliott 1986, 80–83).

The debate over how to understand the function of the household code highlights the question of whether Christians were encouraged to attribute religious value to norms that are conventional in the larger culture. Churches today debate the problem of acculturation in their global mission. Countries in which Christians are a minority, like Pakistan or Senegal, present examples of the problem facing 1 Peter. The larger culture is not religiously neutral. It has been shaped by other religious traditions. For 1 Peter, civic religion required honoring the gods of the city, and private religion included such things as visits to oracle shrines and participation in cults devoted to various deities. Conversion requires a challenge to the local religious ethos. At the same time, Christians remain part of their local culture. Since the addressees of 1 Peter are "aliens," some of the cultural ties that bind citizens to the local towns and villages were not open to them. In that sense, it may have been easier to be a religious "outsider" than for someone who was also a citizen of the area. On the other hand, private devotion to gods or goddesses from one's homeland often provided resident aliens with ties to others from the same region. In that case, conversion to Christianity might intensify the separation between individuals and their ancestral traditions. Something has to take their place. The opening section of the letter depicted the new community of believers as the family, the inheritance, the household, and the temple that substituted for what had been abandoned. The household code sections speak to sociocultural realities that believers cannot remake. They are not taken into the new community as Christian ideals. The suffering that results from slavery is acknowledged. Christians are given examples of how to live in those situations.

1. Slaves, Obey Masters (2:18–20)

The opening verse presents a number of exegetical questions. Those addressed are "house slaves" (Gr. *oiketai*). The expression does not indicate whether the author envisages a large household in which the slaves themselves occupied different ranks or a small household with only a few slaves. In either case, the slaves addressed do not show the identification with their masters as a source of personal status that we find in inscriptions (D. Martin, 46–48). The masters are apparently not Christians. Slaves are exhorted to obey "in all fear" (NRSV: "accept authority . . . with all deference"). Does "in all fear" describe the conduct of the slave toward his or her master, as the RSV translation suggests? Or does the expression refer to an individual's relationship to God? In that case, the passage has picked up the image of Christians as "free persons" who live as "slaves of God" from verse 16. Since verse 19 refers to one's conscience or awareness of God while suffering unjustly, the latter understanding of "in all fear" appears to be correct.

The reference to harsh masters (v. 18) and beatings suffered by slaves who had done no wrong (v. 20) shows that 1 Peter is conscious of the brutality endured by slaves. Physical punishment is the usual response to the disobedient slave. That is not questioned (v. 20a). The benefit of suffering unjust punishment lies in the *charis* (vv. 19, 20b) that results. *Charis* was used earlier in the letter in its conventional Christian sense of "grace" (1:2) or "salvation" (1:10 [present], 1:13 [future]). It also appears to refer to Christian salvation in the advice to husbands in 3:7. The NRSV translates *charis* here as "approval," which fails to capture the connection with God's gift of salvation that the term has elsewhere in 1 Peter. Good conduct should be rewarded. In the cases where "good conduct" becomes suffering unjust abuse, God will extend goodwill or a gift to such persons. First Peter 2:19 speaks of suffering "through *syneidēsis* of God." *Syneidēsis* usually means "moral consciousness" or "conscience" in such contexts. Acting according to conscience, that is, in such a way that individuals were not accused of evildoing by their conscience, might serve as a defense when an individual's behavior was challenged by others (cf. Rom. 2:15; 9:1; 2 Cor. 1:12). First Peter 1:17 warned Christians to conduct themselves "with fear" during their time of exile because they appeal to God as judge. Translations such as the NRSV, "being aware of God," do not carry the sense of divine judgment and moral obligation evident in this passage.

2. Follow the Example of Christ (2:21–25)

An extended depiction of Christ as the suffering servant (Isa. 53:4–12 LXX) supports the moral requirement that Christians accept unjust suffering. The example is framed by two references to the readers' conversion (vv. 21, 25). Those who have been redeemed by Christ's blood (1:2, 19) must follow the example that he set. The example also illuminates the metaphorical possibilities of the exhortation to household slaves. All Christians can be spoken of as "slaves of God" (2:16). They all face situations in which others harass them unjustly simply because they are Christians (2:12). Therefore, they should apply this example to those situations.

The example expands 1 Peter's earlier reference to the prophetic testimony concerning Christ's sufferings (1:11). In that context, the eschatological consequence of suffering was Christ's glory and the inspired preaching of the gospel that converted the readers. Here, the eschatological consequence of Christ's suffering is the gathering of a straying flock under its shepherd and overseer (Gr. *episkopos*) Christ (2:25). Verse 22 quotes Isa. 53:9b LXX. The term "sin" has been substituted for Isaiah's "lawless" in the citation. The substitution ties the citation together with the allusion to Isa. 53:4, 12b in verse 24, "he bore our sins" (Michaels, 145–47). Other echoes of the suffering servant occur throughout the section.

Verse 23 has reformulated the silence of the sheep before its slaughterers (Isa. 53:9) so that the example can be directly applied to the experiences of persecuted Christians. They do not respond to insult with insult or to suffering with threats but wait for God's judgment. This formulation is a variant of common early Christian exhortations to love the enemy (cf. Rom. 12:14–19; 1 Cor. 4:12). It reappears in 1 Peter 3:9. Verses 24 and 25a return to more direct allusions to Isaiah 53. Where Isa. 53:12 speaks of the servant who bears the sins of many being handed over to death, 1 Peter 2:24 refers to Christ's bearing sins bodily on the tree (of the cross). Since the phrase has been expanded with the link between Christ's bearing sin and the Christian's "having no part in" (Gr. *apogenomenoi;* NRSV: "free from") sin in order to live righteously, the whole expression may have been early Christian liturgical language (cf. Rom. 6:4–5). The phrase "by whose wounding you have been healed" (v. 24) cites Isa. 53:5b but shifts Isaiah's first-person plural into the second person. This shift is continued in the identification of the readers as the "straying sheep" of Isa. 53:6 in verse 25a.

Although 1 Peter depends on Isa. 53:4–12 for the descriptive images in this passage, the allusions do not follow the order found in Isaiah itself. The order of verses 22–24 might have been dictated by the events of an early Christian passion narrative (so Achtemeier, 180). For 1 Peter 2:21–25, the passion/exaltation pattern is not in view. Rather, the result of the passion is the healing of those who are now the people of God. The image of Ezek. 34:5–16 that promises that God will shepherd the neglected sheep underlies the transition from straying sheep to the injunction to return to the shepherd in verse 25. First Peter 5:1–2 uses the combination of elder and shepherding to describe the author and the activity of leaders in the community. The term "overseer" (Gr. *episkopos*) that is coupled with shepherd in verse 25 appears as a term referring to persons who shepherd the community in Acts 20:28. Although Christ is the shepherd and overseer in verse 25, the audience must recognize the pastoral presence of shepherds in the Christian community. Indirectly, the conclusion of this section encourages readers to accept the instruction conveyed in the letter from Peter.

The dynamics of this passage do not leave the Christian with a life of unjust suffering. Christ did not heal the flock in order to sacrifice the sheep. The concrete examples of suffering that Christians must endure point to episodic forms of harassment. For many the abuse is verbal. Slaves are at the greatest risk because their masters can physically abuse them. The example of Christ's suffering permits those who are slaves to recognize a value to their own experiences of injustice. At the same time, the sufferers know that they have a value to God, which has been expressed in Christ's death on their behalf. The negative words and deeds directed at believers will not shake their confidence in the salvation that they have already experienced. Suffering without belonging to this new community would be senseless. Even so, many Christians today feel that passages like 1 Peter 2:21–25 derail Christian opposition to social injustice and leave the oppressed as silent sufferers.

Certainly, in many parts of the world, Christians as a community are not "resident aliens" dependent on the whims of others. They are responsible for conditions in society. There is no reason for Christians to copy the silent Christ by not responding to speech designed to wound others. We must oppose unjust actions and words—especially when our silence might imply consent to such behavior. But we also know that at times we should walk away rather than respond to the violence directed against us. On the secular level, violence reduction programs in schools often teach such techniques. Christians also must raise challenges to the assumption that self-interest should come first in all situations. "When you try to sacrifice for others and show love rather than fighting back, people call you a fool," a parishioner protested. She did not mean that she would stop trying to follow the example of Christ. The edge of pain in her voice showed that the "name calling" was close to home and painful. That's why we have a church, a community. Christians must support those who are suffering.

3. Wives, Defer to Husbands (3:1–4)

The general exhortation to Christian women married to unbelievers follows conventional patterns (cf. 1 Tim. 2:9–10). The format of the section parallels the previous segment: (a) those addressed should be subject to those with authority (2:18; 3:1); (b) their conduct seeks to please God, "in fear" (2:18–19; 3:2); (c) an example follows the advice (2:21–25; 3:5–6). Unlike the previous section, this passage holds out the possibility that the women's behavior will convert unbelieving husbands (3:1–2). First Peter 2:12 suggested that conduct might convert suspicious outsiders (Michaels, 158).

Plutarch exhorts a young husband to teach his wife restraint in desire for finery by exhibiting the same virtues himself:

> You must not think that your wife will refrain from immoderate display and extravagance if she sees that you do not despise these things in others, but, on the contrary, find delight in gilded drinking cups, pictured walls, trappings for mules, and showy neckbands for horses. For it is impossible to expel extravagance from the wife's part of the house when it has

> free range amid the men's rooms. (Plutarch, *Advice to Bride and Groom* 145C; Malherbe 1986, 108)

Similarly, Plutarch says that a husband who expects his wife to be sexually restrained should not engage in wanton behavior himself (*Advice to Bride and Groom* 144F–145B). Neo-Pythagorean texts also emphasize the contrast between a simply dressed, virtuous wife and one whose extravagant clothing makes her appear no different from a prostitute:

> The temperate, freeborn woman must live with her legal husband adorned with modesty, clad in neat, simple, white dress. . . . She must avoid clothing that is either entirely purple or is streaked with purple and gold, for that kind of dress is worn by hetaerae when they stalk the masses of men. . . . You should have a blush on your cheeks as a sign of modesty instead of rouge, and should wear nobility, decorum and temperance instead of gold and emeralds. . . . She must please her husband by doing what he wishes, for a husband's wishes ought to be an unwritten law to an orderly wife, and she should live by them. (Pseudo-Melissa, *Letter to Kleareta* 160–62; Malherbe 1986, 83)

The image of a "virtuous wife" in the philosophical texts has been formulated from the perspective of males. These texts do not tell us about women's experience or desires. First Peter 3:1–4 adapts the pattern by coordinating the outward finery that is renounced with what is precious in God's sight. The formulation in verse 4 echoes Matt. 5:5 and Matthew's characterizations of Jesus (Matt. 11:29; 21:5). In the Pythagorean example the wife replaces her jewels with virtues that were outwardly admired in males as well as females: nobility, decorum, temperance. In this Christian example, the wife's inner, Christian virtue remains invisible to her pagan husband. He recognizes the conformity of her outward behavior to cultural norms of "good behavior." The true value of his wife's behavior can only be perceived by believers. The faith tested by trials proves more valuable than precious metals. It results in glory and honor when Christ returns (1:7). Only if the husband becomes a Christian will he discover the grace that she already knows.

First Peter does not suggest that the women are subject to harassment or abuse by their husbands. Balch uses examples in which males attack women converts to Judaism or women who were devotees of Eastern cults (Balch 1981, 84–86). Although some philosophers claim that wives should follow the opinions of their husbands, women's religious activities were not dependent on those of their husbands. First Corinthians 7:12–15 indicates that Christian and non-Christian could live together in concord. Paul presumes that the pagan partner will divorce a spouse if he or she is unwilling to live with a Christian. The assumption that women will not attempt to win over their husbands verbally (v. 1) could be no more than the cultural stereotype of a decorous wife. If the Jewish proselyte experience is reflected in the passage, then the assumption may have been a strategy to lessen the tension over proselytizing. Therefore, there is no reason to presume that because this passage begins with the "be subject" that is characteristic of the household code, abuse or violence is implied. In the case of slaves, physical abuse was a possibility. First Peter referred to that situation explicitly. Though women are enjoined to be subordinate to their husbands, this passage does not suggest that they are to endure abuse in silence.

The cultural assumptions about relationships between husbands and wives in these ancient texts are foreign to the personalist definitions of marriage characteristic of modern societies. Initially, the critique of hairstyles, clothing, and jewelry appears to be antiquated misogyny. However, questions of behavior and dress do concern modern Christians. The pressures on young people, both boys and girls, to conform to culturally defined body images can lead boys to damage bones and muscles by "working out" and girls to eating disorders that are life threatening. Cultural definitions of the "right clothing" can be equally severe. Adults discover unspoken codes concerning acceptable bodily appearance and dress in the work environment. Christians have to ask serious questions about the values these pressures are teaching their children. They also need to ask whether clothing accumulating in the house should be given away to those in need. A more general question focuses on the contrast between esteem based on external appearances and that which stems from a person's inner relationship to God.

4. Follow the Example of Sarah (3:5–6)

Unlike the Christian wives addressed in the exhortation,
the wives of the patriarchs were not married to unbelieving husbands (Michaels, 164). The opening statement refers to the

wives of the patriarchs in general as persons who adorned themselves by obeying their husbands. Obedience (NRSV: "accept authority of") is substituted for external cosmetics, clothes, or jewelry. This comment does not fit any particular Old Testament story. Earlier in the letter, "obedience" is linked to faith (1:2, 14, 22). Perhaps because these women had husbands who were obedient to the Word "obedience" is singled out as their virtue. (The RSV: "used to adorn themselves and were submissive" misses the point of the participle, "being obedient," which has been picked up from verse 1. It indicates how it is that these women adorned themselves.)

Sarah is said to be obedient to Abraham because she called him "lord" (Gen. 18:12 LXX). The text does not make the correspondence between Sarah and the women in its audience clear. To push the parallel too far would lead to the uncomfortable conclusion that women should also follow the religion of their husbands. Abram's wife and family depart with him from Haran and their ancestral land (Gen. 12:4–9). Balch suggests that the example aims at instilling the virtue of domestic concord (Balch 1981, 103–4). Hebrews 11:11 introduces Sarah as an example of faith after Abraham and his offspring. She may have been a stock example for women proselytes. The final exhortation not to fear anything (v. 6; Prov. 3:25 LXX) is also unclear. Since fear of God is recommended (v. 2), the cause of fear must be human beings. Proverbs 3:25–26 promises the Lord's protection against storms that afflict the wicked. The phrase may have been conventional encouragement for converts who could not be sure how others would respond to their conversion. People who join the church today often express anxiety over the reaction of family or friends, especially those who are not religious. The situation is even more difficult for those who are dependent on others economically. Converts in countries where Christianity is a minority and where extended family ties still dominate most areas of life face an even more daunting prospect. One young man from a Hindu family was completely ostracized when he became a Christian. No one from his family will speak to him when he passes them on the street.

5. Husbands, Honor Wives (3:7)

As in the other New Testament examples, exhortation to husbands follows the instruction to wives (Eph. 5:25–33; Col. 3:19). The formulation is unclear. Husbands are to live with their wives "according to knowledge." The content is not specified. The rest of the section suggests that "knowledge" must refer to knowledge of God's will. The relationship described follows a pattern sometimes referred to as "love patriarchalism." The wealthy or powerful care for those who are weaker or subject to them. The "weaker" are thought to be morally inferior to their superiors. Consequently, their flaws must be anticipated and dealt with compassionately. The remarks on "how to handle a woman" from the *Letter of Aristeas* provide an example:

> "How can one reach agreement with a woman?" "By recognizing," he replied, "that the female sex is bold, positively active for something which it desires, easily liable to change its mind because of poor reasoning powers, and of naturally weak constitution. It is necessary to have dealings with them in a sound way, avoiding provocation which may lead to a quarrel. Life prospers when the helmsman knows the goal to which he must make the passage. Life is completely steered by invocation of God." (*Letter of Aristeas* 250–51; *Old Testament Pseudepigrapha,* 2:29)

The word "vessel" (Gr. *skeuos*) was used in an exhortation to males in 1 Thess. 4:4. In that context, honorable conduct toward one's "vessel" referred to restraint in sexual behavior. We have seen that philosophic moralists encouraged husbands to set a suitable example for their wives.

Unlike the previous example, this exhortation assumes that wives will share their husband's beliefs. The "honor" given is not merely a function of her weaker status. It also reflects that she is a fellow believer. Both husband and wife will participate in prayer without hindrance (cf. 1 Cor. 7:5). The more egalitarian view of marriage today has no place for the presumption that either party is "of poor reasoning powers," essentially a child. But the respect that honors the individuality of each person—including acceptance of that person's weaknesses—is essential to any marriage. Engaged couples often complete a form of personal inventory as part of their marriage preparation. When their responses suggest a lack of respect, a severe clash of values, or presumption that the other person will certainly change once they are married, pastors often recommend counseling before the couple goes ahead with the marriage. Christians have a special responsibility to share the process of growth in their faith.

1 Peter 3:8–12
Relationships with Others

The reference to wives as coreligionists and to shared prayer in 1 Peter 3:7 provides a transition to a passage on communal concord addressed to all members of the Christian community. The opening, "and finally," suggests that 1 Peter considers this passage to be the conclusion to a section of the letter. The quotation from Ps. 34:12–16 in verses 10–12 also provides a transition to the next section, which expands the discussion of suffering. The themes in verses 8–9 appear in a different order in Rom. 12:9–18 (Goppelt, 224). Verse 8 consists of a list of virtues characteristic of a community that calls itself a "brotherhood"—love, compassion, humility. This list concludes with the exhortation to nonretaliation. Verbal harassment that is answered with a blessing (cf. 1 Cor. 4:12; Luke 6:28a) will receive a blessing from God. (First Peter 2:23 made this point in its description of Christ's suffering). The virtues listed in verse 8 may also be applied to how Christians speak with others. The psalm text begins with the requirement to control the tongue, moves to a list of verses that refer to seeking peace, and concludes with a promise about the prayer of those who do good. They can be confident that the Lord listens.

The psalm text explains how 1 Peter 3:7 understands the unusual expression "that your prayers may not be hindered." Those who do not live as God intends cannot expect God to attend to their prayers. In contemporary American society, restraints imposed on speech generate intense conflict. Verbal attacks that fall under the category "discrimination," "racial or sexual harassment" and the like are punished with increasing severity. Most other forms of speech are losing even the formal restraints of respect and courtesy that would have been standard several decades ago. Older members of the church think that I should use "Dr." before my name at the end of my weekly column. To younger people that would be an assertion of authority as though I were telling them what to believe rather than sharing reflections on a common faith. In a more serious situation, we are learning from those devoted to nonviolence that appropriate speech is often the best way to deal with a potentially violent situation. The suggestion to respond with a "blessing" need not mean that we suddenly spout prayers. It could mean quiet words of respect, sympathy, or even disagreement. The psalm text presents a challenge. It suggests that God hears not only how we pray but also how we speak to others.

Do Not Fear Suffering

1 PETER 3:13—4:19

The strong internal relationships that 1 Peter 3:8–12 depicts were particularly important for a church facing external pressure (Goppelt, 228). The reference to God's rejection of the "wicked" in verse 12 provides the transition from community interactions and the difficulties posed by external harassment. God's care for the righteous should relieve believers of the fear caused by outsiders. This distinction between the righteous and the wicked in God's eyes can be read as a universal principle as in the wisdom traditions. It could also take on an eschatological coloring. The distinction will be applied at the judgment. The discussion of suffering in this section moves from general examples of suffering to an eschatological description of the situation as the "fiery ordeal" of the last days (4:12). Other themes already sounded in the letter reappear in this section. Those who are innocent will shame their persecutors. Christians look to the suffering of Christ as an example. They should remember that baptism meant a regeneration of their moral lives. Relationships within the community have a heightened significance for those facing the trials of the end time.

1 Peter 3:13–17
The Righteous Accept Unmerited Suffering

This section begins with an apparent paradox, "who is there to harm you if you are zealous for what is right?" (v. 13). The stock exhortation to civic loyalty held that the emperor's agents were to punish wrongdoers and praise those who do right (2:14). Believers know that they can be falsely accused as wrongdoers (2:11–12). Slaves may face physical abuse (2:20). The injunction to prefer suffering for doing right rather than be punished for wrongdoing that was originally addressed to the slaves reappears in general form at the conclusion of this section (v. 17). The next verse echoes the beatitude on those who suffer for righteousness (v. 14; cf. Matt. 5:10). The "harm" described in this section appears to be the fear and anxiety caused by verbal attacks (v. 14b). First Peter proposes the remedy for both the anxiety caused and for the verbal confrontation: for the heart, Christians reverence Christ, the Lord (v. 15a); for the verbal confrontation, the gentle answer that defends the Christian hope that shapes a believer's life (v. 15b). This response resembles the earlier exhortation to return blessings for curses (v. 9).

Verses 14b–15a use the words of Isa. 8:12–13 LXX to formulate the advice to replace fear with reverence for the Lord. By inserting "Christ" before "Lord" in the Isaiah text, 1 Peter demonstrates the Christian meaning of the prophets (1:10–11). Verses 15b–16 turn from general statements to the concrete experiences of the readers. They must be ready to make a defense (Gr. *apologia*). The Greek term can be used of a defense made in a legal proceeding. Since the passage does not refer to legal charges, 1 Peter must be using the term as a general expression for responding to any demand for an explanation of the "hope" that Christians possess. Earlier in the letter, the "lifestyle" of Christians was the primary form of witness to others (2:15; 3:1–2). Now a verbal response includes more than a blessing, it engages the outsider in a conversation. The apology must do more than "explain." Its ultimate goal must be conversion of the other party. Two adjectives describe the demeanor of the individual who makes such a defense, "humility" or "gentleness," and "fear," that is, "reverence." Since the Isaiah citation encouraged the faithful not to fear (v. 14b), some interpreters presume that these adjectives describe a Christian's attitude before God (see Michaels). However, these adjectives are suited to the situation of alien residents who must take care not to offend a local populace. Though enemies should not cause fear and distress to believers, they must exhibit "fearful" and "humble" behavior in such situations.

Throughout the letter, 1 Peter reminds readers that they cannot provide others with any legitimate reason for hostility. In the instruction to slaves (2:19), the Christian's "conscience before God" testifies that the punishment is unjust. Here, the conscience of the believer has an eschatological function. Those who harass the faithful will be "put to shame," that is, they will be condemned at the judgment. The images of legal defense and "conscience" as testimony to an individual's life refer to the setting of the heavenly court. This suffering does not undermine God's love for believers, since it occurs according to God's will. In this instance, opponents are not converted by the Christian's behavior or words. That possibility should not keep believers from testifying to their faith when challenged.

Many adults today are inarticulate when asked to explain their Christian faith. If a challenger is not silenced by a few Bible verses or religious phrases, people will shrug and change the topic. Such reactions would hardly serve as a "defense" of the faith. One ABC News reporter said during an interview that people are quite willing to reveal the most intimate details of their sexual lives, but most mainline church members have nothing to say about their religion. First Peter indicates that all believers, not only clergy and theologians, should be able to give an account of what they believe.

1 Peter 3:18–22
Christ's Suffering Made the Unrighteous Holy

The example of Christ as suffering servant once again reminds readers that their present difficulties are trivial compared to what Christ has done for them. The passage itself appears to have been composed of a series of creedal formulas describing the death of Christ (v. 18); a legend about the "spirits" at the time of the flood (vv. 19–20); an application of the flood story to Christian baptism (v. 21); and a creedal formula depicting the resurrection as Christ's exaltation to the right hand of God (v. 22). The opening and closing formulas fit the "two-membered" formula depicting Christ's death and resurrection found in the Pauline letters (18a, 22; cf. Rom. 4:25). The contrast, "dead to the flesh, alive to the Spirit" (v. 18b), depicts the new life of the Christian in Rom. 8:6. The Spirit is identified as the Spirit operative in raising Jesus from the dead (Rom. 8:11). The final exaltation formula echoes common early Christian motifs (Ps. 110:1; Rom. 8:34; Ps. 8:7; Heb. 2:5–9).

These formulas would be sufficient to establish the motif of the suffering righteous person. The standard pattern for depicting the suffering righteous (cf. Wisd. Sol. 2—5) concludes with exaltation to divine glory. Those who are righteous have been made so by Christ's death for sin (v. 18; cf. Rom. 3:24–26). The legend about "preaching to the spirits" (vv. 19–20), together with its application to baptism (v. 21), is awkwardly inserted into that context. The word "spirit" connects the statement about the resurrection, "made alive in the spirit" (v. 19a), to the statement that Christ preached to the "spirits in prison" (v. 19b). The sequence—death, "made alive," "preached to the spirits in prison," exaltation—suggests that the legend concerned the period between Jesus' death on the cross and Easter.

The New Testament contains two other examples in which Christ's death and resurrection are associated with "the spirits." Matthew 27:52–53 has many of the righteous raised at the moment Jesus dies and then appear around Jerusalem on Easter. The opening of the tombs reflects Ezekiel's prophecy concerning the dry bones (Ezek. 37:12–13). The phrase "made alive in the Spirit" echoes the process of resurrecting the bones in Ezek. 37:5b–6, "I will give my Spirit to you and you will live." Ephesians 4:8–10 associates the ascent into the heavens with taking a host of captives (Ps. 68:9). Ephesians explains that Christ had first descended into the earth. In both cases, the "spirits" who are freed at the death and resurrection of Christ are the righteous. First Peter 4:19 appears to be a formulaic variant of that tradition. First Peter confuses the sequence by providing a different interpretation of the "spirits." They are "disobedient" and are connected with the time of the flood. The legend of Gen. 6:2 concerning the angels who mated with human women and who were responsible for corrupting the human race had undergone considerable elaboration by the first century (cf. *1 Enoch* 6—19; *T. Reuben* 5:2; see Dalton). Jude 6 and 2 Peter 2:9 allude to the tradition of the imprisonment of these angels. Gnostic mythology considers them to be the cosmic powers that keep humankind imprisoned. The Savior's triumphant ascent destroys the foundation of their rule.

First Peter appears to think of the "spirits" as humans rather than as fallen angels, since they are described as those who once were disobedient, when the Lord was patient during the time of Noah (Goppelt). Divine patience typically refers to a delay in the punishment that sin deserves (cf. Rom. 3:24–26). As an example applied to the Gentiles who were completely cut off from God prior to their conversion, patience refers to God's tolerance of their former ignorance (cf. Acts 17:30–31). Rather than exploit the common parallel between the flood and divine judgment (2 Peter 2:4–5), 1 Peter exploits a different typology, the flood refers to the waters of baptism (v. 21). The typology was popular in the early church. This text appears in the lectionary cycle of Year B for the First Sunday in Lent. In Roman Catholic churches, catechumens who will be baptized and received into the church during the Easter Vigil begin a period of intense preparation. The application makes the "disobedient" recipients of Christ's preaching analogous to the Gentiles in 1 Peter's day (Michaels). Some continue to be disobedient, but the persecuted believers belong to the small group who have been rescued from the flood.

The explanation returns to the theme of conscience. The echoes of judgment remain in the background as they did in verse 16. Josephus explained John the Baptist's baptism to his audience as moral renewal, not physical cleansing (Josephus, *Antiquities* 18.117). The contrast between a Christian conscience that has been cleansed of sin and that of nonbelievers plays an important role in the argument of Hebrews (9:9, 14; 10:2, 22). There the sacrifice of Christ, unlike those in the law, guarantees a pure conscience. Hebrews 10:22 parallels the bodies washed in baptism and the consciences purified by sprinkling. Exhortations to "good conscience" appear in the pastoral epistles (cf. 1 Tim. 1:5, 19; 3:9), while false teachers are said to have corrupted consciences (1 Tim. 4:2; Titus 1:15). First Peter 3:16 reminded readers that their clear conscience implies that persecutors will be shamed, an indirect reference to God's judgment. Similarly, the "good conscience" in this passage looks toward judgment. Baptism does not create such a conscience irrevocably. God finally determines what a person's "conscience" is. Verse 21 speaks of baptism as an "appeal" (NRSV) (Gr. *eperōtēma*) to God of a good conscience. This expression echoes the psalm text of 3:12. God listens to the righteous, not the wicked. Since the exaltation of Christ and subjection of the powers (v. 22; Ps. 8:7b; 110:1; Phil. 2:10) signals the coming judgment and vindication of the faithful, the "appeal" may refer to the conscience that comes before God in judgment. People do not create their own "clear conscience" but receive it as God's gift. They are the "unrighteous" for whom Christ died (v. 18). At the same time, 1 Peter has consistently reminded its audience that their conduct must conform to the baptismal renewal they have experienced. The concluding vision of Christ exalted as Lord over the powers should inspire the reverence that is to guide the believer's lifestyle (v. 15).

As an introduction to the season of Lent, this passage echoes dramatic highlights in the story of salvation. The passion, resurrection, and exaltation of Christ demonstrate God's triumph over the powers of the universe. The cosmic reach of that salvation extends back to beginnings of humankind at the time of the flood. As Christians use the time of fasting and penance during Lent to renew their lives, they should remember God's grace that was given to them in baptism. First Peter also reminds believers that their hope extends beyond this life to reunion with the heavenly Lord, whom they do not yet see (1:8).

1 Peter 4:1–6
Suffering Is Preferable to Past Immorality

Having reminded readers that they must come to God with a pure conscience, 1 Peter returns to the situation in which the readers find themselves. Imitation of Christ's suffering should inspire their willingness to overcome passions (vv. 1–2; cf. 1:14; 2:11). The general introduction (vv. 1–2) is phrased awkwardly. Mindful of the physical suffering that Christ endured, the audience is to "be armed" with the same thought. The image of armor suggests conflict with demonic powers, a motif that returns in 5:9. In this context, the attack is mounted by human passions. Readers have already been reminded of their dangerous hostility to the soul (2:11). Elsewhere virtues serve to arm the believer against loss of their salvation (Eph. 6:13–16; 1 Thess. 5:8–9). In the Old Testament, God takes up this armor to oppose the wicked (Isa. 59:17; Wisd. Sol. 5:18). Philosophical exhortation depicts the philosopher as one who launches an attack against the souls of the ignorant (Malherbe, 1986, 59). In this case, the armor is provided by having the same "thought" (Gr. *ennoia;* v. 1). The term may be intended in its philosophical sense of insight or wisdom. The following clause states the content of this wisdom, "whoever has suffered in the flesh has ceased from sin" (v. 1b). The sentence continues in verse 2 by applying the general expression to the conduct of Christians: live according to the will of God, not human passions.

The maxim in verse 1b is awkwardly juxtaposed with the opening reference to Christ's suffering in the flesh, since it might appear to state that Christ had once been "in sin" prior to his suffering. The earlier use of suffering servant imagery makes it clear that 1 Peter does not intend to depict Christ as sinner. He is the righteous one who died for the unrighteous (3:18). Christ's "suffering," that is, his death, frees believers from their previous life of sin. First Peter uses the expression "suffer" in 3:18 to refer to the death of Christ. Therefore, the maxim could be rendered, "one who has died, has ceased from sin." Just as 1 Peter 3:18–19 moves from the death of Christ to the baptismal renewal of Christians (v. 21), so this passage repeats that transition. Believers, mindful of Christ's suffering, will live the rest of their lives according to God's will. (The baptismal language in Rom. 6:2–14 employs a similar juxtaposition of baptism as participation in the death of Christ and new life free from sin.)

The "before" and "after" language of conversion appears more concretely in verses 3–5. Since 1 Peter treats its audience as the people of God, outsiders are designated "Gentiles" (v. 3). A list of vices points out vices typically associated with idolatry in Jewish texts. Philosophical appeals for conversion also dramatize conversion to a life of virtue by depicting the drunken, dissolute youth who is transformed by the philosopher's wisdom (Malherbe 1986, 56). The descriptions of a past life of drunken licentiousness should not be taken as evidence for the particular vices that the audience had abandoned. They are part of the stock language of conversion stories. Such stories also include the surprised reaction of an individual's former companions (v. 4). However, the note that former associates now abuse (literally: "blaspheme") believers echoes the persistent theme of harassment. Again, new converts to philosophy might expect mockery from former associates. First Peter has returned to the trials of verbal harassment so frequently that the motif cannot be merely a stock theme. This variation on the theme makes the element of judgment that we have found in the background of earlier passages quite explicit. Persecutors will answer to God (v. 5).

The parenthetical explanation in verse 6 seems to refer back to 3:19, Christ's preaching among the spirits. Michaels attempts to avoid the implication that the gospel is being preached to persons who died prior to the coming of Christ by reading "the dead" as a reference to persons who had heard the preaching of the gospel and since died (p. 238). Verse 5 stated that persecutors must face the one who is "ready to judge the living and the dead." The most natural reading of the phrase would not limit "the dead" to any particular group. Consequently, the conventional view that the explanation is intended to explain how universal judgment occurs remains the most persuasive. Admittedly, the logic of this section remains murky. The phrases *kata anthrōpous* ("according to humans"; "like men," RSV; "by human desires," NRSV) and *kata theon* ("according to God"; "like God," RSV; "by the will of God," NRSV) mark a contrast between two standards of judgment. They are attached to separate modes of existence: to be "judged in the flesh" and to "live in the spirit." We have seen that 1 Peter used "suffer in the flesh" in verse 1 to refer to death. Therefore the simplest explanation of this cryptic expression appears to be that even those who were only subject to human standards during their lifetime are subject to divine judgment. The contrast between human and divine evaluation of the lives of the righteous and the wicked in Wisd. Sol. 3 might have influenced this formulation.

Condemnation of the persecutor forms a fixed element in the stories of righteous sufferers or martyrs. Divine judgment has to demonstrate the merit of fidelity to the Torah. In 2 Macc. 7:14 the martyr dies confident that human judgments will be reversed when God raises him to new life. The wicked have no such hope. Though verse 5 promised condemnation of those who blaspheme its audience, verse 6 may have been formulated to encourage believers. First Peter is restrained in its application of judgment imagery to the experiences of the audience. The contrast with the speeches of the martyrs in 2 Maccabees is striking. Second Maccabees highlights the divine punishment that will strike down the persecutor. First Peter does not provide its readers an opportunity to dwell on the condemnation of unbelievers. Christians still live among those who are harassing them. Their responses to verbal abuse may still lead others to convert. The primary function of references to divine judgment is to confirm the faith of the audience so that it will not be shaken by hostility.

1 Peter 4:7–11
Relationships within the Community

Because the end is near, Christians must strengthen the elements of communal life that characterize the people of God. Prayer, mutual love, hospitality, and the ministries of prophecy and service (vv. 7b–11a) describe the activities of the household of believers. The love command (v. 8; cf. 2:17) governs the other relationships between believers (v. 8). The explanation for the priority of love, "love covers a multitude of sins," is proverbial.

It appears in the Hebrew text of Prov. 10:12b, though not in the Septuagint. Mutual love reflects the purity of the newborn Christians (1:22). To "cover" sins suggests that they will not be brought before God at the judgment. The concluding doxology (v. 11b) would ordinarily mark the conclusion of a major section in a letter. However, 1 Peter has already reminded readers that their goal is a share in the glory of God (1:21). When directed toward outsiders, Christian conduct hopes to bring them to glorify God (2:12).

The activities of prophecy and ministry referred to in verses 10–11a are directed toward fellow-Christians, not toward unbelievers (Michaels). Since the prayer and speech described take place in the setting of communal worship, the doxology exemplifies the liturgical context for this exhortation. Some commentators have suggested parallels between the exhortation in verses 7–9 and the preceding depiction of the suffering righteous (T. Martin, 236–40; who begins the new section with v. 7b). Those who are "sane and sober" in order to pray (v. 7) have left behind the drunken carousing of their pagan past (v. 3). Similarly the virtues of mutual love and uncomplaining hospitality, that is, "love of the stranger," contrast with the abuse Christians suffer when they refuse to join in the "wild profligacy" of their former associates. The description of service within the community employs a familiar metaphor, that of good stewards (Luke 12:42; 1 Cor. 4:1, as a description of the apostle). Since some of the addressees were household slaves (2:18), the term "steward" may have carried important overtones. A slave who was the master's "steward" in the household exercised authority over the others. An *oikonomos* ("steward") might also be the manager of a business or serve as the disbursing agent for public funds. The majority of persons designated as *oikonomoi* in inscriptions are either slaves or freedmen (D. Martin, 16f.). The designation showed that the individual was an important person.

In this section of 1 Peter the wealth of the Christian household consists in gifts given by God. The author suggests that they are diverse and given to many members of the community. The term *oikonomos* does not refer to a limited group of "officials." For those who are household slaves subject to abusive masters, this image is a sign of new status within the Christian household. There is more at stake in this section than transforming vicious habits into the virtues of a Christian.

There is more at stake than simply enduring suffering until God's judgment rights the injustice. The Christian community provides new relationships that break apart the abusive hierarchy of power and the fellowship in passion-driven excess that its audience knew from bitter experience. Many Christians read these verses as though they only referred to individual conversion and virtues practiced by each person as an individual. The biblical vision of salvation focuses on the community, the people of God, rather than on isolated individuals. Passages like this one remind Christians today that faith requires community. Believers should be active members of local churches that are gathered for prayer, for mutual support, for celebration. They are also reminded that local churches should be places in which all members of the church share the particular gifts that God has given them.

1 Peter 4:12–19
Rejoice in the Time of Trial

First Peter returns to the trials that Christians suffer once again. The term *peirasmos* ("trial") was introduced in the blessing that opened the letter (1:6). The term has not been used to describe the various sufferings endured by Christians earlier in the letter. Now that 1 Peter has begun to describe the experience of Christians as evidence for the approaching end time, the opposition faced by Christians is described as "a fiery trial" (NRSV: "ordeal"). As in the opening section, readers are reminded that these trials prove the worth of their faith (1:7). The second half of the letter developed the example of Christ, the suffering righteous one as a model for the faithful. Readers are reminded that those who share in the suffering of Christ also participate in his glory. First Peter 4:13–14 describes that participation from two perspectives. The eschatological point of view anticipates the glory that the righteous enjoy when Christ is revealed as judge (v. 13; cf. 1:7–8; 3:21–22). The present experience of Christian suffering also contains elements of glory. First Peter 4:14b expands the beatitude on those who suffer for Christ's sake (14a; 3:14) with a statement of the consequence such as we find in the Synoptic beatitudes (cf. Luke

6:22): the Spirit rests on such persons. The formula "spirit of glory and of God" has added the phrase "of glory" to Isa. 11:2a LXX. That somewhat awkward expression indicates that the sufferer already possesses something of the glory that is to be revealed with Christ.

As in the earlier examples, 1 Peter immediately qualifies the statement about suffering to exclude those who are not suffering "for Christ." Persons who are being punished for evil they have done cannot treat their suffering as a sign of glory (vv. 15–16; 2:20; 3:16). The list of evildoers reflects stock examples arranged in descending order. The expression *allotriepiskopos,* which the NRSV translates "mischief-maker," is not attested elsewhere. It may be the author's neologism for a "busybody" (Gr. *polypragmōn*) or "meddler" (Gr. *periergos*) from the expression for "other people's affairs," *allotria,* and the word *episkopos* (Michaels). Such persons are generally condemned in Greco-Roman moralists (Plutarch, *Moralia* 516E–517A). Cynic philosophers claimed that it was their duty to meddle in the affairs of others, since they are acting as physicians for the soul (Epictetus, *Discourses* III 22, 97; Balch 1981, 93).

Like the injunctions to live quietly in the Pauline letters (1 Thess. 4:11; 2 Thess. 3:11), the warning not to meddle in the affairs of others could be taken as a way of avoiding conflict with a suspicious society. Unlike the first three items in the list, murderer, thief, evildoer, some might think that they had a cynic-like responsibility to challenge the folly and vice of others. The peculiar word suggests that 1 Peter may have intentionally added this particular expression to the stock list because it expressed a real problem for the community. Verse 16 contrasts those who can be tagged as evildoers or busybodies with the one who suffers "as *christianos.*" The only other two examples of the expression appear in Acts (11:26; 26:28). The term is always used by outsiders. Acts 11:26 notes that believers were first called "Christians" in Antioch. Agrippa uses the expression in Acts 26:28. Therefore, the expression in 1 Peter 4:16 probably represents what outsiders called the addressees. It must have been intended as a term of ridicule or contempt. Since outsiders had an expression for members of the movement, they are clearly distinguishable from "Jews" and are recognized as an established group. The correspondence between Pliny and Trajan (c.110 C.E.) established that the mere name "Christian" was not criminal. First Peter 4:16 encourages readers not to be ashamed but to glorify God when they suffer because of that name.

The final verses turn the issue of judgment away from outsiders to the community itself. God will judge the chosen people, the house of God, before the condemnation of unbelievers. Ezekiel 9:6 depicts executioners going through the city cutting down all the wicked in Israel beginning at the Temple. The messenger of Mal. 3:1 also begins at the Temple. First Peter 2:5–6 used temple imagery to describe the Christian community as God's house in which a holy priesthood would offer spiritual sacrifices to God. Since Christians are the "house of God" the time of judgment will begin there. The rhetorical question that concludes verse 17 reminds readers that the fate of unbelievers will be much worse than any sufferings they might endure. That observation is supported by a citation from Prov. 11:31 LXX. This reminder that the time of judgment is at hand does not lead to condemnation of evildoers in the community. Rather, it supports those who are righteous sufferers. They are reminded that the God to whom they have entrusted their lives is the faithful Creator.

By depicting the sufferings of Christians as their participation in the sufferings of Christ who brought them salvation and of the time of testing before the final judgment, 1 Peter invites readers to recognize their situation as part of a great history of salvation. The first question that anyone faced with suffering asks is "why?" Why should others persecute or harass believers who have done nothing wrong? Many apocalyptic texts explain that the persecutors are embodiments of satanic hatred for everything that belongs to God. First Peter does not exploit early Christian apocalyptic convictions to demonize those who are harassing believers. First Peter has left open the possibility that in some cases persecutors may become believers. Although those who persist in hostility and disbelief will be condemned in the judgment, 1 Peter does not use that apocalyptic scenario to encourage a sharp division between an inner-directed Christian community and outsiders. Baptism has drawn a line between Christians and their former associates when they clash over good behavior. If the church had drawn boundaries that isolated members from contacts with outsiders, slaves and women married to non-Christians would not be able to be part of the community. Even resident or visiting aliens would have difficulty remaining in their cities without contacts with citizens and other patrons.

In order to make the case for Christianity, the author employs the gentle defense, assuming that outsiders must also recognize "doing good" when they see it. As we have seen, 1 Peter does not hesitate to exploit ethical topoi that would have been familiar from popular philosophical exhortation. Christians were not the only ones to recognize that a life driven by random and excessive devotion to the pleasure principle was not truly human. The case for Christianity is exhibited in the behavior of those derided as *christianoi.* They live the virtues that others talk about without being philosophers. This strategy was inherited from Judaism. Those who were sympathetic to Judaism or who had become converts to that tradition acknowledged the virtue of that way of life. Jewish writers like Philo and Josephus depicted the patriarchs and Moses as examples of true wisdom and virtue.

First Peter's concern with the relationships between Christians and the surrounding culture raises an issue that always faces believers. For some who are a minority within a larger society, the letter could be describing their situation exactly. They must support one another within the community of faith that has given each member a special place in the larger people of God. At the same time, they must cope with the tensions generated by their conversion. Some parts of their former way of life must be rejected. In other cases, they continue to live and work among non-Christians. That will mean taking particular care not to merit a "bad name" by some wrong that they have done. Many more Christians have the opposite problem. They are the dominant majority. Two questions face us. First, the issue of cultural criticism. What elements of our lifestyle are an obstacle to the gospel? They may seem so familiar that we accept them without reflection. Second, how do we treat religious and ethnic minorities in our midst? Do we subject them to the same sufferings that these Christians endured? First Peter reminds us that judgment begins with the house of God. For Christians in a dominant culture, the question may not be "Were you among the suffering righteous?" but "Did you cause others to suffer just because of their name?"

Shepherding the Flock of God

1 PETER 5:1–14

Letters often concluded with final instructions, details of future plans, and personal greetings (cf. Rom. 15:14—16:23; 1 Cor. 16:1–24). The sudden transition back to the first-person singular in which the author begins to speak in his own voice marks the concluding section of 1 Peter (5:1). For the first time since the opening of the letter (1:1), biographical details link the instruction in the letter to the figure of Peter. Peter was remembered as the shepherd to whom Jesus had entrusted the flock (v. 2; John 21:15–17). He had suffered for the Lord (v. 1; John 21:18–19), and according to later tradition, he had been martyred at Rome (= Babylon, v. 13). Paul had also died there, and two familiar figures from the Pauline mission, Silvanus and Mark, appear in the final greetings (vv. 12–13). Despite these details, which establish the identity of the voice behind the exhortation in the body of the letter, no concrete information about the sender or addressees emerges. Since Peter is not referred to as a presbyter or elder elsewhere in the tradition, some exegetes think that a slip of the pen has revealed the actual author to be a presbyter of the Roman church. Even so, the conclusion provides no names or other details about the addressees in Asia Minor.

The final words of encouragement continue to alternate emphasis on communal relationships with advice on living through the end-time sufferings. New elements are introduced in each section. For the first time, 1 Peter speaks to persons in charge of the local churches about their ministry. Earlier descriptions of worship and ministry were addressed to all members of the church without distinction. Beginning with the apostle Peter himself, the range of suffering Christianity has been extended beyond the churches of Asia Minor and Jesus. Christians everywhere are undergoing the same suffering. Therefore the situation that those in Asia Minor face must be part of God's universal plan of salvation. Since the reference to

Peter's participation in the sufferings of Christ is indirect, one cannot tell if the letter came to Asia Minor along with the news that the apostles, Peter and Paul, had been martyred. If so, the letter may have been received there with the particular authority attached to the final instruction of a hero who was about to die. Certainly, the recipients cannot brush off the letter's advice with the assumption that the author has nothing to say about their situation.

1 Peter 5:1–7
Humility Governs All Relationships

Deciding where the advice to the community ends and concern with external relationships begins is difficult. The advice to "humble yourselves" (v. 6) could be taken as a repetition of the household code (2:18). Since the household code material was directed toward outsiders some prefer to divide the section after verse 5. However, the advice to humble oneself is not directed toward human authorities in this section. Verses 6–7 enunciate theological maxims about one's relationship to God. The sentence is linked to the previous verse by the word "humble." Both the leaders of the church and those under their authority must be humble and trust in God if they expect to attain the glory that is promised to them.

1. Elders, Be Examples (5:1–4)

Since the previous section warned readers that judgment was beginning with the house of God, the turn toward those responsible for the church follows naturally (Michaels). Elders appear as leaders of the local church in Acts (14:23; 20:17–38) and the pastoral epistles (1 Tim. 5:1–2, 17, 19; Titus 1:5). Titus 1:5 refers to installing presbyters in the cities of Crete who will reflect the model of Paul and Titus. First Peter presumes that presbyters exist in the churches of Asia Minor. However, they are encouraged to remember the apostolic witness. References to the glory that will be revealed with Christ (vv. 1, 4) as well as the description of their ministry as shepherding the flock (vv. 2–4) show that Peter is the example for the elders. Paul refers to the "imperishable crown" as the goal of his apostolic ministry (1 Cor. 9:25). His congregations are the "crown" that he expects to receive (Phil. 4:1; 1 Thess. 2:19). The "crown of glory" promised faithful presbyters (v. 4) might simply refer to the eschatological reward expected by all Christians (Rev. 2:10; 3:11). However, Peter is presented as "a partaker in the glory that is to be revealed" (v. 1). The Pauline use of "crown" as a particular expression for the fruit of apostolic ministry may be intended here. Those who have been faithful shepherds will receive the special reward that Peter has already attained. A similar concept of a special place in the end time for those who teach the people to remain faithful to the Lord appears in Dan. 12:3. They are exalted to heavenly glory, where they shine like stars.

The conduct required of those who care for the flock is briefly stated in verses 2–3. Second Corinthians 9:7 applies the distinction between willing and unwilling service to the question of giving for the poor. Only what is done willingly pleases God. Paul used that argument to explain why he did not charge for preaching the gospel (1 Cor. 9:16–17). Other dangers attendant on the position of leadership, greed and domineering behavior, are also noted. The Pastorals warn against choosing as deacons (1 Tim. 3:8) or bishops (Titus 1:7) persons who are greedy. In a hierarchical society, persons who held authority in a religious group might well copy the style of other authorities (Mark 10:42–43). The household codes indicate that Christians were familiar enough with domineering authorities, masters, and husbands. Christian leaders must set a different example for the believers. Paul (Phil. 3:17; 2 Thess. 3:9), Timothy (1 Tim. 4:12), and Titus (Titus 2:7) were held up to Christians as examples of the virtues embodied in their teaching. Philosophical exhortation also expected the philosopher to be a living example of his teaching. The exhortation to elders in these verses is conventional wisdom. The ultimate example for both the author and his readers is Christ, the chief shepherd.

These verses pose a challenge to anyone who undertakes to minister in the name of Christ. Most clergy and lay church workers will never get rich in ministry. The warnings about greed often draw mild laughter from seminarians. Yet clergy who live in poor urban parishes often point to other churches in the same area served by ministers who live in the suburbs, drive late model cars and wear expensive clothes. When those ministers appear on TV as experts on the problems of the urban poor, those who actually live with the poor are incensed. The larger question posed by the passage concerns the way in which ministers are expected to be examples for the rest of the community. The burden that such expectations place on ministers and their families are familiar to us all. It is easy to feel that others should not expect clergy to be better than the rest of the community. On the other hand, we are quite willing to insist that sports figures and others idolized by young people ought to provide examples for them. Certainly all members of the community seek the holiness described in the opening of 1 Peter. While ministers may not be saints, they can model the effort of Christian living for others. We all learn from watching others as much as we learn from books, sermons, and lectures. Some things can only be learned by watching and doing. Probably our most important images of Christian discipleship are embodied in people we have known. Ministers are not asked to act the part of a holiness that they do not possess. They can show others ways in which they struggle to put Christ at the center of their lives.

2. Defer to Those Who Shepherd the Flock (5:5)

The exhortation to defer to the elders (2:18; 3:1) begins as though it were part of a household code. However, it continues with a general exhortation to humility on both sides (cf. 3:8). A quotation from Prov. 3:34 LXX supports the advice. Ordinarily, the "elder" and "younger" pair would make the opening a piece of advice to those who are actually younger in relationship to their elders. However, as 1 Tim. 4:12 indicates, leaders in the local churches were not necessarily chronologically older than others in the community. *First Clement* sought to resolve a conflict that broke out in Corinth when a group of younger people displaced the older presbyters of the community (*1 Clem.* 3.3; 44.3–6; 47.6). It is not clear what 1 Peter 5:5 means by the "younger." Does he mean a particular group within the community, those who are more recent converts? Or does the expression encompass all those in the church who are not presbyters? The exhortation to mutual humility suggests that the pair elder/younger must embrace the whole community.

Humility moderates the hierarchical exercise of authority implied in the subjection of younger to elder. In churches today a different model of egalitarian responsibility and mutual support makes more sense to believers than the language of subordination and humility. In any case, the message is clear. Churches are not to be a chaotic free-for-all. Those who are charged with public care for the church do deserve respect. However, that respect does not mean that church leaders can exalt themselves. God cares for the humble, not the proud.

3. Show Humility to Each Person (5:6–7)

Further sayings on humility reinforce the citation from Prov. 3:34. Humility is not humiliation in human terms. Rather humility describes the position of every human being before God. The eventual goal of this humility is the final exaltation experienced by the faithful. This pattern of humility and subsequent exaltation reminds readers of the initial example of Christ (1:6–7). The few hints about the socioeconomic status of the audience that we can find in 1 Peter suggest that all those addressed are from the lower ranks of society. Resident aliens would have to exhibit humility before patrons and other citizens on many occasions. The promise that humble believers will be exalted should moderate the tensions inherent in their daily lives.

The exhortation to trust in God also reminds readers that Christian life continues to be difficult. The imperative "throw your anxiety on the Lord" echoes Ps. 55:22. Sayings of Jesus also encouraged believers not to be anxious (e.g., Luke 12:11, 22–32). The idea that God exercises universal care over all things was commonplace in Jewish circles (e.g., Wisd. Sol. 12:13; Philo, *Flaccus* 102; Josephus, *Antiquities* 7.54). In that context, universal providence belonged to the understanding of God as Creator. First Peter has a more practical concern. Christians must be assured that their suffering has not escaped God's notice (Michaels).

1 Peter 5:8–11
Resist the Devil and God Will Reward Your Suffering

The exhortation concludes with a final eschatological note. The apocalyptic overtones associated with the conviction that the time of judgment is beginning emerges with the injunction to "resist the devil" (vv. 8–9). Other New Testament passages contain more elaborate use of the imagery of Christians locked in combat against Satan (Eph. 6:10–17; 1 Thess. 5:6–8). The trials that Christians are experiencing throughout the world are evidence of a satanic desire to undermine the righteous. Ravenous lions are a common image of affliction (cf. Ps. 22:13). The end-time evils would be so difficult that even the righteous could not survive without God's assistance (cf. Mark 13:12–20). The conclusion to the Lord's Prayer asks that believers not be subjected to the trials of the end time and that they be delivered from the Evil One (Matt. 6:13). Neither the Lord's Prayer nor this passage of 1 Peter demands the full scenario of apocalyptic judgment to be effective. This passage in 1 Peter is used in the liturgical Office of Night Prayer. Christians have used it along with the Lord's Prayer for centuries.

In fully developed apocalyptic texts like Revelation, the satanic dimensions of Roman imperial rule demand that Christians refuse to accommodate with any elements of that order (e.g., Revelation 13). First Peter has no hostility toward Roman rule. Its attitude toward the larger society is mixed. The sufferings that Christians endure were caused by random individual attacks against them. There is no evidence of a single anti-Christian policy. However, the author underlines the solidarity between Christians in Asia Minor and those in Rome. Christians everywhere experience the sufferings of the end time. For 1 Peter the universality of suffering does not serve to demonstrate a growing evil in the world. Nor is the apocalyptic image of Satan seeking to destroy the righteous evidence that the world cannot last much longer.

The author's primary concern is consolation. The churches in Asia Minor can take comfort in the knowledge that others share the same suffering with them. They are reassured that whatever they experience now, the goal is not destruction but glory. Christians can face their life without fear because God supports and strengthens the faithful. Christians who have used this passage in Night Prayer recognize its power to evoke the saving, sustaining power of God.

1 Peter 5:12–14
Final Greeting

The final greeting fits the formal pattern characteristic of ancient letters. Verse 12 commends Silvanus through whom the author has transmitted the letter. He may have been responsible for delivering the letter to Asia Minor (as in Acts 15:23). As we have seen, both Silvanus and Mark were associated with the Pauline mission. Later traditions concerning the author of the Gospel of Mark may be related to the notice in this letter that Mark was a close associate of Peter in Rome. The relative status of the two associates is indicated by the expressions "faithful brother" for Silvanus and "my son" for Mark. Both have antecedents in the Pauline letter tradition. Some prominent Christians, like Sosthenes (1 Cor. 1:1), and apostles, like Apollos (1 Cor. 16:12), are referred to as "brother." Timothy and Titus, who were subordinate to Paul, are referred to as "my brother" (2 Cor. 1:1; 2:13; 1 Thess. 3:2; Philemon 1), as are "fellow-workers" like Epaphroditus (Phil. 2:25). The term "child" (Gr. *teknon*) is used for Timothy and Titus in the pastorals (1 Tim. 1:2, 18; 2 Tim. 1:2; Titus 1:4). Paul himself used that designation for the slave whom he converted in prison (Philemon 10). When the pastorals shift from Paul's use of "brother" to the expression "child" in addressing Timothy and Titus, they make the recipients successors to the apostle. They are entrusted with his final words. First Peter 5:13 projects a similar relationship between Peter and Mark.

Since 1 Peter uses the symbolic name "Babylon" to refer to Rome (cf. Rev. 14:8; 18:2), he and his associates become the primary example of a church in exile. This designation throws the opening reference to its addressees in the "Diaspora" into a different light. Ordinarily, a letter to those in the Diaspora would have to come from Jerusalem (as in Acts 15:22–29). Here the political center of the empire that controls the provinces of Asia Minor is also the epitome of a place of exile. Since the author shares the situation of his addressees, they can be confident in his advice. This warm greeting also reminds readers today of their responsibility to other churches around the world. No church that remains isolated in local or even national boundaries incarnates the vision left by the apostles. Christians must reach out to their brothers and sisters around the world with the same love and support demonstrated in this letter. The sufferings of Christians in distant regions of Asia Minor were acknowledged by their fellow believers in the capital of the empire.

THE BOOK OF

James

Introduction

Authorship

The opening refers to "James, a servant of God and of the Lord Jesus Christ" (v. 1). There are no other references to the author in James. Readers must have been able to identify the author with a familiar figure in early Christianity. The New Testament mentions a number of persons named James: the son of Zebedee (Mark 1:19), the son of Alphaeus (Mark 3:18), the brother of Jesus (Mark 6:3), James, the younger (Mark 15:40), and James, the father of Jude (Luke 6:16). Of that group, only James, the son of Zebedee, and James, the brother of the Lord, could be described as well-known figures. Acts 12:1–2 indicates that James, the son of Zebedee, was martyred by Agrippa I (d. 44 C.E.). Since Paul indicates that James, the brother of the Lord, was one of the leaders in Jerusalem along with Peter and John (Gal. 2:1–14), James, the brother of the Lord, appears to be the individual referred to as the sender of the letter. In Acts 15:13–29, James determines the conditions under which Gentiles can enter the church. This decision is set down in a letter to be circulated among the Gentile Christians of Antioch, Syria, and Cilicia. According to 1 Cor. 15:3–8, James became an apostle when he saw the risen Lord.

Josephus contains a brief notice that refers to the death of James (*Antiquities* 20.200). The high priest, Ananus the younger, executed several persons for transgressing the law during the period between the Roman governors (c.62 C.E.). A much more elaborate story appears in the church historian Eusebius (*History of the Church* 2.23.4–8). That account pictures James as a model of righteousness and devotion to God. His knees are calloused like those of a camel from praying for the sins of the people. James is taken to the pinnacle of the Temple on Passover where he is to deny Jesus. Instead, he confesses Jesus as Son of man and is cast down from there. Since he had not died but was praying for his enemies, James was stoned as he continued to pray for his enemies, and then he was clubbed. Finally, Eusebius's source alleges that Vespasian laid seige to Jerusalem immediately after the execution of James (c. 69 C.E.). The legendary elements in Eusebius's account are obvious. Gnostic writers in the second and third centuries produced several works in which James received true Gnostic teaching from his half brother and wrote down the teaching of the risen Christ secretly for later generations. These examples make it clear that James was the focus of considerable speculation in the earliest centuries.

The reference to James in Jude 1 may be the first example of an attempt to use the apostolic authority established by this letter to support the teaching of a lesser-known figure (Dibelius and Greeven, 12). However, most exegetes recognize that James can hardly be traced back to the actual brother of the Lord. Its careful, well-schooled Greek style could not have been composed by a Galilean craftsman. Despite the author's emphasis on the necessity of deeds as the logical outcome of faith, the requirements of the law are formulated in Hellenistic Jewish terms. None of the debates over the ritual requirements of the law appear in James. Martin has attempted to defend James's authorship by assuming that earlier material had been edited by a later hand. He then attempts to interpret the letter as though James addressed the turmoil caused by the outbreak of the Jewish revolt against Rome (R. Martin, lxiii–lxix). Though ingenious, the text lacks explicit details that would make such a precise determination of its historical setting probable. Martin's secondary setting, the reworking of James's original text by a Hellenistic Jewish editor in Antioch, provides a more likely account of the origin of the letter as a whole.

The few allusions to teachings of Jesus that can be found in James are closest to Matthew and are largely confined to the Sermon on the Mount. The style of exhortation found in James follows conventions of Hellenistic school rhetoric, such as replies to imaginary interlocutors (diatribe) and the use of rare or elegant terms. Although James follows the pattern of some of the wisdom literature (e.g., Sirach) and has individual units that comprise discussions on particular themes, the repetition of material within the letter as a whole creates a literary unity for the work (Cargal). The author of James appears to have been a Greek-speaking Jewish Christian. Like other Hellenistic Jewish writers, he understands the significance of religion to be worship of God and a commitment to superior moral conduct. His appeal to James, the brother of the Lord, was probably based on the tradition that James had sent a letter to the churches in Syria setting the conditions for admitting Gentiles to the community.

Occasion

Hints about the addressees are as rare as hints about the author. They are described as "the twelve tribes in the Diaspora" (1:1; NRSV: Dispersion) and are said to gather in a synagogue (2:2). The community is guided by elders (5:14). Although "diaspora" could be applied metaphorically to Gentile Christians (1 Peter 1:1), there is no reason to assume that the term is purely metaphorical. James is a general exhortation to a way of life that is in accord with true piety. Since it lacks specific greetings at the conclusion, some interpreters have doubted the appropriateness of referring to James as a letter. The repeated reference to the addressees as "brothers," which divide the text (1:2, 16, 19; 2:1, 5, 14; 3:1; 4:11; 5:7, 12, 19), could be found in a speech of exhortation as well as in a letter. However, the concluding instructions on communal relationships (5:12–20) reflect a common practice of concluding letters with assorted instructions to the addressee.

If James is not merely a general exercise in exhortation, then the clues to its occasion must lie in unusual features of the advice given. The warning against those who think that faith can save those who have no works (2:14–26) suggests that a misunderstood Paulinism might have led to the composition of James. Although there is no evidence that James opposed Pauline theology directly, the "faith/works" pair may have been a slogan taken from Paul. The division between "faith" and "works" found in James differs from that in Paul. Paul speaks of "works of the law." The problem addressed concerns Gentile converts, who are not required to adopt a way of life that would mark them out as being "Jewish." James never uses that expression. The concrete examples of works, such as acceptance of the Ten Commandments and charity toward fellow Christians in need, have an equally strong place in Paul's ethical exhortation (cf. Rom. 13:8–10). However, Paul and James make very different use of the Abraham figure. Paul appeals to Abraham's faith; James to his works (James 2:21–23; Romans 4). If the slogan that "faith saves" created problems in the church, the problems may have been a lack of communal solidarity.

Divisions between rich and poor also caused some difficulties in the community (2:1–13). Since this example appears before the comments about faith and works, concern for the poorer members of the community may have been the primary difficulty that James had in mind. Deference toward the rich and dismissive or scornful treatment of the poor were acceptable attitudes in the larger society. James consistently rejects that position, since God exalts the poor and humbles the rich (1:9–11). Concern for the poor had an important place in the Jerusalem church. Paul states that when the leaders there agreed that Gentile converts did not have to observe the law, they also expected him to take up a collection among the Gentiles for the poor in Jerusalem (Gal. 2:10). Paul spent considerable effort in meeting that obligation (Rom. 15:25–33; 1 Cor. 16:1–4; 2 Cor. 8—9). The early chapters of Acts praise the exemplary sharing among Christians (2:44–45) even though disputes over distribution of alms threatened to divide Hebrew and Greek-speaking Christians from each other (6:1). James does not refer to the concrete situations described in Paul or Acts. Since Christianity challenged the conventional stratification of rich and poor, the topic would continue to be addressed in early Christian exhortation.

Lack of detailed references to the situation in which its ethical advice should be applied makes it impossible to determine the particular occasion that led to the composition of the epistle. Laws notes that even the Jewish Christian character of James should be challenged. The ritual details of Jewish law are nowhere in evidence. Nor is the author familiar with more than the Greek text of the Old Testament. Therefore, she concludes that its author was not a Jewish Christian at all. Rather, she suggests that the author and the churches to which he writes were "God-fearers," Gentiles with a respect for Jewish monotheism and ethics, who had converted to Christianity (Laws,

36–37). This observation correctly identifies the Hellenistic Jewish context of much of the letter but does not explain why its actual author chose to adopt the teaching of the apostle James as his authority. Both as a historical figure and as a figure in later legend, James, the brother of the Lord, is the champion of Jewish Christianity. Evidence from inscriptions and synagogue architecture in the Greco-Roman period shows that one cannot define Judaism by a single criterion. Outsiders generally identified circumcision, Sabbath observance, and dietary laws with Jews. These items are contested in Paul's letters, since they concern Gentile converts. The fact that they do not appear in James tells us nothing about its setting except that such details of practice were not matters of controversy. The concluding verses of the letter suggest that readers are to view its contents as "the truth" to which erring members should be encouraged to return (Cargal).

The apodictic character of the moral exhortation in James often offends modern readers. In James, unlike other epistles in the New Testament, exhortation is never connected to the experience of becoming a Christian, nor to the death and resurrection of Christ, as in 1 Peter. James 2:7 may allude to the invocation of Jesus' name when persons joined the community. For a Jewish Christian audience, the language of conversion, which implies a sharp break between a pre-Christian past and a new Christian life, is hardly appropriate. References to Jesus as "Lord" (1:1; 2:1) show that James assumes that Jesus has been exalted to divine glory. His authority stands behind the teaching of those who are Jesus' servants. If the addressees recognize the passages with parallels in the Sermon on the Mount as words of Jesus, then the letter as a whole may have been perceived as instruction for those who would also be servants of the Lord.

A final difficulty for many readers lies in the repeated reference to the audience as *adelphoi* ("brothers"; RSV: "brethren"). The NRSV has adopted the policy of translating the word *adelphoi* "brothers and sisters." However, when James refers to the obligation to care for the poor in the community, it speaks explicitly of a "brother or sister" who is in need (2:15). This alteration indicates that James uses *adelphos* in the singular as a designation for males. Does he also use the plural in that sense? If so, then the word *anthrōpos* (1:19–20; RSV: "man"; NRSV uses "everyone" in v. 19 and shifts to a second-person "you" in v. 20) may have been intended as a reference to males rather than to human beings in general. All the examples of activities and occupations in the letter were associated with males. The only other reference to a woman is the example of Rahab, the whore (2:25). Much of the wisdom literature to which James can be compared also presumes the androcentric perspective of teachers and male disciples or fathers and sons. James 2:15 shows that women belonged to the community and were recipients of its charity. Were they also recipients of its wisdom? Or does James assume that they will be guided by husbands and male relatives? The complete lack of exhortation addressed to or concerning women suggests that they are not envisaged as recipients of the teaching in James.

However, studies of Jewish inscriptions show that women participated in synagogue life and that some were even described as "elders" in their respective communities (Kraemer). The community James addresses gathers as a synagogue (2:2; NRSV: "assembly") and is led by elders (5:14). Though the readers projected by the epistle do not include women, they may have been present when it was read. Certainly, the exhortation in the letter can be applied to both men and women. The inclusive rendering of James facilitates its application to Christians today.

Theological Themes

James opens with a series of injunctions that identify central themes in the exhortation (1:2–11). Readers should rejoice in trials that will produce endurance (RSV: "steadfastness") and finally perfection (1:2–4). God will give wisdom to those who ask for it without doubting (1:5–6). The status of rich and "lowly" will be reversed (1:9–11). Convictions about God play an important role in James. Humans do not define perfection but receive it as a consequence of their relationship to God. Prayer links human beings to God. The humility that they show toward God redefines human relationships, since God exalts the lowly and humbles the proud. Further instructions about speech seek to order relationships between human beings (1:26).

God

Although James refers to Jesus as Lord, the term "Lord" usually refers to God the Father. The name of Jesus, the Lord, was used in anointing the sick (5:14–15). Otherwise "Lord" means God the Father. Even references to the Parousia of the

Lord (5:7–8) are followed by references to the Lord that clearly refer to the God of the Old Testament (5:10–11). Although most readers today assume that "Parousia of the Lord" refers to the coming of Jesus, the context in James suggests that God is the one whose coming is anticipated. Faith, prayer, and good works are the basis of an individual's relationship to God. James refers to God as "father" (1:17, 27; 3:9). The term indicates God's activity as creator and ruler of the cosmos (1:17). Christians are the first fruits of a new creation that God is bringing into existence (1:18). Believers anticipate God's future gifts of salvation (1:12).

God is the source of the gifts that Christians need to achieve the perfection that God has promised them. Wisdom comes from God (1:5). So does the righteousness that should govern human conduct (1:20). God's holiness requires purity of humans. For James, holiness stems from ethical conduct, not from ritual practices (1:27; 4:4). Without that holiness, the believers' monotheism, which is the basic confession about God, does not differ from the demons' acknowledgment of divine power (2:19). Holiness also presumes that humans worship God (3:9). God favors the lowly and humbles the proud (4:6). Humility indicates that humans acknowledge God as Lord (4:7).

James underlines the unchanging holiness and goodness of God. This emphasis reminds readers of the security of God's promises. The major source of doubt about divine goodness appears to be the "trials" and testing of their faith that believers suffer. James insists that we cannot treat God as the source of testing or temptation because God is the unchanging Creator (1:13–14). The unchanging stability of God contrasts with the variable passions of human beings. Consequently, those who are steadfast while undergoing trials achieve perfection (1:2–4). Similarly, those whose prayers demonstrate a single-hearted trust in God can expect a divine response (1:8). God's perfection provides a model for human behavior.

This emphasis on the unchanging stability of God as the model for those who possess wisdom can be compared with the Stoic vision of the wise. Human vices such as lust and lack of self-control are the sources of evil (cf. Malherbe, 87–88). However, James highlights the significance of God's stability in biblical terms. God is faithful to the promises of salvation and mercy (1:12, 18; 4:8, 10; 5:11). God's concern for the oppressed will bring judgment against their oppressors (5:1–8). Therefore the believer's participation in God's perfection is not demonstrated simply by freedom from the passions. It requires active evidence of a similar concern for the poor and suffering (1:27).

Rich and Poor

The repeated emphasis on God's concern for the poor (1:9–11, 27b; 2:1–7, 14–17; 5:1–6) has been seen as evidence for the situation of James's audience. Although they know what it is like to be subject to the power of the rich (2:6), Christians still fawn over wealthy patrons (2:2–4) and neglect the poor in their own community (2:15–16). A similar division between persons of wealth within the community and "the rich" who appear to be outsiders appears in James 4:13–17: 5:1–6. In the first instance, readers are warned not to be self-confident in the security of their financial activities. They are described as merchant traders. In the second, the rich are landowners who violate the law by defrauding their laborers of wages owed. The merchants are advised to remember the fragility of life. The wealthy landowners are castigated with prophetic threats of judgment. The readers are encouraged to remain patient until the Lord's coming (vv. 7–8). They do not appear to belong to the group that is condemned. However, James 1:9–11 refers to both the lowly Christian and to the rich one. Like the merchants of James 4:13–17, the rich will vanish in the middle of their activities.

The descriptions of rich and poor in James highlight three elements in the relationship between the two groups: honor or dishonor; justice or injustice, and charity or neglect. Two other characteristics of the rich also appear in these passages: their false sense of security and their conspicuous displays of wealth. By exhibiting their wealth in clothing, jewelry, or feasting (2:2; 5:5), the rich were able to elicit expressions of honor from others (2:3). The conviction that wealth provides security made them suppose they were impervious to divine justice (5:3). Even if James's readers were not rich landowners, they were liable to adopt the social ideology surrounding wealth and poverty. Despite the fact that God exalts the humble, they were willing to honor the rich and treat the poor with contempt. They thought that merely acknowledging the poor brother or sister with a greeting was sufficient evidence of pious fellowship. Attention to their need for food or clothing was not necessary (2:15–16).

The obligations of charity for the widow, the orphan, and the poor, and justice in payment of laborers are grounded in the law. The prophets denounced the rich for neglecting the law (Isa. 5:8; Jer. 5:26–28; Amos 5:12; Micah 2:2). No Israelite could claim to be righteous without caring for the poor. Job, whom James describes as a model of steadfastness (5:11) was a model of charity and justice as well (Job 31:16–23, 38–40). Nor did Job place false confidence in wealth (31:24–25). The law requires justice and charity of the rich. Those like Job who met such requirements are entitled to the honor that others give them. James understands the tradition differently. The rich as a class are guilty of amassing their wealth by oppressing their laborers. God's concern for the poor carries with it a corresponding demand that wealthy believers humble themselves. Consequently, exegetes look to postexilic Jewish traditions that celebrated the piety of the "lowly ones" in Israel (e.g., Pss. 86:1–2; 132:15–16; Matt. 5:3; Luke 1:47–54; 6:20; see Dibelius and Greeven). Within this context "the poor" does not refer to the economic status of an individual but to membership in a community of the pious who remain faithful to God despite the adversity caused by the wicked. A similar use of "the poor" appears in some of the Dead Sea Scrolls (e.g., 4QpPs 37:3, 10–11; 1QM 11:8–13; 14:7). The "poor" are God's elect (1QpHab 5:4).

Though James shares the view that God's chosen are the poor and humble, the letter does not use the terms "poor" or "humble" as terms for the members of the community as a whole. The general picture of the lowly as God's elect and the requirement that Christians care for the poor in James resembles the treatment of rich and poor in the teaching of Jesus (so Mussner). However, James does not appeal to Jesus as the basis for its injunctions (contrast 2 Cor. 8:9). They are presented as the will of an unchanging Creator.

Prayer

Prayer plays an important role in both individual and communal life. Those who seek wisdom from God without doubts or wavering will be rewarded (1:5–8). James reminds readers that God is the source of everything good that comes to human beings (1:16; 3:17). Confidence in prayer shows that believers recognize the blessings that they have already received from the Lord. Consequently, petitions are not the only form of prayer. Christians use the power of speech correctly when they bless God, the Creator (3:9). They misuse it when they curse others, who are made in God's image, and indulge in anger or other evils of speech (3:9–10). James 4:4–10 encourages readers to turn away from the passions and desires typical of the world and to "draw near to God" (v. 8). This process of humbling oneself before God (v. 10) suggests some form of penitential prayer.

Another example of humility before God emerges in the admonitions to tradespersons and merchants (4:13–17). They are to substitute recognition of God's will for boasting in their own success. The statement "if the Lord wills, we shall live and we shall do this or that" (4:15) employs a common element in ancient petitionary prayer, namely, recognition that God's will governs all things.

The most concrete examples of prayer come in the concluding instructions (5:13–18). Communal prayer and anointing will heal the sick (5:14–15). However, physical illness is not the only difficulty faced by Christians. In order to heal the effects of sin, communal confession and prayer are to be employed (5:16). In response to those who might doubt the extraordinary claims being made for prayer, James points to the example of Elijah (5:17–18). This example demonstrates the power of a righteous person's prayer (5:16c). When the example is transferred to the church, the righteous one cannot refer to an individual. Instead, the prayer of the church as a whole serves the same purpose as the prayer of the prophet. It can heal the afflicted and reconcile the sinner with God.

OUTLINE OF JAMES

Learning Perfection	1:1–27
Greeting	1:1
Trials Lead to Perfection	1:2–4
God Gives Wisdom	1:5–8
Only the Humble Can Boast	1:9–11
God Gives Good Things Not Trials	1:12–18
Learn to Control Speech	1:19–21
Be Doers of the Word	1:22–27
Be Doers Not Hearers	1:22–25
True Piety Cares for the Lowly	1:26–27
Faith Must Produce Works	2:1–26

Do Not Show Partiality toward the Rich	2:1–7
The Royal Law: Love of Neighbor	2:8–13
Faith without Works Does Not Save	2:14–26
Perfection Governs Speech	3:1–12
Not All Should Be Teachers	3:1
Unrestrained Speech Causes Evils	3:2–12
Wisdom from Above	3:13—4:12
Seek Heavenly Not Earthly Wisdom	3:13–18
Passions Cause Strife	4:1–5
Humble Yourselves before God	4:6–10
Do Not Judge Others	4:11–12
The Lord Governs Human Life	4:13—5:12
Do Not Be Confident in Future Plans	4:13–17
God Condemns the Rich for Injustice	5:1–6
Await the Lord's Judgment with Patience	5:7–11
Do Not Swear Oaths	5:12
Final Exhortation to the Community	5:13–20
Prayer Heals the Sick	5:13–15
Prayer Heals the Sinner	5:16–18
Seek Out Erring Christians	5:19–20

Learning Perfection

JAMES 1:1–27

Most Christians share Luther's skepticism about James. It tells us nothing of Jesus, so it cannot have much to contribute to the development of Christian faith. Luther referred to James as an "epistle of straw." At the end of the nineteenth century, the German commentator, Johann Gottfried Herder replied that the nourishment of unthreshed grain could be found within the straw nonetheless (Dibelius and Greeven, 1). Modern interests in liberation theology have drawn some attention to the treatment of rich and poor in James (Maynard-Reid).

However, most Christians find the assumptions of an ancient economy structured on the hierarchical authority of a wealthy, landowning elite far removed from their own experience. Like Proverbs and Ecclesiastes, and like other first-century writings that embody the generalities of ancient wisdom, James gathers advice on how to live that is difficult to translate into modern experience.

Some interpreters emphasize the connection between a community undergoing trials of faith and the view that such a testing of the righteous would be a feature of the end of the age. In that context, James reminds its readers that they must seek God's wisdom and not waver in their devotion because God will soon come to vindicate the lowly. Ralph Martin even suggests that James, the brother of the Lord, formulated the teaching that lies behind the present letter to respond to the unrest in Judea during the mid-60s A.D. Roman misrule and alienation between the people and the wealthy aristocracy would fuel the outbreak of violence led by the zealots. Martin argues that James was remembered for advocating a piety of single-minded, humble waiting for God's intervention (lxix). This advice was recast in a more generalized form of wisdom by disciples of James in Antioch where parallels with Matthew could easily have been taken into the work (R. Martin, lxx–lxxvii). This proposal attempts to explain the apostolic source of the work but must admit that the letter itself does not speak to the concrete situation of Judea.

James does represent an experience of Christian faith quite different from that of most believers even in the New Testament. On the title page of his German commentary, Franz Mussner cites a comment of Pope Pius XII: "We Christians are also Jews." That is a striking comment from a pope who has been accused of not using his office to expose Nazi attempts to exterminate the Jewish people. The lessons that Christians today have to learn from James are perhaps better stated by Pope Pius XII than by Luther. We need to listen to the Jewish heritage of our faith. We often think of that Jewish heritage in the same way as 1 Peter and much of the New Testament does, as the heritage of a few Old Testament heroes, of the psalms, and of the prophetic texts that point to Jesus. James is Jewish Christian in a much different sense. It has a vision of what it means to do the will of God. Perfection does not stem from detailed observances of Jewish ritual and custom that would separate some persons from others. Nor does it presume that its ethic only applies to the crisis of an evil age that lives in anticipation of God's judgment. Rather, James claims to present a wisdom that comes from God as the unchanging Creator who has called a people into existence. God promises salvation to those who learn this perfection.

James 1:1
Greeting

Readers must have been expected to recognize that "James" was the brother of the Lord. Later traditions about James consistently refer to his piety. He remained a leader of the Jerusalem church until his martyrdom. Although the phrase "servant of God" appears in Paul (Rom. 1:1; Gal. 1:10; Phil. 1:1), James may have taken the expression from the Old Testament (Deut. 34:5; 2 Sam. 7:5; Jer. 7:25; Amos 3:7). By adding "and of the Lord Jesus Christ," James converts the older Jewish formula into a Christian designation.

James refers to the addressees as "the twelve tribes in the Diaspora." First Peter referred to the churches of Asia Minor as "the exiles of the Diaspora." There the expression "diaspora" was metaphorically applied to Gentile Christians who now claim to be God's elect. James shows no consciousness of Gentile Christians as its addressees. The term "diaspora" could refer to the geographical location of the addressees. They live outside Judea. However, the metaphorical significance of the term "diaspora" can indicate that the Christian community understands itself as the new gathering of the people of God that was expected in the messianic age (Jer. 3:18; Ezek. 37:19, 24; Sir. 36:13; 1QS 8:1; *2 Bar* 78:5–7). Though Christians still live in the Diaspora, they are the restored people of God, the "twelve tribes."

James 1:2–4
Trials Lead to Perfection

The immediate injunction to rejoice in various trials depicts a significant fact of life in the Diaspora. Past heroes had taught Jews that they would be tested by those who govern their lives (Judith 8:25). First Peter 1:6–7 describes concrete experiences of Christians as a persecuted minority. However, James does not describe specific situations in which such trials may occur. Instead, it focuses on the effect of trials for believers. A faith tested by trials produces endurance (*hypomonē*; RSV: "steadfastness"). Those who exhibit patient endurance under trial will be perfect. The language of this chain of virtues expresses a common sentiment. Matthew 5:48 concludes the section on love of enemies with Jesus' injunction to "be perfect as your heavenly Father is perfect." The Lord's Prayer instructs disciples to pray that God will not lead them into trial (Matt. 6:13). Mark 13:13 warns disciples that they will be hated by all for Jesus' sake, but that those who endure to the end will be saved. Read in an eschatological perspective, the chain in verses 2–4 would be telling believers to rejoice in trials because those whose faith has been proved by enduring to the end will be among the elect at the judgment.

The same chain of virtues can be read in a more general sense. *Testament of Joseph* 2:4–7 describes the sufferings of Joseph during his imprisonment. The question is whether such trials show that God is unreliable. The author insists that God does not abandon the righteous, but the trials demonstrate the character of an individual's soul:

> For a brief time he may stand aside in order to test the disposition of the soul. In ten testings he showed that I was approved, and in all of them I persevered, because perseverance is a powerful medicine and endurance provides many good things. (*T. Jos.* 2:6b–7)

This example presents the perfection of the patriarch in terms familiar from ancient Stoic ethics. The wise person can endure any external circumstances (Dibelius and Greeven, 71–74). The expression "lacking in nothing" echoes a common Stoic argument that the wise person must possess all the virtues.

In the eschatological reading of this chain of virtues, the perfection achieved lies in the future, when God's judgment establishes the new creation. Christians are its "first fruits" (1:18). If the chain is understood as an example of general ethical teaching, then perfection is an achievement that individuals should realize in this life. As they did for the patriarch Joseph or for Job, the trials will end. Those who have been faithful during that period will emerge with the character exemplified by such heroes. Most people are suspicious of claims to perfection in ancient moralists. We operate on the assumption that human beings are not perfect. Therefore, the deferred perfection of the eschatological reading seems more plausible than the Stoic reading. Asked to discuss the meaning of perfection in Matt. 5:48, an adult faith-sharing group became very uneasy and even angry. Most of the thirty participants had very negative reactions to the word "perfect." Childhood demands of parents and teachers, which individual persons felt that they had failed to meet, often surfaced as examples of why "perfect" was an oppressive expectation. On an earlier occasion members of the group had no difficulty identifying difficult times in their lives that had shaped their faith. After the fact, most would agree that they had come out the other end stronger and better Christians.

Since the next section of the letter will instruct those who are lacking perfection to turn toward God, James does not present Christians as a group of moral superheroes. Trials remind them that they depend on God (Cargal). However, there is a danger of apathy in the modern acceptance of "things as they are." James opens with a striking reminder that Christians are not willing simply to get through life. Disciples look to God for standards of behavior that challenge the conventional standards of society. The "perfect work" that stems from endurance under trials (NRSV: "let endurance have its full effect") is a characteristic that will be exhibited in the good works described in the letter (R. Martin).

James 1:5–8
God Gives Wisdom

The catchword "lack" links this section with verse 4. Those who claim that such perfection is impossible should remember that wisdom is a gift of God, not a human achievement (Wisd. Sol. 7:7; 8:21). There is no true human perfection without God's gift of wisdom (Wisd. Sol. 9:6). Two obstacles may stand between believers and God. The first is a suspicion about God's nature. Perhaps only a few are blessed with wisdom. The second is a flaw in those who claim to have asked for wisdom. They are ambivalent in their choice. Wisd. Sol. 7:8–10 reminds its readers that wisdom must be loved more than all other goods. James contrasts the integrity of God's character with the hesitant wavering of human beings.

God gives *haplōs* (NRSV: "generously") and *mē oneidizontōs* (RSV: "without reproaching"). The term *haplōs* has a range of meanings from "integrity," "without ulterior motives," "without reservation" to "generously." The human virtue of *haplotēs* is described in *Testament of Issachar* 3:3–8 as integrity of life. Issachar does not meddle in the affairs of others, do evil, or slander others. Issachar's integrity is also exhibited in generosity toward the poor (*T. Iss.* 3:8) and love of God and neighbor (*T. Iss.* 5:1–2). The second characteristic of God's giving *(mē oneidizontōs)* is a negation of a verb that means "to insult or revile someone" (1 Peter 4:14) or to "reproach" a person (Wisd. Sol. 2:12). Human beings often accompany gifts with some element of reproach that suggests some fault in the person asking for aid. Sirach 18:15–18 reminds readers not to spoil their gift with words of reproach. God does not exhibit the flaws that attend human gift-giving. God is more than ready to answer the request for wisdom.

However, there is human responsibility evident in the prayer that is addressed to God. A series of verbs describe the *dipsychos* (RSV: "double-minded") person. Such individuals do not ask God in faith but are wavering and doubtful (cf. Mark 11:24). The image of a storm-tossed sea was popular in moral exhortation for the inner turmoil of a person without virtue

(Philo, *Giants* 51; Dio Chrysostom, *Orations* 32.23), but the primary focus of the imagery in this section can be related to the commandment to love God with all one's heart (Deut. 6:5; 18:13; Ps. 101:2). One must obey the Lord wholeheartedly (Sir. 1:28). The Dead Sea Scrolls refer to the wholehearted love of God among members of the sect (1QH 14:26; 16:7; CD 1:10). The wicked are "double-hearted" in their quest for God and are not steadfast in obedience to God's will (1QH 4:14; cf. Ps. 12:2; 78:37). The final description of those who are "double-minded" (*akatastatos;* RSV: "unstable") in all their ways employs a verb that is used for "storm-tossed" in Isa. 54:11 LXX. Thus the image of the wavering, uncertain Christian as a storm-tossed wave governs this section.

This section presents a paradox. On the one hand, those without wisdom are to ask God for it. On the other, God only responds to the prayer of those whose hearts are committed to God's way. Such single-hearted devotion already exhibits the perfection that is the object of praying for wisdom. Such paradoxes are inherent in the life of faith. Matthew 6:8 enjoins Christians not to heap up prayers like the pagans because a loving God already knows their needs before they ask. God's grace is already active in those who pray faithfully to receive it.

James 1:9–11
Only the Humble Can Boast

Exhortations in wisdom literature frequently shift quickly from one topic to another. The division between the faithful and the double-minded in the previous section may have suggested the contrast between the lowly and the rich. This section introduces one of the basic themes in the epistle: God exalts the lowly and humbles the proud. The initial parallelism between the two is expanded with an explanation of the fate that attends the rich. The exposition shifts from an exhortation to the lowly and to rich Christians (vv. 9–10a) to sayings that condemn the rich in general. They apply more directly to the rich who are not believers. Similar ambiguity appears in the treatment of partiality in the community in James 2:2–7. The community as a whole can be described as humble or lowly ones oppressed by the rich. Yet distinctions of rich and poor also make themselves evident within the church.

The eventual humiliation of the rich often attaches to divine judgment (Isa. 40:6–8). "Boasting" is often a negative characteristic of the wicked whom God will strike down (Ps. 49:6; 94:3). Consequently, the boast of the rich might be taken as ironic. So long as they pride themselves on their wealth, they will perish. The metaphor of grass that dominates this section has been taken from Isa. 40:6–8 LXX. Isaiah contrasts the abiding word of God with the fragility of human glory. James inserts the scorching sun as the agent responsible for the withered grass (v. 11a). The final phrase of verse 11 speaks of the rich fading away in their *poreiai* (RSV: "pursuits"). The word can mean "journey" and creates a link between this verse and the conclusion of the previous section that referred to the "ways" (= roads, paths; v. 8) of the double-minded. The castigation of the rich in this section parallels the words addressed to the double-minded in the previous one. Both represent a way of life that is contrary to God's word. The self-absorbed preoccupation with wealth and its consumption leaves no room either for God or for their "lowly" brothers and sisters. Yet riches cannot even secure the individual's life on earth, let alone status in God's judgment.

James 1:12–18
God Gives Good Things Not Trials

A beatitude shifts the readers' attention back to those who are undergoing trials (v. 12; cf. vv. 2–4). Once their faith has been "proved" (RSV: "stood the test"), they receive the "crown of life" (1 Peter 5:4, "crown of glory"; Rev. 2:10). The beatitude also reintroduces the theme of verses 5–8. Sirach 6:31 describes wisdom as a glorious robe and crown. The crown is promised to "those who love God." They are the opposite of the wavering, double-minded persons in verses 6–8. With this introduction, James moves to counter two false views of God: (a) that God is the source of trials (v. 13), and (b) that good gifts might come from some source other than God (v. 16).

The value that James attributes to trials in generating the tested faith of those who receive salvation might easily give rise to the suspicion that God is responsible for the trials that believers undergo. The Bible does speak of God "testing" the righteous (cf. Wisd. Sol. 3:5). Both Abraham (2:21) and Job (5:11) were said to have been tested by God. The logic of the counterthesis in verse 13 is unclear. James says that God is "*apeirastos* of evils" (RSV: "not tempted with evil"). The word does not occur elsewhere in the New Testament or Septuagint. It could mean that God is inexperienced with evil, since God has no contact with anything evil. It could mean that God cannot be brought to do evil. Or it could mean that evil persons cannot test God. Sirach 15:11–20 contains an extended reflection on evil and human choice. Sinners cannot blame God for the evil they do, since God does not do evil (v. 11) and has no need of sinful persons (v. 12). Rather, God created humanity with freedom to choose between good and evil, life and death (vv. 14–17). Wisd. Sol. 1:12–16 contains a similar meditation on death. Sinners summon death by their way of life. God did not create it and does not delight in the destruction of the living.

James 1:14–15 gives a slightly different explanation of evil. Its origin lies in the power of desires to entice persons into sin. Those who persist in sin receive the antithesis of the crown of life. They experience death. With the explanation in terms of desire, James has shifted the meaning of "trial" from some form of outer suffering inflicted on the individual or community by others to an inner struggle. Paul uses the conjunction of desire awakened by the commandment and human weakness to explain how the law was coopted by sin to produce death (Rom. 7:7–24). James has a more straightforward genealogy of death. Desires use their power to entice individuals to give birth to sin. Sin grows up into death. By underlining that the desire that initiates the process is the person's *own desire,* James focuses on individual responsibility for the result of the process much as Sirach insisted on human freedom to choose between life and death. James does not suggest that humans are trapped into sin and death by some irresistible power.

Verse 16 uses a common expression in ancient exhortations, "do not be deceived." It usually marks a point of transition as it does here. The exposition returns from reflections on what humans do to what God does (vv. 5, 12). Since the discussion about the origins of sin and death in wisdom literature often turned to the question of God's actions as Creator, James too turns to creation. Readers already know that God gives generously (v. 5). Now they are reminded that the Creator is responsible for good and perfect gifts. Since the origin of these gifts is with God, whose nature does not change, the gifts could not be otherwise. Several astronomical terms describe the nature of God. The "father of lights" created the stars (*Apoc. Mos.* 36:38; cf. Ps. 136:7). In God there is no *parallagē* ("variation") or *tropēs aposkiasma* ("shadow of turning"). The exact reference of these expressions is unclear. The term *parallagē* can refer to any change or succession of events including the revolutions of the stars (Epictetus, *Discourses* 1.14.4). *Tropē* can refer to the apogee of a heavenly body (Wisd. Sol. 7:18). Therefore the expression appears to refer to the revolution of the fixed stars and to the different lengths of shadow cast by the sun depending on the time of year. In antiquity the motions of the stars were thought to be eternal and, unlike earthly things, never subject to decay or alteration. God is greater than the eternal astronomical bodies because no type of change occurs in God. Consequently, God's goodness will never change (R. Martin). This argument may have been directed originally against ancient belief in astrology. The "stars" cannot cause evil things to come down from heaven because of the unchanging goodness of their Creator.

The final verse in this section turns to humans. James returns to addressing the readers who are described as "first fruits of God's creation." The expression "first fruits" refers to individual converts (Rom. 16:5; 1 Cor. 16:15) and to the risen Christ as the "first fruits" of many brothers and sisters (1 Cor. 15:20). God's word has been instrumental in bringing this new creation into being just as it brought the original creation into existence (Gen. 1:3; Ps. 33:6; Sir. 43:26; Wisd. Sol. 18:15). Thus the only things that come from heaven are the blessings that enable the addressees to belong to this new creation. James may be reminding readers of their own rebirth as members of the Christian community (cf. 1 Peter 1:23). However, James never elaborates on peculiarly Christian images. The primary referent of the perfect heavenly gift must be wisdom. Those who possess her possess all other good things besides (Wisd. Sol. 7:11–12). She dwells in their souls and makes them friends of God (Wisd. Sol. 7:27–28). Since God has brought believers forth through the "word of truth," they must already possess some part of the divine wisdom that they are to seek from God. No one knows what God wills without wisdom (Prov. 14:33; Wisd. Sol. 9:11–13).

The message of this section insists that humans take responsibility for the evils that come about through disordered desires. This emphasis raises questions about the modern culture of "evil as disease." Though we are less likely to blame God or the fates than people were in the first century, we constantly look for explanations that mitigate individual responsibility. But James does not pose this challenge in a morally chaotic framework. Its readers are Christians who know that the unchanging Creator of all things gives wisdom to those who are already part of a new creation. Christians are not waiting for the "crown of life" before receiving a good and perfect gift from God. Therefore it would be foolish for them to live as persons being led about by the chaos of desires.

James 1:19–21
Learn to Control Speech

The first example of how persons exhibit wisdom in their lives touches an area that most Christians today never think of, attention to speech. Matthew 5:21–22 contains a saying of Jesus that moves from the legal prohibition against murder through anger to name calling. James 1:19b–20 opposes anger by exhorting readers to be ready to listen and slow to speak. Angry speech is a sure sign that a person lacks wisdom in both Jewish and non-Jewish moralists (Prov. 15:1). *Testament of Dan* 2:1—4:7 describes the evils that anger creates in the soul. It creates an alliance with falsehood that continually disturbs the soul. God withdraws from such persons and Satan becomes their ruler instead (3:5–6; 4:7). James does not provide the reasoning that associates anger and injustice. Verse 20 merely reminds the reader that human anger can never become the vehicle for divine justice. Justice (*dikaiosynē;* RSV: "righteousness") reappears in the description of the fruits that come from heavenly wisdom (3:17–18). There righteousness results from efforts to make peace.

Ralph Martin has proposed that the original formulation of

this instruction was addressed to the violence of the zealots in and around Jerusalem prior to the outbreak of the revolt against Rome. James, the brother of the Lord, opposed the claim that violence could be used to establish God's rule (R. Martin, 48). The epistle, itself, does not contain any concrete references to social and political events in Judea. Anger appears to be taken as the primary example because it exemplifies the way in which the passions as a whole distort the soul. The final verse in this section (v. 21) calls on readers to put away all vices in order to receive the "implanted word" *(emphytos logos).* The phrase has been formulated to parallel the earlier reference to the "word of truth" through which believers have been brought into the community. The word *emphytos* can be used for something that is "inborn" or "innate." Wisdom of Solomon 12:10 refers to an innate evil found in the idolatry of the Canaanites whose land God gave to Israel. Since this word is received from God, the term *emphytos* cannot refer to something that is a given in human nature.

It is treated as another heavenly gift from God that brings salvation. However, there is a catch. The soul must be prepared. Every *"ryparia"* (RSV: "filthiness") and *perisseia kakias* ("abundance of evil"; RSV: "rank growth of evil") must be put aside. The imagery suggests cleansing and clearing away evil so that the *emphytos logos* can bear fruit. Some interpreters presume that James is referring to baptismal catechesis (Mussner). However, that interpretation departs from the wisdom exhortation that has been characteristic of this section of James. The verb can be used of something that is "implanted" or "deeply rooted" in something else. This appears to be the sense in which James is using the adjective, not of an innate or natural quality of the soul. God is the agent who implants the word in those who receive it "in meekness." Presumably, the "implanted word" saves the soul by keeping it clear of the evil that is found in souls driven about by passions. Consequently, the "implanted word" must be a variant expression for the gift of divine wisdom. Wisdom cannot enter souls subject to deceit and sin (Wisd. Sol. 1:4). On the other hand, nothing but sin can take wisdom away from the souls of those who are devoted to it (*T. Levi* 13:7). *Testament of Levi* 13:5–9 equates doing righteousness with sowing good things in the soul. Joseph is the exemplar of the power of wisdom to deliver the wise from their enemies. Those who teach and practice good things will be enthroned with kings (*T. Levi* 13:8–9).

James 1:22–27
Be Doers of the Word

Jewish wisdom traditions always connect possession of wisdom with its practice as specified in the law. The final section of the opening exhortation to seek perfection turns to the question of practice. It opens with a general metaphor of someone looking into a mirror. That image concludes with a blessing on those who put what they hear into practice. The second half of this section defines true piety as the concrete practice of virtue. Holiness does not require physical separation from the world but rejection of its values.

1. Be Doers Not Hearers (1:22–25)

Lest the previous reference to the "implanted word" (v. 21) suggest that Christianity dispenses believers from the practice of virtue, James warns that they must practice what they hear. The example used to describe the two types of person is not entirely clear. Wisdom can be described as a spotless mirror that reflects God (Wisd. Sol. 7:26). That image explains how the believer can be described as looking "into the perfect law, the law of liberty" (v. 25). But the opening image speaks of a person regarding his face in a physical mirror and then forgetting what he looks like as soon as he leaves the mirror. We are so used to glass mirrors, instant photographs, video, and photo ID cards that the comment seems impossible. How could anyone forget what he or she looks like? Only very young children are unable to recognize themselves. Most ancient mirrors were made of polished metal. The image was much less clear than those we are familiar with. Even so, the forgetfulness of the first individual is intended to strike the readers as somewhat absurd.

The desirable mirror is not a blemished work of polished metal but the law of God, "the perfect law of freedom" (v. 25). Stoic philosophers would have understood the expression as a reference to the "law" of divine reason that governs the cosmos. The wise are free because reason governs their souls. Greek-speaking Jews made a similar argument about their own law (Philo, *Life of Moses* 2.48). This law is equivalent to the "implanted Word" in the previous section. Since it is perfect, those who follow it will be perfect as well. Ralph Martin observes that James involves all parts of the body in the schema of perfection. The tongue speaks rarely and never in anger (vv. 19b–20). The ears hear the word (v. 23). The eyes see and remember true images (vv. 24–25). The hands and other parts of the body will carry out the deeds that are the practical evidence that a person knows the law of freedom (v. 25; R. Martin, 54–55). The next section will mention the heart, which must not be deceived by a religion that is never put into practice (v. 26). Readers might also remember Jeremiah's prophecy that the covenant would be written in the hearts of the people so that instruction would no longer be necessary (Jer. 31:31–34). By working together references to all parts of the body, James presents a picture of "the implanted Word" governing all our activities.

2. True Piety Cares for the Lowly (1:26–27)

The concluding verses of this section pick up from verse 22 the reference to deceiving oneself. What constitutes true piety? A concern with being "pure and undefiled" (v. 27) is typically linked with the idea of purity attached to cultic activities. Those who serve God directly as priests must maintain standards of purity not required of ordinary people (Ezek. 22:26). Mark 7:14–23 reports a saying of Jesus in which external purity rules are rejected as evidence of holiness. Instead, the vices that come out of the heart defile a person. Though James is not citing this tradition directly, his comments here clearly exhibit the same spirit. The religious activity that is pleasing to God requires putting a bit on the tongue (v. 26) and caring for the widowed and orphans. Concern for widows and orphans frequently appears in the Old Testament as righteousness (Exod. 22:21; Deut. 10:18; 24:17–13; Ps. 68:5; Isa. 1:10–17; Jer. 5:28; Ezek. 22:7; Zech. 7:10; Sir. 4:10).

When James admonishes readers to keep themselves "unstained" from the world, he does not assume that Christians will cease to have anything to do with the affairs of ordinary life. The few details that are given about the community, the rich and poor and the traders, and perhaps persons employed by the rich landowners, all point to persons who lived ordinary lives. The phrase must be intended in the metaphorical sense of a reorientation of values so that the individual no longer lives according to the standards of the world (cf. Rom. 12:2). The examples of true piety, control of the tongue, and concern for the afflicted will be spelled out in the following chapters.

Faith Must Produce Works

JAMES 2:1–26

James turns from general exhortation to warn its readers that discrimination against poor brothers and sisters must not exist within the church. The earlier contrast between those who merely hear the word and those who put it into practice has been replaced. "Faith" takes the place of hearing the word. The "perfect law of freedom" (1:25) reappears as the "royal law" that is summarized by the love command (v. 8). Readers have just been told to keep themselves "unstained by the world" (1:27). These concrete examples demonstrate that they still accept social conventions concerning the treatment of rich and poor. Partiality toward the wealthy and powerful is a common feature of any society. In societies that bestow honor and privilege on the rich in exchange for their patronage and material support for communal projects, the behavior described in this section would have been second nature. Though self-sufficiency was frequently presented as an ideal, most people's lives were enveloped in a complex web of obligations to benefactors. If one seeks assistance from a very powerful person, then it will be necessary to enlist the aid of a mediator. Recipients were expected to show public marks of honor to benefactors (Neyrey, 1993, 7–9).

This system generated patterns of flattery that were often challenged by moralists. The Cynics castigated other philosophers who depended on wealthy patrons for caring more about their own comfort than benefiting the souls of their patrons. By living as antisocial itinerant beggars, Cynic philosophers could claim independence from the social network of patronage. The satirist Lucian (c.120 C.E.) attacks some philosophers for their love of luxury disguised under exhortations to virtue and moderation. The Cynics, on the other hand, correct and abuse their fellow citizens but contribute nothing to society:

> But if you were to ask the very man who is straining his lungs and bawling and accusing everybody else: "How about yourself? What do you really do, and what in Heaven's name do you contribute to the world?" he would say, if he were willing to say what was right and true: "I hold it unnecessary to be a merchant or a farmer or a soldier or to follow a trade; I shout, go dirty, take cold baths, walk about barefoot in winter, and . . . carp at everything the others do. If some rich man or other has made an extravagant outlay on a dinner or keeps a mistress, I make it my affair and get hot about it; but if one of my friends or associates is ill abed and needs relief and attendance, I ignore it." (Lucian, *Icaromenippus* 31; Malherbe 1986, 40)

This selection from Lucian illustrates the form of exhortation that James employs in these sections of the letter, the diatribe. In the diatribe a fictional sparring partner is created by the use of question and response. Vivid examples of the type of behavior being condemned also form an important part of the philosophic diatribe. As in this case, examples are sharpened and exaggerated. The audience would recognize typical situations and persons in the stock figures and episodes. Since James has adopted the diatribe form, readers must be careful to distinguish between reality and the exaggerated generalizations characteristic of the genre (Dibelius and Greeven, 129).

The example from Lucian also illustrates the logic that connects the two segments in this section of James. The Cynic philosopher who gives up wealth and castigates others for devoting their lives to material pursuits has other vices. He is a busybody butting in where he has no place, and, even worse, he shows no concern for his friends when they are in need. James moves from partiality shown the rich to the failure to aid the poor brother or sister. Listeners who might have held themselves aloof from the first example can be caught in the trap of the second. The requirement that a philosopher's life exhibit the truth of his teaching has been translated into the demand that one's faith be demonstrated in deeds. The Cynics defended their detachment from normal social relationships by claiming that they benefited others by pointing out their evil and folly. Such benefits, Lucian implies, ought to be exhibited in concern for one's friends.

Early Christians went beyond the language of benefaction and friendship to speak of one another as "brothers" and "sisters." The family was the only sphere in which benefits did not come with a corresponding obligation attached (Neyrey 1991, 9). Two important consequences follow from this shift. First, everyone is obligated to aid another when he or she has the means to do so. Benefaction is not at the discretion of the donor. Second, benefits do not create corresponding obligations. If they did, the honor and privilege suggested by the seating arrangements in the Christian synagogue would be entirely appropriate. Honorific titles and inscriptions should also designate prominent patrons as "father" or "mother" of the synagogue (see Kraemer, 118–23). Instead, Christians are to treat one another as siblings. Their charity has no strings attached.

James 2:1–7
Do Not Show Partiality toward the Rich

The statement of principle (v. 1) that the example will illustrate (vv. 2–7) suddenly refers to the Lord Jesus as the basis for the faith that readers are to put into practice. The term *prosōpolēmpsia* ("partiality") is rare in non-Christian writings. It may have been formulated in early Christian circles. It commonly refers to God's evaluation of human beings. Status and accomplishments in this world will not change the individual's standing in the sight of God (cf. Rom. 2:11; Eph. 6:9; Col. 3:25). The faith that requires not showing partiality as its practice is described by an awkward phrase, "of our Lord Jesus Christ of glory." It could be a variant of the designation that Jesus is "Lord of glory" (so 1 Cor. 2:8) or an attempt to identify Jesus with the "glory" of God. If the phrase is taken as adjectival, then "glory" simply describes Jesus. Although James rarely refers to Jesus, this expression shows that Jesus is the object of Christian faith. Anyone who claims to be a believer must reject partiality. The advice in this section poses a greater challenge to conventional standards than that in the opening comments on perfection. By introducing it as a condition of faith in "our glorious Lord Jesus Christ," James underlines the importance of what follows.

Verses 2–3 provide an example of partiality: the rich man is honored, the poor dishonored. Persons who are seated or shown special, prominent seats are commonly superior to others in antiquity (cf. Matt. 23:6). Those told to stand or to sit by someone's feet are of lower status or even captives (cf. Ps. 99:5; 110:1; Isa. 66:1). Defining the context in which this discrimination occurs is problematic. The word *synagōgē,* "synagogue" (NRSV: "assembly"), has usually been understood as a gathering of the community for worship. The difficulty with that assumption has been the statement that those who show partiality have become "judges with evil opinions" (v. 4). That comment suggests a legal setting in which the church had gathered for judgment (Matt. 18:16–18; 1 Cor. 5:3–5; 6:1–4). Since later Jewish law contains stipulations requiring those who come before a judge to be treated equally and to dress in a way that does not emphasize their relative status, some scholars suggest that James has a legal setting in mind (Ward).

The legal overtones of the example may be determined by the second half of the argument, the assertion that Christians run the risk of becoming like those who persecute them (vv. 6–7). That persecution takes the form of court proceedings in which the superiority of the rich enables them to oppress the Christian. James suggests that this hostility stems from the fact that the weaker party is a Christian (v. 7). The rich were able to use legal proceedings to oppress the poor (Amos 8:4–6; Wisd. Sol. 2:10–11). "Blaspheming the name" need not imply a persecution of Christians as such. Rather ridicule of "the name" may have been no more than a mocking reference to the individual's beliefs in order to undermine the reliability of someone's character.

Although the example opens with deference paid to the rich, James refers to the dishonor shown to the poor as the real problem facing the community. Verse 5 reminds readers that God has chosen the poor to inherit the kingdom (cf. Matt. 5:3; Luke 6:20). James 1:9–10 stated a generalized version of the same principle, which contrasted the lowly and the rich. In this version, the poor are rich in faith as a result of God's choice. Since God's choice has overturned the partiality that was typical of ancient society, no one who behaves differently can claim faith in Jesus Christ. When James turns the table on his readers, he challenges any tendency to consider themselves "the poor, heirs of the kingdom." Though Christians have experienced oppression by the rich, they have learned from their oppressors, not from God! The tendency of the oppressed to adopt the behavior of their oppressors frequently emerges in revolutionary movements. The lowly may prefer the limited power they can exercise against others to the exaltation that comes from God. Religious leadership must insist on the equality of all persons as children of God.

James 2:8–13
The Royal Law: Love of Neighbor

A third argument against partiality draws on the law. The law itself warns against partiality in judicial proceedings (Lev. 19:15). The law provides the basis for God's judgment against those who dishonor the poor. The same law that prohibits partiality requires love of neighbor (Lev. 19:18; Deut. 16:19). The "royal law" (vv. 8, 12) reminds readers of the "perfect law of liberty" that guides the actions of the wise (1:25). In this section, the identification of wisdom with the commandments of God (cf. Sir. 2:15–16; 15:1–3) is expressed by references to Leviticus and to the commandments from the Decalogue not to kill and not to commit adultery (v. 11). The command to obey all the words of the law indicates the wholehearted devotion to God's will that characterizes true piety in James (cf. Deut. 26:16—27:1). The *Testament of Asher* describes the single-minded person's devotion to God as the rejection of all forms of evil, including that created by an individual's desires (*T. Asher* 6:1–5).

The section ends on a note of judgment. The "law of freedom" is the basis for God's judgment. By shifting back to the general term "law of freedom," James indicates that judgment does not consist in cataloging individual transgressions. No one who is devoted to God would violate any of these fundamental precepts of the law. Speaking and doing must conform to the "law of freedom" inasmuch as they are the foundation of true piety (1:26–27). A further saying on judgment concludes this section on a different note. The severity or mercy of judgment is a function of the mercy that individuals show. Mercy is another way of fulfilling the law of love. *Testament of Zebulun* 5.1–3 promises that the Lord returns the mercy shown to others:

> Now my children, I tell you to keep the Lord's commands; show mercy to your neighbor, have compassion on all, not only on human beings but to dumb animals. . . . Have mercy in your inner being, my children, because whatever anyone does to his neighbor, the Lord will do to him.

Mercy moderates the apparent harshness of the earlier warning against disobeying a single command in the law. Since the injunctions to love and mercy fulfill the law, the readers should pay special attention to the lowly and suffering who need assistance. Again, the tradition in James reflects similar emphases in the Sermon on the Mount. God's forgiveness is a function of the forgiveness shown to others (Matt. 5:7; 6:14–15; 7:12; 18:22–35).

James 2:14–26
Faith without Works Does Not Save

The diatribe style shifts back to the requirements of faith. Just as faith cannot exist in conjunction with partiality (v. 1), so it cannot exist without works (v. 14). The particular formulation of the slogan being rejected in this section, "faith without works," seems to be dependent on the Pauline assertion that people are made righteous through faith in Christ, not through works of the law (Gal. 2:16). However, James is not concerned with the particular Pauline arguments about the salvation of non-Jews. The slogan appears to reflect a secondhand Paulinism that is put to quite a different use. The first example returns to the issue of the poor Christian. It depicts another form of dishonor, greeting them with the standard wishes for good health and ignoring their physical needs. Readers are expected to recognize that those who behave in this fashion will not merit salvation (v. 17). Such dead faith is equivalent to the persons who hear the word but do not put it into practice (1:22–24).

James pursues the argument with the imaginary opponent in typical diatribe style. The first counterargument is an ironic appeal to the basic confession of the Jewish tradition, that God is one (Deut. 6:4). By itself, that confession of faith will not save, since even the demons can recognize the unity of God, but all the demons can do is shudder. They cannot fulfill the second part of the confession in Deuteronomy, "You shall love the LORD your God with all your heart . . ." (Deut. 6:5–6). Jews living in the Diaspora were certainly familiar with outsiders who admired the monotheism, antiquity, and moral seriousness of Judaism but who did not convert. Some of these persons even appear as benefactors of local synagogues. Others may have been useful mediators when Jews had to deal with local officials. Some Jews thought that it was better if sympathetic Gentiles did not convert, since such conversions often sparked hostility against the Jewish community. The activities of Christian missionaries sparked controversy in the Jewish community because they threatened this delicate balance.

Although this section of James deals with relationships between Christians, the attitude it seeks to eliminate may have been developed among those who sought an easy accommodation with outsiders. "Faith without works" spares individuals the embarrassment of radical disruptions in their lives or relationships. The danger becomes evident in this example. People will not remember their obligations to Christian brothers and sisters. Our churches today contain many people who agree with the imaginary challenger in James. Not only does "faith" not require any relationships or obligations to others, but any suggestion that it does is met with resistance. Twice as many Americans explicitly claim to be members of churches or synagogues as actually participate in the activities of those groups. Attempts to form bonds between wealthy suburban churches and inner-city congregations often meet great resistance.

James addresses the imaginary interlocutor again in verse 20. He will prove the necessity of works by appealing to Old Testament examples. Abraham demonstrates that works are required by faith. The sacrifice of Isaac constitutes the work that demonstrates the faith of Abraham (Heb. 11:17). James links the sacrifice of Isaac in Genesis 22 with the earlier statement that Abraham was considered righteous because of his faith (Gen. 15:6). In the Jewish tradition, Abraham is the exemplary "friend of God" (*Jub.* 19:9; 30:20; 2 Esd. 3:14; Philo, *Abra-*

ham, 273). Elsewhere Wisdom dwells in the souls of those who are friends of God (Wisd. Sol. 7:14, 27). As he has done earlier, James insists that faith must be perfected by works (v. 22; 1:25). Works are not independent of the faith that gives birth to them. Consequently, James adds the word "alone" to the summary statement in verse 24. "Faith alone" does not justify a person.

While Abraham was a familiar example in Jewish and early Christian circles, the second example, Rahab, is less familiar (Josh. 6:17, 23). However, she was considered a type of the proselyte. She saved herself and her family by assisting the Jews in entering the promised land (Heb. 11:31; Mussner). She is celebrated in the genealogy of Jesus (Matt. 1:5). The combination of Abraham and Rahab as figures may have been based on their appeal to proselytes. Another early Christian tradition considered them both examples of works of hospitality (*1 Clem.* 10—12). The conclusion that sums up the section requires an odd juxtaposition. "Works" are coordinated with the soul and faith with the body because "works" and the soul keep the faith and the body alive. The awkwardness of the juxtaposition results from the fact that faith lives in the soul whereas works are performed through the body. However, the statement that "faith without works is dead" makes good sense within the framework of covenant theology. Religion is a matter of practice, of obedience to God's will. Life and blessing depend on faithful observance of God's commandments (Deut. 7:12–14). Faith and works cannot be separated in this understanding of religion (2 Esd. 9:7; Dibelius and Greeven, 177). Today many Christians run the risk of thinking that faith means nothing more than private, individual views. Even the commitment to gather with others to worship God regularly seems unnecessary to some people. James certainly would wonder if faith without community could survive.

Perfection Governs Speech

JAMES 3:1–12

James 1:26–27 established two conditions for true piety: proper speech and concern for the poor and afflicted. The previous section highlighted the latter. It reminded readers that works that exhibit love of neighbor, "the royal law," are not an optional complement to faith. Without them, faith would not be alive at all. Now James turns to the first condition, control of one's speech. The previous section contained three examples of misused speech: (a) words that honor the rich and dishonor the poor (2:3); (b) greeting a poor brother or sister without providing assistance (2:16); and (c) claiming to have faith without works to show for it (2:18). Those examples dealt with what we would call "empty words." They contradict the reality of faith. This section turns to speech itself as a "work." James 1:26 pointed to the need to put a bridle on the tongue. This section returns to that metaphor (v. 2).

Although this section of James often strikes people today as strange, we are in the middle of one of the most intensive social debates about speech in modern times. Protection of "free speech" was an essential element in the emergence of modern, liberal democracies. When students read this passage or the sayings of Jesus about angry speech in Matt. 5:21–22, they usually react by saying, "Everyone has a right to say whatever they want," or "It's better to let it out and say what's on your mind when you're angry with someone." Yet as a society we have come to wonder whether all forms of speech should be permitted in public, on rap records, in the media, and the like. Speech that expresses hatred toward or demeans others because of their racial origins, sexual preference, gender, or religion is being restricted. Courts are recognizing some forms of speech as sexual or racial harassment. Therefore, Christians today have a special reason to reflect on the advice in this section.

James 3:1
Not All Should Be Teachers

The first saying speaks of a particular group within the community, those who are teachers. The introduction to the next section (v. 13) makes it clear that teachers are among the "wise and understanding." Presumably, James has those persons who teach wisdom to fellow Christians in mind. Martin suggests that conflict among persons who claim to teach was causing difficulty in the churches (R. Martin, 104). Daniel 12:3 described the function of "the wise" as leading the common people to righteousness (cf. Dan. 11:33). Those who succeed are exalted like angels at the resurrection (Collins, 393). In that case, the stricter evaluation of teacher/leaders gives special honor to those whose teaching and example enabled the people to remain faithful during the persecutions and turmoil of the Maccabean period. Their position may have made such teachers targets for persecution and martyrdom under Antiochus. According to Josephus, Agrippa arrested and executed John the Baptist because of the popularity of his teaching among the people (Josephus, *Antiquities* 18.5.2; sec. 116–19). The Dead Sea Scrolls indicate that the Teacher of Righteousness, the founder of their sect, was persecuted by religious authorities in Jerusalem (1QpHab 8:9–12:6). If, as seems likely, the epistle was written by a later, Greek-speaking Jewish Christian, then its readers may also know that the teacher on whose authority the letter rests had also suffered persecution and martyrdom.

When the author tells his audience, "you know that we who teach will receive a heavier *krima* ("judgment"; NRSV: "be judged with greater strictness"), he may have had two courts in mind. The human court singles out teachers in the community hoping that if they are silenced, their followers will be intimidated. The heavenly court, on the other hand, holds those who teach God's word accountable for the righteousness of the people. Those who prove to be faithful teachers will receive special honor. Paul expressed this sentiment when he described his churches as the evidence for his heavenly reward (Phil. 4:1; 1 Thess. 2:19). Those who fail in their responsibility must expect stricter judgment from God. By associating this saying with earlier examples of righteous teachers who were persecuted, one can understand the instruction as further evidence for how Christians should behave during periods of testing or trial (1:2).

Like much of the teaching in James, this injunction can also be read as a general piece of wisdom. Teachers whose lives do not benefit from their own instruction should be avoided. They may even be hated or mocked by others. Sirach 37:17–26 situates this teaching in connection with a reflection on the power of the tongue, since the tongue governs whatever comes forth from the mind. Those teachers whose wisdom benefits both themselves and others will be honored forever (Sir. 37:22–26).

James 3:2–12
Unrestrained Speech Causes Evils

James immediately dissociates himself and his addressees from being among the wise (v. 2). The comment "all of us make many mistakes" represents a common response to the ethic of perfection advocated in much of James. However, James would not accept the spoken or unspokened rider that most modern readers attach to that expression, namely, "so that's okay." Mediocrity has no place in James's vision of the Christian life. Instead, James expects readers to draw two conclusions from the observation, "all of us make mistakes." First, looking back to verse 1, we should not rush to claim the ability to teach others a wisdom that we cannot yet practice. Second, looking at the example of the truly wise or perfect person, we should attempt to make our lives more perfect. If there is someone who never makes a mistake in what he or she says, then that person is able to control the entire body. Such control must include the passions, which are the source of inner trials (1:14). The reference to putting a bridle on the body (v. 2b) introduces the metaphors that will be used to describe the tongue (cf. 1:25).

The tongue is presented as the small organ or rudder that directs the larger whole, the body or the ship at sea (vv. 3–5a). The images of controlling horses and ships were commonplace in ancient writers (Dibelius and Greeven, 185–90). Philo comments that God made humankind to be the charioteer or helmsman of the whole creation (Philo, *Creation of the World* 88). The mind acts as helmsman or charioteer in controlling irrational impulses and directing the life of individuals. Let the irrational impulses take control and the mind is set on fire by the passions (Philo, *Allegorical Interpretation of the Laws* 3.223–24). James uses the images of the horse and the ship to suggest that one can gain control of the whole by concentrating on the small thing that is responsible for giving them directions.

Left uncontrolled, the tongue becomes the source of great evils. They begin with the tongue's power to boast (v. 5a). With it the wicked even turn against heaven (Ps. 73:8–9). Their speech is like a hot fire because it ignites other evils (Prov. 16:27; 26:21). As James observes, a small fire can engulf the entire forest in flames (cf. Philo, *Special Laws* 4.83). The deadly effects of an uncontrolled tongue are described in a grammatically awkward series of expressions that begin with the tongue as fire and conclude by attributing the fire in the tongue to Gehenna (v. 6). This sequence parallels the string that began with desires and leads through them to sin and death (1:14–15). Fire was commonly associated with Gehenna or hell (cf. Luke 16:23–24). Just as the speech of the wicked spreads through the world to attack the heavens itself (Ps. 73:8–9), so James speaks of the tongue as a "world of injustice." It pollutes the entire body. Even worse, James suggests that evils that come from the tongue can infect every area of life. James has an unusual expression for the cosmic reach of its evils, "the wheel of becoming." The phrase appeared in pagan religions for the cycle of rebirth or of nature. Since James refers to the eventual fate of all things engulfed in flames, the metaphor may have been taken from ancient Stoic sources. In Stoicism cosmic cycles are linked to the doctrine of the great conflagration that returns all things to fire. Since James does not exploit either the religious or astronomical meanings of the term, the expression might best be translated "the course of human existence" (Dibelius and Greeven, 198; R. Martin, 115).

This dramatic conclusion leads James to reflections on the lethal power of the tongue (vv. 7–8). On the one hand, God created humankind to govern all creatures (cf. Ps. 8:6–8). Human beings have demonstrated their ability to master nature by taming animals. On the other hand, they are unable to control the poisonous effects of the tongue. One of the most familiar passages in ancient literature appeared in Sophocles's

Antigone. The chorus celebrates the vast mastery achieved by human wisdom, but notes that humans have been unable to conquer death (*Antigone* 342–52). Sirach 28:17–21 describes the extraordinary power of the tongue. Its fetters are as strong as iron and the death to which it leads is worse than Hades. The tongue of the wicked is like the bite of a poisonous snake (Ps. 140:3).

Sirach 28:24–26 uses the negative power of the tongue to support a warning to place the mouth under a heavy guard. Only careful attention to speech can protect one from the snares that lie in wait for the righteous. James takes a slightly different approach to the problem. Most people speak with a divided tongue. They use the same instrument to curse human beings, who are God's image, and to bless God (v. 9). Earlier James reminded readers that they could not be double-minded (1:8). Now they must overcome the human tendency to be "double-tongued" (Sir. 5:13–14; 28:12). Sayings of Jesus also warned believers that what comes out of the mouth is the key to an individual's true piety. Humans will be judged on how they have used the power of speech (Matt. 15:9; 12:33–37). The *Testament of Benjamin* notes that the good person does not speak in a double-tongued way:

> The good set of mind does not talk from both sides of its mouth: praises and curses, abuse and honor, calm and strife, hypocrisy and truth, poverty and wealth, but it has one disposition, uncontaminated and pure toward all men. There is no duplicity in its perception or its hearing. Whatever it does, or speaks or perceives, it knows that the Lord is watching over its life, for he cleanses his mind in order that he will not be suspected of wrongdoing either by men or by God. The works of Beliar are twofold, and have in them no integrity. (*T. Benj.* 6:5–7)

These reflections on speech belong to the overall picture of perfection advocated by this epistle.

Though the initial account of how powerful the tongue is might make the task seem impossible, James insists that a "double-tongued" Christian is unthinkable. The impossibility is linked to the two uses of speech: cursing or praising God. A single spring cannot produce both brackish and fresh water (v. 11). A single tree cannot yield different types of fruit (v. 12b; cf. Matt. 7:16–20; 12:33–35; Luke 6:43–45). The final metaphor, salt water cannot yield fresh, reformulates the original phrase about the spring. It points to the concern that drives this entire section: Christians must learn to control the tongue. Only the fresh water spring is of any use on the natural level. Only blessing God is of any use to bring people to salvation. James challenges the casual attitude that many people take toward speech. The goal of perfect wisdom that it sets before believers should not be confused with a works righteousness, a presumption that human beings can become perfect without God's assistance. The wisdom traditions that James employs insist that wisdom is God's gift, not a human achievement. By underlining the power that the tongue has over human beings, James also reminds readers that any success they have in disciplining speech will also be a gift from God.

Wisdom from Above

JAMES 3:13—4:12

James returns to the discussion of wisdom with which the letter opened. It challenges those who might still consider themselves wise to evaluate their way of life (3:13). The collection of sayings in this section of James focuses on conflicts that arise between human beings. In some cases, the conflict may be selfish ambition that drives a person's actions (3:14, 16). In other cases, covetousness leads to open conflict (4:2). Conflict may be expressed in words when Christians speak evil of others or condemn them (4:11). Each case involves a disordered relationship between the believer and God. Those who acknowledge their dependence on God will receive the grace to overcome the passions that distort human life (4:8). Recognizing that God exalts the lowly and humbles the proud takes the energy out of selfish human ambition (4:10). Judging others is an arrogant claim to exercise a function that belongs to God alone (4:12). The contrast between earthly and heavenly wisdom makes the religious character of ethics clear. Left on their own, human beings would not be able to see beyond the unruly passions that dominate their life.

Anyone can see envy, selfishness, ambition, strife, speaking ill of others, and condemnation of others every day. We do not need to look outside ourselves. This section of James speaks of envy, ambition, and lack of humility as root causes for many of the conflicts we experience. When we catch ourselves making negative or judgmental remarks about others, we might ask what the root of that behavior is. Educators have begun to challenge the use of rewards that make one child's failure or weakness the condition for another's success. Cooperative rather than competitive models of learning and achievement make the school a better place for all students. James might suggest that Christians who see the image of God in all people (3:9) have a special concern for the ways in which children learn to interact with others. The elaborate workshops on conflict management that are being incorporated into many school programs might not be so necessary if Christian parents and churches paid attention to the basic virtues of charity, humility, and peacemaking in everyday life.

James 3:13–18
Seek Heavenly Not Earthly Wisdom

James suddenly challenges its audience to substantiate their claim to possess heavenly wisdom and understanding (v. 13). Paul used a similar combination of vices to challenge those in Corinth who thought they had attained perfection. The jealousy and strife between members of the church proves that the Corinthians are still immature (1 Cor. 3:1–3). Before readers think that they might qualify as the wise, James attacks with a warning not to make such a claim if they discover "bitter jealousy" (*eritheia;* NRSV: "selfish ambition") in their hearts. The word *eritheia* is rare. Aristotle uses it to refer to self-seeking pursuit of political office by unfair means (*Politics* 5.3 [1302b,4; 1303a,14]). The earlier discussion of rich and poor indicated that Christians continued to act out the prejudices of their society. They have not traded in worldly views of power and importance for God's viewpoint. The Christian community should not provide another forum for human jealousy and ambition to work themselves out. James warns its audience not to think that they can claim a wisdom they do not possess. Such an assertion would be false to the truth (3:14). It would also make a mockery of God who has given Christians birth through a "word of truth" (1:18).

James can prove that such wisdom is not from God. Instead, it is described with a list of three adjectives in descending order of severity: "earthly" *(epigeios)*, "sensual" (*psychikē;* NRSV: "unspiritual"), and "demonic" (*daimoniōdēs;* NRSV: "devilish"; v. 15). Of themselves, envy and ambition might not seem to merit this sharp condemnation. James explains that they lead to "disorder" or "anarchy" *(akatastasia)* and "every foul deed" (v. 16). A catalogue of virtues shows that heavenly wisdom provides the antithesis to "every foul deed" (v. 17). Heavenly wisdom is "pure, peaceable, open to reason, full of mercy and good fruits, impartial, sincere" (v. 17). James may have drawn on a conventional list of virtues connected with wisdom (cf. Wisd. Sol. 7:21–28). Wisdom teaches these virtues and makes the one who receives it a "friend of God" (R. Martin). The conclusion to the section associates righteousness with peacemaking (v. 18; cf. Prov. 3:7; Matt. 5:9). The NRSV takes the dative "those who make peace" as a dative of advantage: the peacemakers are those who receive this fruit. Proverbs 11:30 contrasts the "fruit of righteousness" that gives life with the violence that takes it away. Those who follow wisdom's paths of peace gain the fruit of wisdom, the tree of life (Prov. 3:17). James encourages his audience to become peacemakers.

Peacemaking returns to the opening challenge. The wise must demonstrate that they possess wisdom by works done in "meekness of wisdom." No one can pursue peace if he or she is driven by personal ambition and jealousy. What follows indicates that the readers are not exemplary peacemakers. Although the whole list of virtues that flow from heavenly wisdom might seem impossible to attain, peacemaking is not so far-fetched. All Christians can take the initiative in promoting peace, helping to mediate conflicts, and standing up against a culture that glamorizes violence. When we begin to think about the concrete habits of action and mind that are required of peacemakers, the list of virtues that stem from wisdom emerge in a new light. Conflict resolution requires openness to reason, mercy, impartiality, and sincerity. Without such virtues any resolution to a conflict will be a loss or humiliation for one side. Such a forced conclusion contains the seeds of its own destruction. Both sides to a dispute have to feel that the solution is a fair one or there is no peace.

James 4:1–5
Passions Cause Strife

The tone shifts sharply to castigate those who are driven by their *hēdonai.* The word generally means "pleasures," but its negative effects suggest that James uses the term as a synonym for "desire" *(epithymia).* Earlier James insisted that desire entices people to sin (1:14–15). The passions cause two types of conflict. The first is internal, a warfare within the individual (v. 1). The second is external and consists of passions and covetousness that lead to wars between humans. The association between passion and war was a common theme in the moralists. Bodily passions cause war (Plato, *Phaedo,* 66c). Philo traces all the famous wars of history to *epithymia* (Philo, *On the Decalogue,* 151–53). James has inserted "murder" into the chain of destructive passions as a pair with "covet" in verse 2. The verb appears out of place in the chain, so the NRSV attached it to the opening pair, "you want something and do not have it; so you commit murder." The connection between covetousness and murder may have been inspired by the story of Cain. The *Testament of Asher* argues that "love of brother" drives out envy. Joseph exemplified that virtue, which his brothers lacked:

> And you, my children, each of you love his brothers with a good heart and the spirit of envy will depart from you. For that attitude makes the soul savage and corrupts the body; it foments wrath and conflict in the reason, excites to the shedding of blood, drives the mind to distraction. (*T. Asher* 4:7–9)

The internal divisions represent the double-mindedness that stands in the way of prayer (1:7–8). James returns to the topic of prayer in the middle of this outburst (vv. 2b–3). The double-minded person cannot expect God to respond to prayers that are aimed at fulfilling such disordered desires. During a television interview, country music star Garth Brooks gave a simpler example of this conclusion. Asked to explain the origin of a song, "Unanswered Prayers," the singer replied that it came to him after he and his wife ran into one of his old girlfriends. When he was going with the first girl, he prayed that they would be together forever. Now, that is one prayer that he is glad God did not answer. "Sometimes the best prayers are the ones God does not answer," he told interviewer David Frost. In the earlier reference to prayer, James sought to encourage readers to pray for heavenly wisdom. The previous section reminded readers that wisdom leads to peace.

The vehement outburst, "Unfaithful creatures!" (v. 4), makes conversion of the audience seem unlikely. Their affection for the world makes such individuals enemies of God. "Unfaithful creatures" in the RSV translates the term *moichalides,* that is, adulterers. James takes on the tone of the prophets who condemned Israel for its infidelity to God (Isa. 1:21; 50:1; Jer. 3:7–10; 13:27; Ezek. 16:23–26; 23:45). Ralph Martin thinks that this entire section was originally directed against those who had been swept up in the political turmoil that led to the revolt against Rome (R. Martin, 145). However, the text as it stands remains at the level of general exhortation. The sharpened conflict between God and the world often appears in apocalyptic contexts. James 1:27 speaks of true religion as avoiding the world. James uses the expression "world" to refer to those values of human society that are hostile to God (Laws).

Verse 5 introduces a citation that is identified as from Scripture, though it does not correspond to any known passage. Its translation is also problematic. What is the subject of the verb "long for" or "desire" *(epipothein)?* What is the reference of the opening phrase "with regard to jealousy" *(pros phthonon)?* The NRSV takes "God" as the subject of the verb and treats the prepositional phrase as adverbial. Then the clause that modifies "spirit," namely, "which dwells in us," is treated as though the verb were transitive, "which he [= God] has made to dwell in us." Although "spirit" could refer to God's Spirit, the only other use of the term "spirit" in James clearly means the human spirit (2:26). The dualism between those who are attached to the world and those who are friends of God in the previous verse suggests an apocalyptic dualism of two spirits at war within individuals and for the allegiance of human beings. The Dead Sea Scrolls describe the "two spirits," truth and falsehood, in which human beings will walk until the judgment. Those who follow the angel of darkness are led astray into vice, haughtiness, deceit, abundant evils, cruelty, ill-temper. The angel of truth leads the righteous in charity, humility, zeal for the law, steadfastness (1QS 3:18—4:26). God has allotted the two spirits to battle it out in the hearts of all humans until the end.

The *Testament of Simeon* describes envy as a spirit that dwells within individuals prodding them to destroy those who are the object of envy. The only solution is to flee to the Lord for refuge. Then the spirit of envy will depart and those afflicted by it will learn compassion and love of others (*T. Sim.* 3:1–6). Since verses 1–4 depict the internal and external divisions caused by passions, specifically envy or jealousy, the citation in verse 5 should probably be interpreted along the lines of the *Testament of Simeon.* In situations that imply conflict, the preposition *pros* with an accusative can designate what is being opposed. The *Testament of Simeon* instructs those whose minds are wracked by envy to seek refuge in God. The citation in James makes a similar point. God desires the spirit that dwells within humans to be opposed to jealousy, not to be its slave. The verse indicates God's displeasure with the behavior described in the previous verses (R. Martin). The ethic of perfection that runs throughout James depends on the power of God's wisdom to transform the double-minded, vacillating, pleasure-seeking drives of human beings into the integrity of devotion to God's will. Evidence of that transformation is to be found in concrete actions such as loving the afflicted and peacemaking.

James 4:6–10
Humble Yourselves before God

The next section develops the maxim employed in the *Testament of Simeon,* the evil spirit [of jealousy] will flee if a person turns to God (vv. 7–8a). The injunction to draw near to God in order to drive out the devil or a particular vice appears frequently in the *Testaments of the Twelve Patriarchs.* These verses describe what the audience must do to transform their lives from the double-mindedness of sinners to holiness and integrity before God (v. 8b; Mussner). The exhortation begins with a citation of Prov. 3:34 LXX. Readers already know that God favors the lowly (1:6, 12; 2:5). James may be telescoping a possible objection posed by the audience of verses 1–5, namely, that despite their prayers (v. 3), God has not eliminated such desires. James suggested that they did not ask God for the spirit of wisdom (v. 2) but only for the means to pursue their passions (v. 3). The introduction to the quotation, "But he gives greater grace" (v. 6a), suggests something greater than the spirit bestowed on humans when they were created (referred to in v. 5; so Mussner).

James implies that the reason his audience has not experienced an end to the conflicts generated by the passions is their lack of humility before God. The rest of the passage consists of a string of imperatives. Humility demands a complete reversal of one's way of life. The turn from laughter to weeping (v. 9) must be understood in the context of wisdom literature. Fools delight in doing wrong (Prov. 10:23; Sir. 21:18–20; 27:13). James is not suggesting that the righteous should go about in a state of morbid depression over their sins. This appeal is addressed to the wicked whose way of life neglects God's will entirely. If such people turn to God, they discover that the things that previously gave them joy are evidence of the distance that separated them from God. Weeping is evidence that their conversion is sincere. Once this transformation has been accomplished, then those who have embraced humility will be exalted by God (v. 10; 1:9–10).

Humility is a difficult virtue for many modern Christians to understand. It often suggests either false claims to a lowliness that the speaker has never experienced or the degradation and lack of initiative that governs the lives of the poor. One Sunday morning the pastor was preaching eloquently about concern for the poor. The woman next to me had worked hard all her life so that her family would not fall into the category sociologists describe as "the working poor." She leaned over to me and whispered, "The trouble with him is that he doesn't know what it's really like." When her comment jolted me out of the mental fog I had lapsed into when the pastor began on one of his pet topics, I thought of how many of the very best Christians I know in the parish must feel exactly as she does. They are the humble, pious, lowly ones. More often than not, they experience the world as a place in which the deck seems to be stacked against them. Things that are merely minor annoyances for the rest of us, like a blown tire or a roof leak caused by snow and ice or a doctor's prescription, are a serious setback to those families.

James knows that God's word to them is not humility but exaltation. God has not written them off because of their socioeconomic position. God does not take pleasure in their suffering.

What about the rest of us? Isolated in middle-class comfort and privilege, we can easily become complacent. Because we are not among the rich and powerful who control society, we may think of ourselves as humble. Or we may think that we deserve what we have because of our hard work. Other parishioners resent "being constantly picked on about the poor," as someone else put it after the service. The man who made that comment is also a serious Christian. He gets annoyed when he feels that the preacher is trying to "lay a guilt trip on us from the pulpit." This section of James appears to be that sort of preaching. If there were real, harmful divisions in the community, then such harsh language might be appropriate. But for the average congregation, James appears to be hostile to a legitimate pride that people take in the way of life they provide for their families. The key question is, What is legitimate pride? Does it recognize how much we owe those achievements to God's grace and to gifts we have received from others along the way? A modern spiritual writer suggests the following definition of humility:

> Humility is not a false rejection of God's gifts. To exaggerate the gifts we have by denying them may be as close to narcissism as we can get in this life. No, humility is the admission of God's gifts to me and the acknowledgment that I have been given them for others. Humility is the total continuing surrender to God's power in my life and in the lives of those around me. (Joan Chittister, O.S.B., *Wisdom Distilled from the Daily;* HarperCollins, 1990, 65)

We can all learn the humility that recognizes God's presence in our lives.

James 4:11–12
Do Not Judge Others

The harsh tone of the previous section vanishes as James returns to speaking to his audience as fellow Christians (Dibelius). Rhetorically this shift in tone indicates that the call to return to the Lord has been successful. But there is still the possibility of a conversion that has not completely transformed the lives of believers. James has already warned readers that true piety demands attention to what we say about others (3:9–10). The "royal law of freedom" does not condemn or judge others (2:12–13). The *Testament of Simeon* made compassion and love of others the result of driving out the spirit of envy. If James has been drawing on that tradition of exhortation, then this injunction not to speak evil of or to judge another would be a natural conclusion to the section. Slandering others is frequently condemned in the Old Testament (cf. Lev. 19:16; Ps. 50:20; Prov. 18:8; 20:13; 26:22).

The *Testament of Gad* associates the spirit of hatred with envy. Such persons publicize the sins of others and try to see them punished to the full extent of the law (*T. Gad* 4:3–6). The righteous, on the other hand, will never denounce others:

> Righteousness expels hatred; humility kills envy. For the person who is just and humble is ashamed to commit an injustice, not because someone else will pass judgment on him but out of his own heart, because the Lord considers his inner deliberations. He will not denounce a fellow man since fear of the Most High overcomes hatred. Being concerned not to arouse the Lord's anger, he is completely unwilling to wrong anyone even in his thoughts. (*T. Gad* 5:3–6)

James makes a similar point. Those who speak evil against others have violated the fundamental law that we are to love others as ourselves (2:8). Only God is able to act as judge (Ps. 9:21; Isa. 33:22) because only God has the power to save or condemn (Deut. 32:39). Like the righteous person in *T. Gad,* believers should be concerned with doing the will of God, not with passing judgment on the behavior of others. Those who are truly righteous recognize that they will answer to God both for their actions and for what is in their heart. This exhortation may have played an important role in churches that combined Jewish and non-Jewish Christians, since it prohibits judging or condemning others because of the particular details of their religious practice (cf. Rom. 14:1–12; Mussner).

The Lord Governs Human Life

JAMES 4:13—5:12

Recognition that God governs human life is a basic element in the humility of the righteous. Those who lack such humility assume that their success is the result of their own achievements. The final section of general exhortations in James applies this insight to familiar themes: the relationship of rich and poor; the need for patient endurance until the judgment, and integrity in speech. Although most of the section speaks to the letter's Christian audience, the sharp denunciation of oppressive landowners (5:1–6) does not speak to Christians but to outsiders. They are responsible for the death of God's righteous one (5:6). Throughout the letter, James reminds its readers that God's judgment will establish true justice. The final segment of this section encourages them to remain patient until the Lord comes (5:7). Just as no one can tell where he or she will be a year from now (4:15), so no one can rush the Lord's coming. Nevertheless, James confidently assures readers that the judgment is at hand (5:8–9).

James 4:13–17
Do Not Be Confident in Future Plans

Prosperity brings arrogance, a false confidence in our ability to secure the future. James returns to the diatribe style of responding to an imaginary interlocutor. The opponent confidently asserts his plans to make money by journeying abroad to trade for a year. Traveling merchants and tradespeople were the backbone of early Christian missionary success. Paul was able to ply his trade of leatherworking while he went from one city to another preaching the gospel. James does not object to the occupation of trading as such. Nor is he concerned about the merchant's desire to make money. The problem lies in the arrogant confidence that conceals the fact that we really depend on God for success. Jewish wisdom traditions contain numerous variants of the maxim expressed in verse 14a that human life is fragile. We cannot count on what the next day will bring (Prov. 27:1; Sir. 11:18–19). Greco-Roman moralists also warned their audiences against undue confidence in the future (Seneca, *Letters* 101.4; Epictetus, *Discourses* 1.1.17; 3.21.12). James highlights the transitory character of human life by comparing it to a mist or smoke that appears for a short time and then disappears. Hosea 13:3 uses this metaphor to depict the transitory existence of those who had turned away from God to worship the calf idol, "they shall be like the morning mist, or like the dew that goes away early." Psalm 68:2 describes God driving his enemies away like smoke. Wisdom of Solomon 5:14 promises that the wicked will vanish like smoke, while the righteous will have eternal life. Therefore, the image was not a neutral observation. Those who disappear like mist or smoke have ignored or rejected God.

The rejection of God becomes evident when people boast in their wealth. Wisdom of Solomon 5:8 has the wicked confess that the wealth that was the object of so much boasting did not release them from judgment because they ignored the "way of the Lord." The next section will depict wealthy persons who fall into the category of the wicked as it is used in Wisdom of Solomon 5. Here James does not accuse his readers of completely neglecting the ways of God. The danger in this section is stated more gently. The readers may be so caught up in their pursuits that they forget that they are radically dependent on God. James offers two pieces of advice. First, always qualify claims about the future by recognizing that everything is subject to God's will (v. 15). Second, refrain from boasting (v. 16). James may have had in mind Christians who boasted about their wealth (R. Martin).

An independent proverb sums up the first segment (v. 17; cf. 2:13; 3:18). If those who know what is right fail to do it, they sin. Moral exhortation of the sort found in James ensured that its audience could not claim ignorance of what they ought to do. In the *Testaments of the Twelve Patriarchs* the patriarchs often begin the exhortation by saying that they are going to describe sins they had committed so that their sons and brothers will not behave ignorantly (*T. Reub.* 1:6; *T. Dan* 2:1). If the patriarch instructs his children in the ways of God, then he will not be held guilty for the sins they commit (*T. Sim.* 6:1). James had told readers that teachers would be held to a stricter standard (3:1). Now that he has almost completed his instruction, he warns listeners that they too will be held responsible for acting on the knowledge they now possess.

James 5:1–6
God Condemns the Rich for Injustice

With a sudden shift to prophetic condemnation (cf. Isa. 13:6; Ezek. 7:19–20; Amos 8:3, 9), James announces the woes to come upon the rich. For them, the coming of the Lord will mean condemnation and destruction (vv. 1, 3, 5). The woe oracle seals the doom of the rich oppressors. It does not summon them to repentance (Dibelius and Greeven; Mussner). With biting sarcasm, James describes the wealth that the rich store up as both evidence and fiery torment on the day of judgment (v. 3). By using the past tense to describe riches that have rotted, moth-eaten garments, and rusted gold (vv. 2–3a), James suggests that the day of judgment has already begun to fall on the rich. The image of earthly treasures destroyed by moths and rust was traditional. Matthew 6:19–20 uses it to encourage laying up treasure in heaven rather than on earth. "Rusted" money indicates that it has been hoarded, not used to help others. Sirach 29:10 commends using one's money to help relatives or friends rather than letting it "rust under a stone and be destroyed." The charge of permitting one's money to rust was a condemnation of the rich for failing to fulfill the obligation to give alms (Dibelius and Greeven). The benefactor relationships of ancient society created complex relationships by which the wealthy were compelled to give liberally to public needs as well as to private individuals. In that context, hoarding was not only a private vice but also a sin against the larger community.

James turns to more direct charges against the rich. They have violated the law by withholding the wages of their laborers (Lev. 19:13; Deut. 24:14–15; Job 31:38–40; Jer. 22:13). In this instance, the wealthy are not only hoarding what might be shared with the larger community but also actually refusing to give the laborers what is due. God cannot remain deaf to the cries of those who are victims of injustice (Ps. 17:1–6; 18:6; 31:2; Isa. 5:9). The dissolute luxury of the rich has merely fattened them up for the day of judgment (v. 5). James returns to the final charge against such persons: they have killed the righteous person. Wisdom of Solomon 2:12–20 depicts the plot that the wicked hatch against the righteous. They cannot tolerate the reproof that his way of life constitutes. When they die, the wicked see the righteous exalted with God and are overcome with fear (Wisd. Sol. 5:1–8). James stands in this tradition. Christian readers will doubtless recognize that the righteous in verse 5 include both Jesus and the alleged author of the letter, James. James 2:6–7 reminded readers that they had been oppressed and dragged into court by the rich. Therefore the audience could see its own fate reflected in the suffering righteous.

This prophetic outburst against the rich is based on traditional material. Although it might seem to some to express no more than the resentment of those who could never aspire to be wealthy landowners, James has been careful to indicate that real injustice motivates the condemnation of the rich. First, they do not understand that wealth is held in trust for the larger community. The rich have an obligation to use some of it to benefit others. Second, they neglect the laws that demand fair treatment of laborers. Consequently, some part of the wealth that the rich enjoy has been gotten at the expense of others. Third, the excessive personal consumption of wealth by the rich shows that they have the means to help the less fortunate. If any person has so much of the basic goods, food, clothing, and money that these goods are rotting away, then that person cannot need or even enjoy what he or she possesses. Finally, the rich may be drawn into activities that actually lead to the death of the righteous. In ancient times, the rich may have actually sought to remove such a person from the scene. In modern times, the situation might be a more subtle matter of neglect. When someone is injured because of defective machinery at work or because of a defective product, the management that knew of the problem but did not want to surrender profits is responsible. Ironically, the legal settlement may cost the company much more than it would have cost to fix the problem when it was first reported.

James 5:7–11
Await the Lord's Judgment with Patience

The previous section appeared to say that the judgment of the rich was at hand. Now James turns back toward the Christian audience and counsels patience until the coming of the Lord. This advice recalls the opening admonition to endure trials patiently (1:2–4). Those who might protest that the Lord is too slow in coming are reminded of the time it takes before a farmer can harvest his crop (v. 7b). Two further commands, "strengthen your hearts" (v. 8) and "do not grumble" (v. 9), are each completed with an assurance that judgment is at hand. The second seems out of place. Grumbling against others appears to be yet another example of "speaking evil" of others (4:11). However, the cause of the grumbling may be linked to uncertainty about judgment. Some may doubt the goodness of God (R. Martin).

Waiting for the Lord with patience in times of trial is the governing theme of the section (v. 10a). James gives two examples to bolster the readers' determination to remain steadfast. The prophets were frequently depicted as martyrs in this period (v. 10). Job was an example of patient endurance under suffering (v. 11a; cf. *T. Job* 27:7). Finally, James takes on the suspicion that the suffering of the righteous and delayed judgment raise. Is God really concerned? James insists that its readers already know what the purpose of God is. God is compassionate and merciful (v. 11b). These are traditional epithets of God (Ps. 103:8; 111:4) that are demonstrated by the outcome of the stories of such exemplary figures as the prophets and Job.

James 5:12
Do Not Swear Oaths

A separate piece of tradition has found its way into the text. The prohibition of oaths resembles a saying of Jesus in the Sermon on the Mount (Matt. 5:34–37). The law prohibited swearing falsely (Exod. 20:7; Lev. 19:12; Num. 30:3; Jer. 5:2; Hos. 4:2). Sirach 23:9–11 warns against overuse of oaths or habitually using the name of the Lord. Persons who swear frequently are likely to engage in some form of falsehood. James and Matthew represent a tradition that prohibits all oaths. The variant in James is less elaborate than the one in Matthew. It lacks the expanded examples of things it is improper to swear by and insists that oaths are to be replaced by truthful speech. Matthew's doubling of the yes and no in situations where an oath is called for may reflect the attempt to develop an alternative form of speech to replace the oath formula (Dibelius and Greeven). However, citations of the saying in later Christian writers follow the form in James 5:12 that places an article before the first yes and no in order to indicate that only the second is what Christians are to say (cf. Justin, *Apology* 16.5; Clement of Alexandria, *Stromata* 5.99.1; 6.67.5; the RSV translates Matt. 5:37a as though it followed this tradition).

This saying belongs to the collection of material on proper speech that appears repeatedly in James. Since oaths were commonly required in court proceedings, one wonders how refusal to swear affected Christians who were dragged into court (James 2:6–7). James concludes the saying with the warning that those who violate the prohibition risk condemnation in God's court. Since James locates this saying just before the concluding advice about relationships within the community (or opens that section; so Cargal, 188), it may have been perceived as a rule governing the relationships between Christians. Christians who were brought before a court by outsiders may have continued to use the oaths that were part of compulsory legal form. Similarly, the merchants would have been expected to use oaths to conclude some of their dealings.

Most Christians from ancient times to the present assume

that the saying aims at honest speech, not the formal oaths required when we are involved in legal relationships. A few groups take the prohibition more literally and refuse to swear any oath. I once saw a superior court judge remove a juror from a panel because he would not swear an oath. When I met him in the elevator a few minutes later, the young man was very angry that he had not been allowed to serve on the jury. Since I had been thrown off by one of the lawyers, I suggested that they did not want religious types of any sort. He would have to recognize that most judges and lawyers would not consider refusal to swear an oath a sign of a person's integrity. Most people also recognize the truth of the statement that people should not have to use oaths to back up what they say. We all deal with people with whom various legal forms are not required. Sometimes we go through the paperwork anyway just to keep the records straight. Sometimes we don't. It is not necessary for the individual to be a friend or longtime associate to demonstrate such integrity. The contractor who works on my house from time to time is a person whose word (and cost estimates!) can absolutely be relied upon. He also knows that he will be paid for his work on time. Sometimes we do not finish the paperwork until after the job has been done and paid for. Even though the prohibition of oaths has little to say about such ordinary experience, the larger question of honesty in dealing with others is important in all our relationships.

Final Exhortation to the Community

JAMES 5:13–20

The typical letter form concluded with details of practical advice or personal plans. James does not contain any personal details or the greetings that normally conclude a letter, but the conclusion does turn toward details of the inner life of the church. The shift in tone suggests an intimate relationship between the author and addressees. Cargal suggests that the letter concludes with the summons to bring back those who have strayed from the truth (v. 19) as a resumption of the opening address to the twelve tribes in the Diaspora (Cargal, 46). As a general conclusion to the letter, the exhortation to restore those who have wandered suggests that the letter has accomplished its purpose. It has called readers back to the truth. James exercises his function as "servant of God" (1:1) by restoring true wisdom about God and the Christian life to the community (Cargal, 213). This section returns to the communal character of Christian life that appeared in the exhortation on love of one another in James 2. Prayer, suffering, and sin all take place within the church community. All its members have a responsibility to aid one another in the trials of life.

James 5:13–15
Prayer Heals the Sick

Most of the concluding instructions concern prayer. The use of prayer or blessing formulas at the end of a letter may have suggested the theme. The first series of sayings is introduced by questions, "Is anyone . . . let that person . . ." The first two (v. 13)—when suffering, pray; when happy, sing psalms [NRSV: "songs of praise"]—might appear to refer only to individuals. However, other passages in the New Testament indicate that the community sang psalms (1 Cor. 14:15; Eph. 5:19–20; Col. 3:16–17). Therefore, James may envisage community participation as well.

The focus of the passage comes in the reference to the sick person (vv. 14–15). There the elders of the church are to pray over the individual and anoint that person in the name of the Lord (v. 15). The expression "elder" designates persons entrusted with leadership and teaching in the church (cf. Acts 11:30; 14:23; 15:2; 16:4; 20:17; 21:28; 1 Tim. 5:17–19; Titus 1:5; 1 Peter 5:1; 2 John 1). Though most references to "the Lord" in James are references to God the Father, this one appears to be a reference to anointing in the name of Jesus. Anointing invokes the healing power of Jesus (Mussner, 220–21). Acts indicates that early Christians healed in the name of Jesus. The power that was active in their healings was associated with the risen Lord (Acts 3:6, 16; 4:7, 10; 9:34; 19:13). James 5:14 indicates that anointing and prayer for healing had become a formal ministry in the church. Clearly, God is the one who responds to the prayer and the invocation of Jesus' name in the anointing rite. The anointing is not some form of medicine. Nor are particular individuals credited with special gifts of healing. In that respect, James differs from the view found in Paul (1 Cor. 12:9, 28, 30) that healing is a gift of the Spirit given to particular individuals. Mark 6:13 refers to the disciples' curing the sick by anointing them with oil.

Verse 15 affirms the saving power of such prayer. The sick person will be raised up. Any sins committed will be forgiven. Some exegetes think that the future verbs, "will save" and "will raise up," are indications of salvation in the judgment rather than present healing. However, there is no indication that the illness ends in death. The verb "raise up" was also used in healing miracles (cf. Mark 5:41). Therefore, physical recovery seems to be what is intended (R. Martin). Forgiveness of sin reflects a common assumption that illness results from an offense against God (cf. John 9:2). Mark 2:1–12 associates Jesus' cure of the paralytic with his power to forgive sin. Physical healing removes any doubt about the restoration of the individual's relationship to God.

As part of its liturgical renewal, the Catholic Church restored the sacrament of anointing from its use for the dying to prayer and anointing of any persons who are seriously ill. The sacrament may be celebrated with the community prior to a hospital admission or other course of treatment. Other churches are also rediscovering the importance of a healing ministry that is carried out within the context of communal prayer. One of the most important effects of healing services that involve the whole community, not just the sick, is breaking the barriers of silence and isolation that illness often imposes on the sick and their families. Members of the congregation feel free to ask people how they are doing, to send cards, or to drop in for a visit even if the person is not a personal friend. People who are in the hospital at the same time have even taken to visiting each other. Although we may think that the assumption that sin and illness are connected is archaic, the association has a modern form that is very real. In our health-conscious culture, many people feel that illness is a fault. If they get sick, it proves that they did not eat right, take the right herb, exercise properly, or whatever. When parishioners insist on being anointed privately, they often feel that there is something "wrong" or "better kept private" about serious illness. Perhaps as public healing services become a more established part of church life, the sick will not feel that they have to hide their illness.

James 5:16–18
Prayer Heals the Sinner

James moves from the special case of sin and illness to sin in general. Communal confession and prayer will heal (v. 16a). Public acknowledgment of sin appears frequently in the Old Testament (Lev. 5:5; Num. 5:7; Pss. 38:4–6; 40:13; 41:5; 51:5–8; Prov. 20:9; 28:13; Dan. 3:27–31). Although the verb "heal" *(iasthai)* usually refers to physical healing, the context suggests that James thinks of the confession that is accompanied by forgiveness of sin (cf. 1 Peter 2:24, citing Isa. 53:6, on the death of Christ; Mussner, 227). The verb appears in the Old Testament as God's healing the sinner (Deut. 30:3; Pss. 6:3; 30:3; 107:19–20; Jer. 3:22). The context suggests a communal ritual of repentance, confession, and healing, not cataloging of individual faults.

After affirming that forgiveness and healing are available in the community, the reference to a "just" or "righteous" person's prayer seems awkward (v. 16b). Does James mean the prayer of the wise, that is, anyone who has attained the perfection described earlier in the letter? Certainly, James assures its readers that God always responds to the prayer of those who are single-hearted in their devotion (1:5). Or is this an indirect reference to the piety of James, the brother of the Lord (R. Martin)? More probably, the phrase is an independent maxim that reformulates the common view that God hears the cry of the lowly or righteous (Ps. 34:15; Prov. 15:29). Lest the reader object that such prayer is not possible for average people, James introduces the example of Elijah as a man "with the same nature" *(homoiopathēs)* as us. His fervent prayer closed and then opened the heavens (vv. 17–18). Though Elijah's prayer is not the agency of shutting and opening the heavens in 1 Kings (17:1; 18:42), he is credited with both their shutting (Sir. 48:3) and their opening (2 Esd. 7:109). James draws on the general tradition about the prophet. Presumably the logic of the argument is from a greater case, Elijah's prayer and the weather, to a lesser one, Christian prayer for healing. If a human being can pray so fervently that God grants the former, surely we can pray with enough faith to receive healing and forgiveness.

James 5:19–20
Seek Out Erring Christians

Matthew's treatment of the parable of the lost sheep (Matt. 18:10–14) highlights the responsibility of community leaders to seek out Christians who have gone astray. First Thessalonians 5 refers to particular individuals entrusted with admonishing members of the community (v. 12) as well as to the duty of all members to exhort one another (v. 14). Galatians 6:1 encourages those who are spiritual in the community to admonish those who sin with gentleness. Clearly concern for winning back fellow Christians who go astray was common in the early church. The description of the erring brother in James fits the Old Testament depiction of those who have rejected God's way. The problem is determining who the subject of the promise in verse 20 is. "Let him know" must refer to the person who brings back an erring Christian. That would seem to suggest that the soul of the one rescuing the sinner is saved from death. In that case, the phrase is a reformulation of the saying about mercy (2:13). However, the earlier sayings about communal forgiveness make it difficult to read in that sense. Consequently, other interpreters conclude that the soul being rescued from death can only be that of the sinner. The "death" from which the sinner has been rescued is God's condemnation (R. Martin).

James concludes with a partial citation of Prov. 10:12b. The Proverbs text speaks of love covering a multitude of sins. If James had the full citation in mind, then the rescue of the sinner might be an example of the love that fulfills the "royal law" (2:8). The conclusion encourages readers to recognize that "mercy triumphs over judgment" (2:13b; Mussner). The perfect wisdom that James encourages Christians to seek from God does not mean perfectionism. Though members of the Christian community should seek out wisdom, single-hearted obedience to God, and love of others, failure to achieve that goal should not cause discouragement. The church that heeds the exhortations in James can find its way to God while it continues to live in the Diaspora.

THE BOOK OF

Jude

Introduction

Second Peter is our earliest evidence for the use of Jude in early Christianity. Jude's apocalyptic condemnation of the false teachers who had infiltrated the community (v. 4) provided much of the ammunition for 2 Peter's attack on similar false teachers (2 Peter 2:1—3:3; see Table 4). Both Jude and 2 Peter employ epistolary conventions, but neither refers to addressees in a specific location. The exhortation is addressed to any who share the apostolic faith (vv. 3, 17). Ancient examples of divine judgment as well as prophecies of future judgment serve as evidence of the fate that awaits the opponents, who have turned away from holiness to impiety. Readers must be careful not to abandon the salvation that God has extended to them. They may even win back some of those who had been led astray by false teaching (vv. 22–23).

Jude secures the allegiance of his audience by framing the condemnation of false teachers with assurances that they are not among those being condemned (Watson). He had apparently intended to write a letter about their "common salvation" (v. 3a). The readers possess a "holy faith" that they can build up with prayer in the Spirit, love of God, and the mercy of the Lord Jesus (vv. 20–21). However, the urgency of the threat led Jude to change his plans and substitute a letter that would enlist readers in the fight on behalf of the faith (v. 3b). The conclusion indicates his confidence that they will succeed (vv. 22–23). They possess the Spirit, which the false teachers, who are only interested in material passions, lack (vv. 19–20).

Jude writes as a Christian to a Christian audience, which

recognizes Jesus as the basis for salvation (v. 1, 25); acknowledges him as Lord (v. 4, 17); recognizes God as Father, Son, and Spirit (vv. 20–21); knows that the apostles made predictions about the end time (v. 17); and expects that the faithful will share the glory of the exalted Jesus (v. 24). Despite its Christian context, the argument against the false teachers never appeals to other Christian writings (Bauckham). The examples of God's judgment are all drawn from Jewish tradition. Since that material includes a reference to Enoch and a tale known only from apocryphal traditions, Jude is not limited to canonical sources. The only direct quotations in the letter come from the apocryphal traditions (vv. 9, 14b–15) and the prophetic words attributed to the apostles (v. 18). Therefore, authority does not appear to reside in the canonical text as much as it does in the testimony of ancient traditions about wickedness and divine punishment.

Authorship

The author identifies himself as "Jude, the brother of James." The name Jude (= Judas) appears frequently in the New Testament. Only two of them (excepting Judas Iscariot) could be referred to as "servant of Jesus Christ": (a) a member of the Twelve (Judas [son] of James, Luke 6:16; Acts 1:13 = Thaddaeus, Matt. 10:3), or (b) along with James, a brother of Jesus (Matt. 13:55; Mark 6:3). The importance of James, the brother of the Lord, in the Jerusalem church (1 Cor. 15:7; Gal. 1:19) suggests that "Jude" must be the brother of the Lord even though one might have expected the author to refer to his own relationship to Jesus. Jude is referred to as the brother of Jesus in the story preserved by Hegesippus that Jude's grandsons were brought before Domitian because they were of Davidic descent and were relatives of Jesus (Eusebius, *History of the Church* 3.19.1–20.7). There are no indications that Jude was familiar with the epistle of James.

However, Jude must assume that its recipients are acquainted with James as an authority in the community. Several internal hints suggest an author who was a second-generation Christian. The well-written Greek with a high proportion of unusual words indicates an author educated in Greek, not merely someone who had picked up the common language of the marketplace. The author never claims for himself the authority of a founder or apostle. Rather he tells readers to remember the predictions "of the apostles of our Lord Jesus Christ" (v. 17). That remark suggests that, like his audience, Jude looks back to tradition preserved from that earlier generation. Like them, he will engage in a struggle for the faith that was "once for all entrusted to the saints" (v. 3). That expression also suggests a deposit of faith that had been inherited from an earlier generation. Since the argument of the letter is based entirely on Jewish material, we may infer that the author was a Jewish Christian.

Occasion

Jude states the occasion for the letter explicitly: false teachers have made their way into the church and have succeeded in gaining a following there (v. 4, 18). Readers may even encounter them at the communal "love feast" (*agapē;* v. 12). The accusations of immorality and greed (vv. 4, 8, 16, 18) are conventional in polemic texts. Jude does not provide other details that might indicate particular teachings or practices that are under dispute. Though Jude speaks of the opponents as denying "our only Master and Lord, Jesus" (v. 4), denial must be a matter of conduct, not confession. The false teachers are able to participate in the communal meals, where they are apparently only noticeable because of their greed. Bauckham suggests that part of their offense consisted in abuse of communal hospitality (Bauckham, 16).

The antithesis, "unblemished" vs. "stains," encourages readers to avoid such persons. They presumably reject the threat of divine judgment, though there is no evidence for a philosophical challenge to Christian teaching such as one finds in 2 Peter. In any event, Jude's primary interest appears to be restoring the faith of those who have been influenced by these teachers rather than engaging in debate with the teachers themselves (vv. 21–23). Perhaps those causing trouble were not permanent members of a particular community but wandering teachers or prophets. Jude charges them with being merely "psychic" (NRSV: "worldly") people, that is, persons who have animal souls. They are without spirit (v. 19) and defy authority (v. 8). The negative images in the description of divine judgment will encourage readers to stay far away from such teachers. They embody mythological examples of evil from the ancient past.

Theological Themes

Jude can hardly present an elaborate theology in such a short letter. The elements of the faith that the author and his audience share emerges from comments made during the course of the argument. Salvation implies a calling by the God of Israel to serve Jesus as Lord in anticipation of Jesus' coming in judgment (v. 1). This message was taught by the apostles (v. 18). Jude's creed resembles Paul's formula in 1 Thess. 1:9–10 except that Jude never speaks of his audience as having been pagans. Either Jude speaks to persons in an entirely Jewish Christian environment, or, by the second generation of Christians, that sense of turning away from idolatry no longer exists.

Believers have received the Spirit as a consequence of their calling (v. 19). Since Jude consistently castigates the false teachers for immorality, slavery to passion, self-interested flattery and the like, Christians must have been taught that life in the Spirit required a serious moral transformation. Those who fall away from that holiness of life will be condemned at the judgment. A few hints of communal life also come through in the letter. Christians celebrate a common meal called a "love feast" *(agapē).* They must also gather for instruction and prayer on other occasions. Such meetings should build up the faith of all in the community (v. 20). Jude assumes that its audience is familiar with a number of stories concerning notorious sinners in Jewish legend and with prophecies of the end time from the apostles. Jude also assumes that the recipients of his letter will have the occasion to hear it read. Jude attributes vices that disrupt communal well-being to the false teachers. They create divisions, grumble, boast, and flatter those from whom they expect to gain some advantage (v. 16).

Unlike the pastoral epistles, 1 Peter, or James, Jude does not refer to particular individuals within the community whose ministry involves teaching. Responsibility for preserving and building up the faith falls to all those who hear the letter. They can win back those who have been led astray by false teachers (vv. 22–23). Second Peter's use of Jude indicates that the letter was preserved, copied, and circulated by its recipients. They must have found it useful for the task of preserving the faith. When 2 Peter reused sections of Jude, the epistle's warnings served to strengthen the faith of an even wider audience. Some readers might say that Jude was too successful. This little known

Jewish Christian teacher was so thoroughly assimilated into the Petrine corpus, that he is fated to trail after the author who reused his work. "Once you've done 2 Peter, you've already done Jude," an editor said to me on the phone one day. The introduction, "brother of James," suggests that Jude was used to standing in the shadow of others. However, the false teachers he opposes are not the quasi-philosophical sophisticates of 2 Peter. As we read Jude, we have the opportunity to watch a small part of the postapostolic church take charge of preserving the faith it has inherited.

OUTLINE OF JUDE

Greeting	vv. 1–2
Resist False Teaching	vv. 3–4
God Destroys the Unfaithful	vv. 5–7
God Condemns the Rebellious	vv. 8–13
Enoch Predicted Their Destruction	vv. 14–16
Remember the Warning of the Apostles	vv. 17–19
Build Up Your Faith	vv. 20–23
Final Blessing	vv. 24–25

Jude

Jude uses the form of a short letter to make its appeal. Since concrete details about the addressees are lacking, the letter genre may have been used because it represented the main form of apostolic exhortation in the early churches. Jude also lacks the usual internal references to the distance between the sender and addressees. The body of the letter employs conventions of rhetorical argument to make its case (Watson). Verbally, numerous catchwords link the sections together, for example, impiety (vv. 4, 15, 18); "keep" or "guard" (vv. 1, 6, 13, 21, 24); "Lord" (vv. 4, 5, 9, 14, 17, 21, 25); "holy" (vv. 3, 14, 20, [24, "unstained"]); "flesh" or "desire" (vv. 7, 16, 18, 23); "love/beloved" (vv. 1, 2, 3, 12, 17, 20, 21); "mercy/be merciful" (vv. 2, 21, 22, 23); "judgment/condemnation" (vv. 4, 6, 9, 15). These catchwords are coupled with parallelism and contrasts that sharpen the impact of the negative image of the opponents painted by the letter (Charles). Charles lists twenty sets of triplets within the twenty-five verses of the letter. Such repetition fixes the author's message in the mind of the audience. Typology provides the primary device for making the argument. By fixing in the hearer's mind the correspondence between the false teachers and negative types from ancient days, Jude undermines the boasting and self-recommendation by which false teachers captured their audience (v. 16). The rhetorical success of the letter lies in the author's ability to make his negative characterization of the rival teachers stick in the reader's mind (Neyrey 1993, 53).

Jude 1–2
Greeting

The sender does not refer to himself as an apostle but merely as a "servant of Jesus Christ." He consistently places himself on the same level as the addressees in regard to the faith that they must defend. "Servant" does claim some honor for the person who uses it (cf. Rom. 1:1; James 1:1). It also appears in exhortations to Christians in general (1 Cor. 7:22; Eph. 6:6). Given the rhetorical skill and traditional learning that the author brings to the task of refuting the heretics, the author of Jude must have been a teacher in the church. The Jude who is named in the greeting is probably the brother of Jesus known by that name. However, he is identified by his relationship to his brother James, a more prominent figure in the early church. Presumably the readers are also Jewish Christians for whom James is a key figure among the first generation of apostles. Though it seems highly unlikely that this letter could have been composed by an Aramaic-speaking Galilean Jew like the historical Jude (*pace* Bauckham), Jude does represent Jewish Christianity.

The normal Christian form of a letter greeting spoke of "grace and peace." Jude expands the formula to produce the first of the triads that dominate the letter, "mercy, peace, and love." This combination recurs in the concluding exhortation. The addressees, "beloved" are to build up their faith by keeping themselves in the love of God and awaiting the mercy of Jesus (vv. 20–21). Thus, the greeting telegraphs the wish that the author has for his readers. If the letter succeeds, then mercy, peace, and love will be multiplied in the community.

Jude 3–4
Resist False Teaching

The opening to the body of the letter highlights its urgency. The author abandons a planned letter expounding the salvation that Christians share to address the crisis of false teaching. By hinting at the letter that he did not write, the author reminds readers of what is at stake, nothing less than salvation itself (v. 3). Another key to the gravity of the situation is the athletic metaphor, "contend," used to describe the action expected of the letter's recipients. Athletic metaphors appear frequently in Paul's letters (Rom. 15:30; 1 Cor. 9:24–27; Phil. 1:27–30; 4:3; Col. 1:29—2:1; 4:12–13; 1 Tim. 6:12). The faith was given to the saints "once for all." The false teachers cannot produce some "new version." If they reject the faith held by the author and his audience, then these teachers have no faith at all. In the athletic contest, there cannot be more than one winner. Jude is confident that his addressees can carry off the prize as long as they remain true to the message of salvation that they inherited.

That the opponents are said to have entered the churches surreptitiously could imply that they were not established members of the community but traveling missionaries. Christians naturally read the expression "our common salvation" as a reference to the salvation that comes from Christ. In the theological framework of the letter, salvation includes a renewed moral life, the gift of the Spirit, and participation in the communal fellowship. The phrase also had a meaning in secular Greek of the period that modern readers do not catch. "Our common salvation" could be used to speak of the welfare of the commonwealth or the security of the state. Thus the comment that such people had crept into the community would suggest that they were acting as spies or foreign agents. If readers think of that metaphor, then the activities of the false teachers in "perverting the grace of God" means destroying the order that the gracious will of the benign sovereign has established for his people. "Denying" the Lord Jesus implies a refusal to live under his rule. Although the opponents do not see themselves as rejecting Christianity, Jude describes their way of life as denying the order established by the Lord.

The imagery of a hierarchical state in which the well-being of the whole depends on the graciousness of the sovereign is also strange to many readers today. We can get some sense of how the ancients felt if we remember that an inscription from 9 B.C. hailed the birthday of the emperor Augustus as "the beginning of good news [= gospel] for the world." Emperors and kings could be described as saviors of their people. If we were to pick a metaphor today that would convey the danger that echoes through Jude's carefully chosen phrases, we might speak of such persons as terrorists. However, Jude also moderates the threat by assuring his readers that the appearance of such persons was predicted in ancient oracles. Their destiny is contained in those same oracles: condemnation. What follows will describe the type of persons involved, the judgment that fell on their ancient prototypes, and the prophetic sentence of condemnation from antiquity (vv. 5–15). Though readers are called to take up the struggle against these people, the eventual outcome is not in doubt. Such people cannot destroy the rule of the Lord.

Jude 5–7
God Destroys the Unfaithful

The formula "I wish you to remember" (v. 5) marks a major transition within the body of an ancient letter (White, 204).

Here it marks the beginning of the argument from ancient examples. Jude uses it again when he turns to the apostles' predictions (v. 17). By emphasizing that he is reminding readers of something they have already learned from the apostles, Jude indicates that their faith is not deficient in some way. They already know how to respond to such false teachers. The series, an unfaithful people in the wilderness (v. 5; Num. 14:11; 26:64–65; Ps. 106:25–26); the rebellious angels (v. 6; Gen. 6:1–4), and the cities of Sodom and Gomorrah (v. 7; Gen. 19:24–25), contains stock examples of wickedness. All three examples appear frequently in the Bible and other Jewish writings of the period. Lists of notorious sinners are also commonplace (cf. Sir. 16:7–10). Sirach uses a similar list to warn its readers against thinking that sin goes unpunished. God's mercy and wrath go together (Sir. 16:11–23). Jude's readers may indeed have been familiar with this list from their earlier catechesis.

The agent responsible for divine punishment is identified in some manuscripts as "the Lord" (v. 5), a reading adopted with some hesitation in the most recent editions of the Greek text. Variant readings include "God" and "Jesus." The latter is taken to be the correct reading in Neyrey's translation (Neyrey 1993, 58). Elsewhere in Jude, "Lord" refers to Jesus (vv. 4, 17, 21, 25). However, it appears awkward for a writer drawing on Jewish tradition to speak of Jesus as saving the people from Egypt. Presumably the ambiguity stems from the author's conviction that Jesus will be the end-time judge who condemns the false teachers. The manuscript readings "Jesus" or "God" reflect attempts to clarify the ambiguity inherent in the term "Lord."

The example of the wilderness generation (v. 5) establishes the principle that Jude wishes readers to draw from all the examples: those who have been saved by God can still be condemned if they are unfaithful. The Essene Damascus Rule uses an extended list of examples to warn its audience that they must observe all the commandments of the Lord perfectly and not "follow after the thoughts of the guilty inclination and after eyes of lust" (Vermes, 84; CD 2:17—3:12). *Testament of Naphtali* 3:1–4 reminds readers of the fixed order in the heavens. They should not attempt to alter the law of God by their actions. The fallen angels violated the order that God established in creation. Both elements of the tradition speak to the situation faced by Jude. Lust and other desires motivate the conduct of his opponents. They are also guilty of trying to unseat the order of things that God has established. God's authority is at stake in the challenge posed by the false teachers. (Neyrey's suggestion that Jude defends his own authority here has no direct support in the text.)

The story of the fallen angels enjoyed great popularity in Jewish lore (cf. *1 Enoch* 6–19; 86–88; 106, 13–17; *Jub.* 4:15, 22; 5:1; 1QApGen 2:1; *T. Reub.* 5:6–7; *2 Bar.* 56:10–14). Lust for human women is commonly cited as the reason for the angels' departure from their heavenly home. Michael is instructed to bind them in chains and darkness until the great day of judgment (*1 Enoch* 10:4–6). On that day, they will be transferred to Gehenna. Jude 6 reminds readers of the basic outline of the story as we find it in *1 Enoch* and other early Jewish sources. Readers were probably familiar with the story. The angels lusted after creatures it was not right for them to have, namely, human beings. The story of Sodom and Gomorrah exhibits a similar passion for what the author calls "other flesh" (v. 7). There the men of the city desire to commit homosexual rape against the angels. Their sin is all the more horrible because it not only violates the general prohibition of homosexual relations between humans (Lev. 18:22; 20:13) and the code of hospitality to strangers but also attacks God in the person of his messengers. Wisdom of Solomon 10:7 notes that the region is still smoking, clear evidence of its extreme wickedness. As in the general summary of the story of the angels, Jude may be drawing on material from Enoch. *First Enoch* 67:4–13 contains an elaborate description of the smoking valleys in which the rebellious angels have been imprisoned forever.

Jude deliberately chooses familiar examples in which the evil committed takes on mythic proportions. To modern readers the emotional impact of these stories is probably minimal since they are unfamiliar to many people. We could hardly point to the smoking steam vents of a volcanic region like Hawaii and tell our children that the smoke comes from the tears of rebellious angels being tormented underneath. After all, we have probably taken them to see models of volcanic action in the science museum. Even if we have lost the mythic sense of nature, we can still reflect on the emotional significance of Jude's examples. Sin represents a complete disruption of the order of the world. We know the feeling when we read the story of a particularly grim and senseless crime. Brutal attacks on young children or on the elderly fill us with a sense of horror, anger, and often evoke cries for the death penalty or worse. Jude's examples are calculated to provoke a similar outrage in its audience.

Jude 8–13
God Condemns the Rebellious

Verse 8 applies the previous examples to the false teachers. They have committed all these sins because they defile the flesh, reject authority, and blaspheme the angels. The first two charges are evident in the comments about the teachers throughout the letter. They will not conform to God's authority nor abandon the immorality of their lives. What Jude means by "blaspheming the glories [= angels]" is not so clear. Perhaps, it implies that they have associated themselves with what comes from the fallen angels. Or it may be no more than a rhetorical flourish that reminds readers that their immorality is rebellion against God, here represented by his angels. Neyrey has suggested that some facet of the angels' role in bringing about divine judgment may also have been under challenge. Since Jude refers to the opponents as "dreamers," they may have claimed a form of divine inspiration for their teaching.

The legend of the fallen angels in *1 Enoch* depicted Michael as the agent who executed God's punishment. Jude returns to legends about Michael (v. 9). The story that Jude is summarizing does not survive in this form in ancient sources. Fragmentary evidence for a *Testament of Moses* suggests that a dispute between Michael and Satan arose over whether Moses deserved burial. Satan contended that Moses did not deserve the honor of being buried by the angels because he had once murdered a man (Exod. 2:12; Bauckham, 60–62). The words Michael speaks, "May the Lord rebuke you," are taken from Zech. 3:2 LXX. The point of the story as Jude tells it appears to be that even the archangel Michael did not take the authority to exercise divine judgment on himself. Instead, he left judgment to God.

Verse 10 turns back to the opponents. Where Michael refused to blaspheme even Satan who deserved it, the false teachers blaspheme what they have no knowledge of. This behavior along with their immoral conduct demonstrates that the opponents are no better than irrational animals. If they act like animals, they will also be destroyed like them. The main function of this description is to prepare the reader for the woe oracle that follows (v. 11). Jude sets out another list of three notorious sinners. Each of these individuals rebelled against specific commands from the Lord. Cain murdered his brother, though he had been warned to master the evil inclination (Gen. 4:5–12). According to later legends, Balaam sought money to curse Israel, contrary to Num. 22:18 in which he refuses to do so. He is also responsible for enticing Israel into sin (Num. 25:1–9; Philo, *Life of Moses* 1. 266–68; Bauckham). Korah rebelled against Moses and Aaron (Num. 16:1–35; 26:9–10; Ps. 106:16–18; Sir. 45:18–19). Jude arranges the series in ascending order from walking on a road, to abandoning oneself to error, to perishing in a rebellion. The suggestion is that the opponents are on a similar course. The Balaam story provides a motive for the destructive behavior of the false teachers, greed.

This segment concludes with a description of the opponents that highlights the serious danger they pose. Their participation defiles the communal meals of the church (v. 12a). Jude does not specify clearly what the offensive behavior is in which they indulge. He merely comments that they eat together "without reverence" *(aphobōs).* Presumably Jude intends readers to associate some form of licentious carousing with the meals at which these teachers are present. He may have been reticent in describing the offensive behavior since his addressees have also participated in fellowship meals with the false teachers. The opponents are also accused of only caring about themselves at the meals. That accusation apparently anticipates the later charge of creating divisions within the community (v. 19). Since the verb is "shepherding themselves," it evokes an accusation in Ezek. 34:2. The false shepherds of Israel do not feed the sheep but themselves. The Septuagint formulates the phrase as a question. In any case, their behavior shows that the false teachers are not seeking "our common salvation."

Images of disordered or useless natural phenomena round out the argument (vv. 12b–13a). Jude has moved from depicting his opponents as misguided humans who take dreams for prophecy to describing them as irrational animals, and now they exhibit the chaotic behavior of some parts of the natural world: clouds without rain (Prov. 25:14); dead, fruitless trees;

waves that drive foam up on shore (Isa. 57:20) and wandering stars (*1 Enoch* 18:13–16; 88:1–3 [the fallen angels were cast from the heavens like meteorites]). *First Enoch* 80:6 describes all of nature becoming lawless and disordered in the evil times before the end of the world. Since Jude is about to invoke Enoch's authority, this imagery may have been taken from that tradition. In antiquity the fixed stars were thought to be paradigms of eternal, divine motion. The planets wandered but did so in predictable fashion. Comets and meteorites were particularly terrifying phenomena because they appeared to be eternal beings that had been jarred loose from their place in heaven. Once again the segment comes to a stern conclusion. The only suitable punishment for such destructive behavior is the eternal darkness of the netherworld.

Jude 14–16
Enoch Predicted Their Destruction

Jude has made extensive use of Jewish apocryphal traditions. Much of the legendary material in the selection of examples comes from sources similar to *1 Enoch.* Now that he turns to demonstrate the fact that all these events were prophesied in ancient times, Jude quotes Enoch (vv. 14–15). The prophecy refers to the end time in which the Lord will come and condemn all those who have opposed him. The angelic hosts who accompany the Lord might be the same angels whom the false teachers were said to blaspheme (v. 8). Jude establishes a sharp verbal contrast between the Lord with his hosts of "holy ones" and the wicked. Throughout verse 15 he repeats the words "all" (4 times), "impious" (3 times; plus "sinners") and "judge/convict." The quotation is derived from *1 Enoch* 1:9, though it is not identical with any of the extant versions (Neyrey 1993, 80–81). Jude leaves no doubt that divine judgment will be executed against such offenders. Since Enoch stands in the seventh generation from Adam (*1 Enoch* 60:8; *Jub.* 7:39), judgment against wickedness was part of God's plan from the beginning of the world.

The charges against the wicked involve both deeds and speech. Jude has already indicated that the opponents blaspheme the angels (v. 8) and whatever they do not understand (v. 10). The description that follows Enoch's prophecy highlights further crimes of speech (v. 16). Grumbling and discontent remind readers of the rebellious Israelites (v. 5) and Korah (v. 11). Balaam also attempted to misuse speech by cursing the Israelites. "Following their own passions" describes the general immorality with which Jude charges the opponents. These passions are expressed in speech. The words in question are no longer merely complaining or grumbling. Such speech would have a disastrous enough effect in the community. The opponents go even further. Jude compared them to shepherds seeking their own pasture. The final two examples of sinful speech refer to ways of manipulating others. They are accused of boasting and showing partiality to those from whom they anticipate some gain for themselves.

After the lofty, mythological sinners of the earlier examples, this list of verbal offenses might seem somewhat flat. However, the sins of speech are associated with the other forms of immorality that the opponents exhibit. They have no respect for God's law. They are corrupting the community, and they follow their own passions. Speech is much more carefully controlled and monitored in a traditional, hierarchical society than it is in modern democracies. We can hardly recapture the sense of horror at blasphemy that ancient society felt because for us words do not have the same power that they do in traditional societies. Words appear to have considerably less consequence than actions. In traditional societies, the word is a form of action. Perhaps the easiest way to recover some sense of the importance of speech is to think of cases where it goes wrong. What happens to the workplace, a church community, or a family when everyone begins to complain, to speak badly about others, or to form factions? Distrust and division set in fairly quickly. I was recently talking to a friend about why people seemed afraid to tell a particular authority what they thought we ought to do. I always found him quite easy to work with. My friend observed that the person in question tended to say negative things about those he did not respect. People become hesitant to speak up because they are afraid of what he might say about them when they are not present. Both of us could see that if things did not change it would be difficult to keep the whole group working together.

Jude 17–19
Remember the Warning of the Apostles

Jude brings his readers back to their own experience. They may not be familiar with the ancient prophecies of Enoch, but they do know what they were taught by the apostles. The expression "scoffer" refers to those who ignore all the precepts of the law (Ps. 1:1; Prov. 1:22; 9:7–8). The Essenes spoke of enemies of the sect as "scoffers" (from Isa. 28:14; CD 1:14; 4QpIsa[b] 2:6–10). The idea that the wicked would gain the upper hand in the last days was such a common feature of both Jewish and Christian apocalyptic literature that Jude does not need to cite a particular prophecy. He has merely created the words attributed to the apostles out of the earlier description of the opponents. Verse 19 adds to the catalogue of their offenses. They create divisions. The earlier charges of self-centered behavior at the communal meal and of partiality belong to this context. Jude also accuses them of being "material" persons and not possessing the Spirit. The Greek word *psychikoi* is derived from the word for "soul." It can mean what is merely natural but in contrast with the spiritual implies that the individuals in question are either immature (1 Cor. 2:14) or perhaps devoid of a fully human soul. Jude may be alluding to the earlier depiction of the opponents as irrational animals (v. 10). Since they have no spirit, such persons cannot be Christians as they claim.

Jude 20–23
Build Up Your Faith

The final exhortation allows Jude to contrast the behavior of faithful Christians with that of his opponents. The exhortation to build up the community probably derives from early catechetical instruction (Rom. 14:19; 15:2; 1 Cor. 14:12, 26; 1 Thess. 5:11). Jude instructs readers to build on their faith. The means for such building are described in a triadic formula: prayer in the Holy Spirit (cf. Eph. 6:18), love of God, and waiting for the mercy of the Lord Jesus (vv. 20b–21). The mercy of Jesus will be demonstrated when he comes in judgment. The series of sinners in vv. 5–7 were used in Sirach 16 as examples that God had to combine wrath with mercy. After an extended account of condemnation, Jude highlights the other side of the coin, mercy for the faithful.

Verses 22–23 contain a further suggestion for communal action. They may be able to restore some of those who were influenced by the false teachers. The Greek text of vv. 22–23a occurs in a number of variants. A long version, the text printed in recent editions, refers to three groups: doubters (NRSV: "some who are wavering") who receive mercy; those snatched from fire, and those to whom mercy is shown. Many commentators think that the original text only had two groups (Bauckham, 108–10; Neyrey 1993, 85–86). An early papyrus, P 72, has a dual-membered form: "snatch some from the fire, and have mercy with fear on those who waver." The dual-membered form becomes a triad with addition of a final participial clause, "hating even the cloak defiled by the flesh" (v. 23c). Bauckham suggests that an allusion to Zech. 3:1–5 explains this peculiar series of images. In this vision, Joshua, the high priest, is plucked from the fire and his filthy clothes exchanged for festal attire. This suggestion does not account for the problematic wording of the text. Presumably the defiled garment is a metaphor for either the opponents or their conduct.

It is hard to determine whether the term *diakrinomenoi* refers to those who "doubt" or those who "dispute." Both translations are possible. Those who opt for "dispute" assume that the persons addressed are going to argue against communal rebuke (so Bauckham). However, the translation "doubt" points to the divisive influence of false teachers on others. Jude's sharp condemnations do not suggest that the opponents can be turned away from their behavior. Those with whom they have been associating may be uncertain about whose account of faith to believe. Such persons can be treated with mercy, not the sharp rejection reserved for false teachers.

Mutual exhortation was a common feature in early Christian communities (cf. Matt. 18:15–17; Gal. 6:1–2; James 5:19–20). The "fear" that believers are to show those whom they snatch from the fire may be a caution about their own conduct such as one finds in Gal. 6:1–2 or in the teaching on forgiveness in Matt. 18:21–34. At the same time, the persistent warnings about defilement that run through the letter suggest that readers should take an active role in promoting the holiness of their community. They are not to let false teaching and selfish or immoral behavior go unchallenged. That message is a difficult one for many Americans who have grown up with a cultural ethos that tells us to mind our own business. In a recent television interview a man arrested for twenty-one bank robberies would have been apprehended the first time if people had paid attention. Instead, he ran several blocks down a busy Boston street with a bag of money that was spewing out red smoke. No one attempted to stop or question him. Our pastor has a good strategy for dealing with those who come up and begin to complain about someone else's behavior. "Did you ever ask why he or she is doing that?" he comments. A question opens the way for conversation whereas condemnation slams the door shut. At the same time, it enables us to overcome the cultural bias toward putting up with everything.

Jude 24–25
Final Blessing

Jude ends with a final doxology that has been expanded to include the immediate situation faced by the letter. Only God's grace can keep the community from falling victim to the evils it faces. Mere human exhortation will not be sufficient to bring an unstained community into God's presence (cf. 1 Thess. 3:13). Jude also expands the time reference at the conclusion of the doxology backward from the usual reference to the present and eternal future (see Neyrey 1993). God's glory, dominion, and power are to be praised from before all time. The mythological examples that formed much of the content of Jude make this expansion a natural development. Jude has instructed his audience that God's power is exhibited in the created order and that God's judgment has been effective from the earliest times. God's condemnation of the wicked and the false teachers who are disrupting Jude's church was decreed in ancient times (v. 4). When it occurs at the judgment, those who have reviled and blasphemed God will discover that they should have honored and praised God. This conclusion also brings the rhetorical agenda of the letter to its close. Jude invites his readers to picture themselves standing with Christ in the heavenly court. Of course, they would desire to be unstained and holy in such a setting. God's eternal power and majesty makes it clear that he can bring the faithful to that glorious destiny.

THE BOOK OF

Second Peter

Introduction

Unlike the Johannine epistles or 1 and 2 Timothy, 2 Peter is not related to 1 Peter in either language and style or in its setting and theological development, a fact recognized by Jerome (*Letters* 120.11). Second Peter 3:1 refers to itself as the "second letter I have written to you." That suggests knowledge of the existence of 1 Peter. However, there are no explicit verbal links between the two. If 2 Peter had been following 1 Peter as a model, one would have expected a reference to the readers as "exiles of the Diaspora" in the greeting and perhaps elsewhere in the text (Bauckham, 143–46). By the time of 2 Peter, a collection of Pauline letters has an authority in the churches similar to that of the Old Testament (2 Peter 3:15–16). But since those letters have been subject to misinterpretation and used to unsettle the faith of believers, 2 Peter will provide an apostolic witness capable of safeguarding the faith as it is found in Paul's letters (3:17). Since Peter was an eyewitness of the transfigured glory of Christ (1:16–17), his testimony to the second coming of Christ takes priority over the false teaching circulating in the churches.

Because Peter, the alleged author, writes the letter as his dying testament, the letter has special authority. Peter has already obtained the divine glory and virtue of those who have escaped worldly passions. He is about to seal that confession with a death that Jesus prophesied for him. The addressees are to consider the apostle a numinous presence watching over their faith in the future (1:14–15). Rhetorically, 2 Peter establishes the spirit of Peter's teaching as the guardian of apostolic tradition. The letter/testament is a witness to that tradition but not its full articulation. Letters generally were not thought to convey the full intent of their author. Often they do no more than substitute for the presence of the author. Second Peter presents its author as the last of the apostolic witnesses. Neither he nor any other apostle will be able to write in the future. The letter guarantees that with his entry into glory, recipients will be able to recall the spirit of his teaching and to use it to guarantee a stable faith in the turmoil of false teaching.

Authorship

The fictive author of the letter is Peter, the apostle. Though speaking in Peter's name, the letter looks back on the generation of apostles. Bauckham tries to maintain some connection between the letter and the apostle by suggesting that 2 Peter was written shortly after Peter's martyrdom (c.80–90 C.E.; Bauckham, 158). This suggestion seems too early for a letter that acknowledges a collection of Pauline letters and a written gospel account of the transfiguration as canonical. Second Peter also used much of Jude in its condemnation of false teachers. Consequently, the best guess for the time at which the letter was written is the end of the first century or beginning of the second (Fuchs and Reymond). No geographical hints about the author or readers are given. The combination of a developing canon that includes Synoptic Gospel material, Pauline letters, and perhaps 1 Peter, with Jewish Christian material from Jude placed under the authority of Peter, is not sufficient to persuade scholars of any particular location for its author: Rome, Asia Minor, and even Egypt have all been suggested. The first clear evidence of 2 Peter in early Christian authors does not appear until the third century C.E. Origen, who refers to 2 Peter by name, doubts that it was written by the apostle (Eusebius, *History of the Church* 6.25.11).

Other hints about 2 Peter's authorship have been derived from its language and style. Rhetorical analysis of the letter suggests an author well-versed in the conventions of Greco-Roman argument. He exhibits a fondness for ornate and unusual words (for a list from 2 Peter see Bauckham, 134–36) and the somewhat inflated elegance that ancient theorists described as Asiatic style. Though 2 Peter is certainly not the best exemplar of all the features of that style, the language and forms of argument in the letter suggest an author who had been educated in its rules (Watson). He lacks the polish of the aristocratic, Attic style favored by theorists like Cicero. If, as Cicero claims, the style was associated with Asia Minor, then it suggests that the author belongs in one of the Hellenistic cities of that region (Neyrey 1993, 120). The combination of Hellenistic philosophical topoi and Jewish lore in a single text is sometimes accounted for by presuming that an earlier letter had been redacted, with the Jewish material taken from Jude or a related Jewish source. More recent rhetorical analyses of the letter indicate that it was composed as a single piece. Therefore, the author probably comes from an educated, Greek-speaking Jewish background.

Occasion

Predictions concerning the evils into which the patriarch's descendants will fall or the emergence of false teachers after the death of the apostles (Acts 20:17–35) are typical of the testament genre. However, 2 Peter's attack on false teachers in the community (2:1–3) is not merely the conventional warning to be wary of those who would lead the elect astray in the end time (3:3) nor a caution against those who peddle false philosophical doctrine (2:2–3). Second Peter indicates that opposing teachers rejected common Christian teaching about the second coming of Jesus (1:16; 3:4). The opponents are Christian teachers who apparently combine both common philosophical arguments and appeals to Paul's letters in making the case against belief in the second coming. The death of the apostolic generation without any evidence of Jesus' return may have played a role in undermining belief in the second coming (3:4, 9). Most of the direct arguments against the opposing views occur in chapters 1 and 3. Second Peter 2 uses apocalyptic topoi developed from the material in Jude to establish the certainty of divine judgment.

Since the topoi in question generally highlight the wickedness of those who will experience God's wrath in judgment (cf. Rom. 1:18–32), it is not possible to conclude that the opponents' rejection of the Parousia was actually responsible for a slackening of morality (*pace* Watson). The general appeal for virtuous conduct in 1:4–11 uses a classic philosophical topos. Virtue brings the soul into conformity with the divine nature (v. 4). Christians who remain stable in the virtue received when they entered the community will be able to enter the eternal kingdom of Jesus (v. 11). Judgment does not concern the righteous, only the ungodly (3:7). Lest readers think that the eternal kingdom already exists in heaven, 2 Peter associates it with the apocalyptic vision of a new heaven and a new earth (3:13).

By tracing debates about divine justice and providence in antiquity, Neyrey locates the discussion of judgment in a philosophical tradition sparked by Epicurean challenges to conventional views about the gods (Neyrey 1993, 122–28). There is—so the Epicureans argued—no evidence that the world is governed by divine providence or that the gods have any concern for administering justice. If the gods did reward the pious and punish the wicked, they should do so in a timely fashion. Epicurean atomism also generated arguments against immortality of the soul; consequently, the claim that the wicked are punished after death cannot be sustained. Epicureans treated the stories about the gods as so many pious fables, a charge 2 Peter promises to refute (1:16). Since these arguments enjoyed wide circulation in antiquity, they often appear as examples of extreme atheism without any peculiarly Epicurean associations. Second Peter may even have formulated the opponents' doctrine as though it represented such "atheist" topoi. However, the parallels make it clear that the challenge 2 Peter seeks to meet stems from the encounter between Christian faith and popular philosophy. The opponents did not represent Gnostic myths concerning the return of the soul to a divine world completely divorced from the material realm of the demonic creator god (Neyrey, 127).

Many Christians today find the doctrine of the second coming and the end of the world difficult to digest for somewhat different reasons. Despite the fact that we refer to Christ's return several times at every service, a sampling of parishioners elicited almost universal agreement that they never thought about the second coming. Older members of the congregation expect to be with Jesus and their loved ones when they die. If God wants to end the world sometime, okay, but it doesn't matter to them. Younger people generally replied that maybe Jesus would come and end the world, but they'd bet more money on scientific theories. If human beings don't destroy the planet first, solar expansion would take care of it. Like their elders, they thought that "getting to heaven" was the main point of religion, and that judgment would be taken care of when people died. Traditional doctrine that separates the postmortem fate of the soul from the "new creation" and resurrection of the body at the second coming also enjoys little support. As one lady put it to me, her deceased husband is with God and when she dies, she's going to join him and that's that. Don't bother her with any further details about Christian eschatology. Of course, she and the others surveyed would not consider themselves opposed either to the general providence of God or to the idea that God judges and punishes the wicked.

Perhaps, the more interesting question for Christians who do not find the questions of Christian eschatology of pressing interest is the argument itself. Neyrey points out that 2 Peter combines two cultures, Jewish and Greek. Defending a traditional belief from the charge of being a "senseless myth" does not mean simply repeating what Christians have always said. Second Peter does seek to make a persuasive case for Christian belief in terms that would be intelligible to an educated audience. As Bauckham observes, though Greek thought represents the natural idiom in which 2 Peter operates, the author will not follow that direction when it contradicts established tradition. He returns to sources close to the apocalyptic spirit of earliest Christianity in order to prevent Christianity from becoming merely another "paganized religion." Christians in all generations have to confront this task: holding on to the tradition while making the gospel intelligible in new cultural contexts (Bauckham, 154).

Theological Themes

Discussion of the occasion of 2 Peter has highlighted the major themes in the letter: God, judgment, and the end of all things. The opening of the letter also highlights the virtues of Christians who remain faithful to their calling and election. That piety (1:3) stands in sharp contrast to the immorality condemned in the apocalyptic section of the letter (2:20–22). Piety also trusts the future salvation that has been promised by God (3:13). Though some critics of 2 Peter find the lack of christological focus in the ethical section of the epistle disturbing, knowledge of God, the key to piety, does not exist without knowledge of Jesus Christ.

God

Divine power is familiar to readers as the source of the renewal of life they experienced when they turned to God in

Jesus, the Lord (1:3). God's powerful word is also reflected in creation and in the continued existence of this world (3:5–7). Other attributes like glory and excellence (1:3, 17; 2:10) indicate the transcendence of God, who should be honored by all people. The gulf between humanity and God is reflected in the contrast between this world, described as the source of defilement (1:4; 2:20) and perishable (3:6–7, 10–11), and the eternity in which God dwells (1:11; 3:8). This separation underlines the honor that is due the divine Lord and the dishonor done him by false teachers (2:1; on honor/dishonor see Neyrey 1993, 3–7, 114). Though 2 Peter does not specify how it takes place, access to God is mediated through the Lord, Jesus Christ (1:2, 14; 3:18), who participates in the honor and glory of his Father (1:17).

The reliability of God's word should be inferred from God's power. Since God has promised believers the great benefit of partaking in the divine nature (1:4), they would be foolish to reject such a benefactor. Yet, the false teachers dishonor God by challenging his word in the prophecies of scripture (1:20–21; 3:9). They have also dishonored God by mistrusting his beneficence (3:9).

Judgment and the End Time

Second Peter begins with the assertion that the "power and parousia of our Lord Jesus Christ" is not some clever myth (1:16). However, 2 Peter does not depict the second coming of Jesus. The transfiguration proves that Jesus possesses divine glory (1:17). The primary descriptions of judgment look back to ancient stories of God's ability to punish the wicked: the fallen angels (2:4); the flood (2:5); the extinction of Sodom and Gomorrah (2:6). In the last two examples, God rescued the righteous from divine punishment. However, these examples merely anticipate the final judgment. The fallen angels, held in the subterranean pits, await the end time (2:4). A similar fate awaits the rest of the unrighteous (2:9).

The Parousia will bring with it a judgment like the ancient flood, complete destruction of this material world (3:4–7). However, the end-time destruction will take place in fire (3:7). Second Peter formulates this description of the judgment so that non-Jewish readers would recognize the parallelism between biblical teaching and the Stoic belief in the great world cycles that reduce all things to fire. Even the elements return to fire (3:10b, 12). A special act of divine providence will preserve the righteous (3:11). Instead of the Stoic doctrine that the destruction of all things would be followed by repetition of the world process, 2 Peter affirms that God will create a new heaven and earth, the inheritance of the righteous (3:13). That new world will not be perishable. Hence, the day of judgment can also be spoken of as the "day of eternity" (3:18).

Piety and Salvation

Knowledge *(epignōsis)* of God echoes throughout 2 Peter as a central term in its description of salvation (1:2, 3, 8; 2:20). The goal of piety is assimilation to the divine nature, since God calls the righteous to share his glory (1:3–4). Nothing that belongs to the changing material world and its passions can belong to the divine world. Consequently, the righteous must seek to be purified from the defiling passions evoked by the world (1:4; 2:2, 12–14, 18–22; 3:11, 14). Another characteristic of the soul attached to God is stability. Such persons cannot be shaken by the ignorant turmoil of the false teachers whose word leads to destruction (1:9; 2:3, 14). Although the idea of virtue or piety as a soul established in divine truth and unshaken by the passions was common in the ancient world, 2 Peter has not merely taken over that view of virtue. No one can become righteous on his or her own. Conversion to Jesus Christ as Lord and cleansing from one's past sins is the beginning of the new life (1:4, 10; 2:20–21). The righteous trust God's promises of participation in the eternal, new creation. Faith is acknowledgment of that promise (1:4). Other virtues supplement that faith (1:6–7). Faith also implies that individuals adhere to the true apostolic teaching embodied in the letter (1:12).

Since the false teachers had also received baptismal forgiveness, their defection shows that knowledge, piety, virtue, and freedom from the passions can be lost (2:20). Second Peter warns that it would be better never to have known Christ than to have known him and turned back (2:21). It tells readers to hold to the prophetic word of God like a light in the dark until day dawns in their hearts (1:19). That image represents the future time of salvation in which the righteous will participate in God's glory themselves. That knowledge of God and the perfection it conveys will never be taken away from the righteous.

OUTLINE OF SECOND PETER

Greeting	1:1–2
Thanksgiving	1:3–4
Confirm Your Faith in God's Goodness	1:5–11
The Apostle's Farewell	1:12–15
True Prophecy: The Lord Will Come	1:16–21
The Lord Will Come in Glory	1:16–18
God Inspires Prophecy	1:19–21
False Prophets Will Be Condemned	2:1–22
False Teachers Will Arise	2:1–3
God's Judgment in the Past	2:4–10a
False Teachers Are Irrational Beasts	2:10b–16
False Teachers Are Full of Corruption	2:17–22
Trust God's Word of Promise	3:1–18
The Power of God's Word	3:1–7
Delay Is a Sign of God's Mercy	3:8–10
All Things Will Be Dissolved	3:11–13
Await Salvation in Holiness	3:14–18a
Concluding Doxology	3:18b

Greeting

2 PETER 1:1–2

Second Peter opens with a letter greeting that identifies the sender as "Simeon" Peter. The form "Simeon" is a transliteration of the Hebrew (cf. 1 Macc. 2:65). "Simon," as Peter is generally known, was the more common form of the name among Jews of this period. The author of 2 Peter might have thought this form more authentic. Acts 15:14 has James use that form during the Jerusalem Council. Second Peter does not recognize the oddity of combining "Simon" with the Greek form of Simon's nickname, "Peter," rather than with the Aramaic "Cephas." The author must have taken the form "Simeon" as more appropriately Jewish, based on traditions familiar to him. The combination "servant and apostle" underlines the special status of the sender. The "servant" who comes in the name of an important figure was entitled to honor appropriate to his master. Important figures in Israel's history were "servants of the Lord" (Exod. 32:13; Deut. 9:27; 34:5; 1 Sam. 3:9–10; 17:32). Thus, the common assumption that "servant" always designates humility should not be accepted (Neyrey 1993, 144). Peter's eyewitness testimony to the glory of Jesus (1:16) and the special revelation of his impending death (1:14) add to his dignity in the eyes of the recipients.

No specific identification is given for the letter's addressees. Instead, they are described as persons whose faith places them on the same level as the sender. Their faith is described as *isotimos,* an expression that can mean either "of equal worth" (NRSV: "as precious as") or "of equal honor" (RSV: "of equal standing"). The latter meaning would suit the rhetorical strategy of this part of the letter. The author wishes to persuade readers to adopt his view of the truth about the Parousia. By attributing "equal honor" to the faith of the readers and that of the famous apostle, the author begins the process of gaining their goodwill (Watson, 88). Neyrey points out passages in Philo where the term refers to the unique honor of God (Philo, *On the Confusion of Tongues* 170; Neyrey 1993, 147). This extraordinary faith reflects the justice (NRSV: "righteousness") of God and of Jesus as Savior. Some scholars have taken the awkward phrase "of our God and [of the] Savior Jesus Christ" (v. 1) as though "God" referred to Jesus (Bauckham). However, the double pair in the next verse clearly distinguishes God and Jesus (v. 2). Therefore the same distinction is probably intended in the previous example.

The expanded greeting formula "grace and peace," which appears in most early Christian letters, has added to it a reference to the "knowledge" *(epignōsis)* of God. Second Peter uses the expression as a reference to the recognition of God that accompanies conversion (cf. 2:20). It implies recognition of who God really is (*pace* Neyrey). Therefore, the greeting formula points to the dynamic process of Christian faith. God's justice has already given believers the same honor in believing as the apostles. Their knowledge of God and of Jesus will bring them increasing grace and peace. The continued benefits of salvation require that the letter's recipients continue to be "of equal honor" with the apostle. To do so, they will have to preserve the truth of Peter's teaching.

Thanksgiving

2 PETER 1:3–4

A thanksgiving usually followed the greeting. These verses do not begin as a thanksgiving, but they can be read as a substitute for the thanksgiving. They express the great benefit of salvation that God has given to believers. Piety (NRSV: "godliness") is a typical virtue in Greco-Roman philosophers, where it indicates proper conduct toward the gods. Such conduct may also include holding proper opinions about them, such as that the gods never cause evil but are anxious to bestow benefits on those who honor them. Those who suffer evil either are being punished by the gods or are merely bearing the consequences of their own vice (see Malherbe 1986, 87f.). These verses make the God who is known by Christians the source of the highest good that ancient moral philosophy could imagine, actual participation in the divine nature itself.

The description of God's promised salvation as flight from the corruption in the world due to passion has the ring of popular stoicized Platonism. The soul's goal is to become united with the divine. It cannot achieve that unity as long as it is associated with the material world and the passions that it awakens. This philosophical commonplace finds its way into Philo's descriptions of the patriarchs and Moses as exemplary "wise men." For example, Isaac,

> who was considered worthy of the self-taught knowledge, abandoned all bodily elements that had been interwoven with the soul. . . . those who have become apt pupils of God, receive free, unlabored knowledge and are transferred to the genus

> of the imperishable and completely perfect. (Philo, *Sacrifices of Abel and Cain* 6–7)

Moses has an even more divine character, since he has been privileged to stand with God. His excellence exceeds the mere control of the passions of the soul. Consequently, Moses' death was also unlike that of other humans, a perfect soul passed to Him-who-is, a soul so filled with the spirit of God that it could not be aware of the transition (Philo, *Sacrifices* 8–10).

The ideal of a soul divinized by detachment from the world and the knowledge that leads it to seek only God forms a staple element in later Christian mystical traditions. The formulation of the Christian hope given in 2 Peter could be embraced both by those familiar with philosophical traditions and by Jews familiar with the type of understanding one finds in Philo (cf. Bauckham). However, the transformation of the addressees is not complete. They could not say that they have already "abandoned all bodily elements" or the exhortation that follows would not be necessary. Participation in the divine nature is the subject of God's promise to believers. Modern biology, psychology, and other social sciences make many readers fairly skeptical about this traditional version of perfection. Passions are often treated as autonomous characteristics of human nature. We are much more comfortable with the perfection that exhausts itself in working for justice, caring for the poor, and the like than with turning away from the world and its passions. God's gift of everything necessary for "life and piety," that is, for the kind of life that would lead to participating in God's nature is the focus of this section, not the particular definition of virtue employed. If participation in God's nature means an outpouring of loving service to others, then that is God's generous gift as well.

Confirm Your Faith in God's Goodness

2 PETER 1:5–11

This section continues the opening thanksgiving by reminding readers to work hard at strengthening the faith they received when they became Christians. If they remain true to that calling, they will enter the eternal kingdom of Jesus (vv. 10–11). This second formulation of the future goal of piety makes its Christian character more evident. Second Peter is not talking about a philosophical enlightenment or about following in the footsteps of Moses or the patriarchs. Its goal is discipleship, entering the kingdom. The author expresses such confidence in God's goodness that he promises his readers that those who maintain their zeal for the faith will never fall (v. 10). The extensive list of virtues contains familiar philosophical terms. Even the traditional command to "love one another" appears here in its Greek philosophical form *philadelphia* ("brotherly love"). However, 2 Peter does not end with the love between brothers but adds the more typically Christian virtue of "love," *agapē.*

The positive tone of this section only contains one jarring note, the reference to those who are blind (v. 9). Christians who do not supplement their baptismal forgiveness of sin with the practice of virtue will wind up being blind. They will not attain the promise of eternal life. When 2 Peter turns to its attack on the false teachers, the consequences of this blindness will become more striking. The false teachers and those who follow them will be destroyed by their instability (2:22). Here the contrast between such persons and the virtues of the addressees serves to consolidate the friendly relationship between 2 Peter and his audience (Watson). Some scholars have seen this section as an imitation of the ancient decrees that were used to honor a patron (Danker). The excellence that Christians are supposed to strive for honors the divine patron who called them into his service. Furthermore, recipients are to recognize that God is the source of all the good things that they have. They should remain loyal to their divine patron and remain separate from the world. Once again, the importance of this strategy will be clearer when the conflict with the false teachers comes to the fore. Since the false teachers are associated with the passions and have turned away from their baptismal promises, the faithful Christian will have nothing to do with such persons. There is no possibility for the false teachers to enter the eternal kingdom.

The Apostle's Farewell

2 PETER 1:12–15

Before 2 Peter introduces the topic that occasioned the letter, it establishes the special relationship between Peter and the readers. At the same time, the audience learns that 2 Peter also enjoys a special relationship with Jesus. The verses are linked together by the expression "remind." At first it appears that this function will cease with the death of Peter (1:13). The standard testament genre has the dying patriarch exhort his offspring to remember the teaching that he is about to give. If they hold fast to that instruction, they will be saved. However, the patriarch can also foresee the fate of his children. When they abandon his teaching, they will suffer divine wrath. Second Peter consistently treats his audience as though they will certainly remain faithful. The false teachers must be resisted, but they will not lead the readers astray.

This positive picture of the audience's future may be linked to another unusual feature of this farewell, namely, that the author's spirit will remain watching over them (v. 15). Peter has received the special privilege from Jesus of knowing that he is about to "put off the body" (v. 14). That phrase points to the philosophical accounts of the wise man's death and the promises in the previous section. Since the testament genre was associated with the patriarchs and Moses, Peter's impending death has been presented as conforming to that model. Thus, 2 Peter makes it clear to readers that no one can challenge

Peter's presentation of true faith. Like the patriarchs, Peter has been "self-taught," that is, he knows the truth through direct experience of God, not through remembering what some other teacher had said. Thanks to the letter, the apostle's presence remains with his readers. They already are "established in the truth." Their stability contrasts with the instability of persons led astray by false teachers (2:14; 3:16). The apostle's eagerness to assure their future stability by reminding them of the truth creates an alliance between the author and his audience prior to the more difficult task of refuting the false teachers (Watson).

Death does not separate readers from the apostle. Today the millennia that separate us from the first generation of Christians lessens the rhetorical impact of the passage. The original readers could sense the apostle's concern for their welfare as well as their participation in a common faith. In addition, we live in a culture that highlights change and innovation over tradition (Neyrey 1993, 166). Sometimes that presupposition carries over into the way in which people think about the apostolic and postapostolic generation. With our greater historical and scientific sensibilities, some Christians feel that we would have gotten more information about the founding events of the faith. This spiritual attitude was parodied by Søren Kierkegaard as the modern demand to always "go further" in matters of faith. Instead, the subjective truth of faith should make believers glad to go as far as the great heroes of faith, and that only after a lifetime of effort (Kierkegaard, *Fear and Trembling*).

True Prophecy: The Lord Will Come

2 PETER 1:16–21

Ordinarily, the testament would continue with reflection on the patriarch's life as an example for his offspring. Second Peter makes that expectation an element in his argument. Peter cannot be charged with making up some clever teaching about the Parousia of Jesus because he witnessed the episode in which God conferred glory on the Son. The testament genre with its emphasis on remembering will return in 3:1–3. This section introduces the crisis that evokes the letter as a series of charges against apostolic tradition that the author must refute. This section introduces two charges: (a) the second coming is a clever myth (vv. 16–18) and (b) prophecy is not secure (vv. 19–21). Both are formulated as though they were spoken by an outsider, someone who sought to demonstrate that Christianity itself is a false religion (Fuchs and Reymond, 67). The next chapter introduces the shocking fact that the enemy is within. False teachers within the Christian movement have taken on the destructive arguments of outsiders (2:1–3). Second Peter highlights the honor and glory of God in developing his argument. Readers know that Peter enjoys a special relationship with Jesus. Jesus, in turn, received honor from God in the presence of Peter and others. The net result of that situation is that those who make these charges are challenging the honor of God himself (Neyrey 1993).

2 Peter 1:16–18
The Lord Will Come in Glory

The opening charge of following sophistic (NRSV: "cleverly devised") myths comes from the stock rhetoric of religious and philosophical polemic. It was commonly used to discredit the teaching of an opponent (cf. 1 Tim. 1:4). "Myth" in this sense has nothing to do with our modern sense of mythology as stories of the sacred or primordial times that embody the religious wisdom and cultural order of a people. Rather "myth" in this context implies a false or pernicious tale. By describing the myths as "cleverly devised" *(sesophismenoi),* the charge indicates that they are used by humans to deceive people. The charge that tales about divine punishment were used by nursemaids and rulers to enforce morality was already voiced in Plato (Plato, *Republic* 2.364–366). Epicureans pressed the case against myths of divine punishment to prove that it was foolish for humans to fear the gods. Lucretius argued that tales of punishment in hell and rewards in paradise merely reflect the anxieties and desires of the mind in this life (Lucretius, *On the Nature of Things* 3.966–1023).

Philo provides evidence that this polemic was felt in Jewish circles. Even the form of the opening statement, "not a myth invented . . . but a sacred oracle," appears several times in Philo (*Flight* 121; 152; see Neyrey 1993, 175). Philo contrasts a humanly fabricated myth with the divine truth found in Scripture. Second Peter follows a similar pattern. Since the argument follows an established apologetic format, it is not possible to tell whether the false teachers employed Epicurean philosophical topoi in their argument against belief in the Parousia. The form as used by Philo leads us to expect evidence from a sacred text. Second Peter turns to a different type of legal argument: the testimony of eyewitnesses, the most certain form of testimony in a legal context. Their evidence, Christ's glory and the voice of God, was intended to establish a proof from Christ's status and role in the judgment (v. 17a; Neyrey 1993, 170–71).

The description of the episode about which Peter is testifying (vv. 17b–18) clearly reflects gospel tradition concerning the transfiguration (Matt. 17:2, 5; Mark 9:2–3, 7; Luke 9:35). The citation of God's word to Jesus is not directly taken from any one of the Gospel accounts. However, the wording is close enough that an audience whose acquaintance with the story came from hearing would recognize them as equivalent (Bauckham). The other comments summarize the story in terms suited to 2 Peter's argument: power, majesty, honor conferred by the deity indicate to readers that God's honor is at stake. Instead of speaking of the voice as coming from the cloud as in the Synoptics, it is brought to him by the "majestic glory" (v. 17). Both majesty and glory are common epithets for God (Heb. 1:3; 8:1; *T. Levi* 3:4). God's voice also has these attributes (Ps. 29:4; Sir. 17:13). Second Peter shows no interest in the other details of the transfiguration story, such as the appearance of Moses and Elijah or the description of Jesus' garments. All the author's argument requires is an audience able to recollect that story well enough to recall that Jesus received glory and that the voice of God spoke about Jesus as God's Son. Consequently, the question of the origins of the transfiguration tradition itself is not an issue. Mark 9:1 prefaces the transfiguration story with a saying that none of those present will die before seeing the kingdom come in power. (Matt. 16:28 has the Son of man coming in his kingdom.) Such a juxtaposition indicates that the story could be understood as an anticipation of the glory associated with Jesus' Parousia. On the other hand, some scholars point to the heavenly glory mentioned in the story and see it, along with the allusion to Ps. 2:7, as a reference to the divine exaltation of the risen Lord. The exchange between Jesus and the disciples after the event (Mark 9:9) also points toward the resurrection rather than the Parousia.

It is impossible to tell whether 2 Peter's audience was familiar with an interpretation of the transfiguration that treated it as evidence for the exaltation of the risen Christ. That understanding conforms to the view that Jesus has an eternal kingdom that believers will enter (1:11). The primary use of the story here is to base the claim about divine judgment on the highest authority, God's word as witnessed by the apostle. As we have seen, Philo countered the charge of human myths by referring to Scripture as the divine oracles or testimony on the heavenly tablets. Second Peter goes beyond the witness of written oracles or engraved statutes to the actual word of God. Indirectly, the argument warns readers that anyone who would reject such testimony contradicts God's authority.

2 Peter 1:19–21
God Inspires Prophecy

The argument moves to a second form of divine testimony, the prophetic word. Once again, the issue of personal, human interpretation over against divine revelation forms the structure of the argument (vv. 20–21). Second Peter refers to a common argument that the Holy Spirit takes over the will of the prophet (Philo, *Life of Moses* 1.283; *Special Laws* 1.65). The Christian apologist, Justin Martyr (d. c.152) explains Old Testament prophecy to his readers. Prophets are not speaking on their own but because the Word moves them (*1 Apology* 1.36; Bauckham, 233). The figure of Balaam, who appears later as an example of judgment (2:15–16) was used in Philo to demonstrate the truth of this principle. God overrides the intentions of the prophet (Philo, *Life of Moses* 1.281; Neyrey 1993). Though the statement about the nature of prophecy is clear, the argument to which 2 Peter responds is less clear. Second Peter 1:20a speaks of the interpretation of prophecy rather than of prophecy itself. This modification may be 2 Peter's adjustment to the particular conflict being addressed in the letter. Second Peter 3:16 charges opponents with distorted readings of Paul's letters. Ancient discussions of oracular prophecy distinguished the words uttered by the oracle from the interpretation given by others (Neyrey 1993, 180–81).

The juxtaposition in 2 Peter 1:20–21 suggests that the truly inspired prophecy does not participate in the ambiguity of pagan oracles with their prophets and prophetesses. The argument may have originated in Hellenistic skeptical arguments against any prophecy. Any divine communication has to be interpreted by its human recipients. Therefore, 2 Peter's opponents might have used this topos in their attack on early Christian belief in the Parousia (Bauckham, 231–32). In either case, 2 Peter wishes to draw a sharp distinction between words inspired by God and the utterances of false prophets (2:1).

These comments on the nature of prophecy are prefaced by the claim that Christians possess a "prophetic word that is more secure *(bebaioteros).*" Readers are told to hold to (NRSV: "be attentive to") that word as a light in the dark until "the morning star rises in your hearts" (v. 19). Hellenistic Greek often uses the comparative "more" to mean the superlative "very." Thus 2 Peter is not comparing Christian prophecy with some other. (Nor does v. 19 speak of making prophecy more secure, as the RSV translation suggests.) The prophecy to which this verse refers must be the transfiguration as a prophecy of Christ's Parousia. The clue to the expression *bebaioteros* lies in Philo's discussion of prophecy. The Balaam episode demonstrates the distinction between the prophet's intent (to curse Israel) and God's action (words of blessing; Philo, *Migration* 113–115). In the case of the transfiguration, God has spoken directly in the presence of witnesses (so Neyrey 1993, 180).

The exhortation to hold on to this prophecy like a lamp in thick gloom forms a striking contrast to the earlier reference to the transfiguration as a shining theophany in which God's glory and majesty were conferred on Jesus. Early Christian texts commonly speak of conversion as a transition from darkness to light (Eph. 5:8, 14). The opening exhortation warned readers that those whose knowledge of God was not fruitful would be blind and shortsighted (1:9). The wicked are condemned to gloomy darkness (2:17) like the fallen angels (2:4). Therefore, the simplest reading of the image takes Jesus as the morning star, whose rising heralds the judgment (Neyrey 1993). However, 2 Peter 1:19 refers to the morning star rising "in your hearts." Normally, as in the Synoptic sayings about the coming of the kingdom, one would expect "seeing" the day or the morning star if the reference were to the Parousia. Bauckham, who thinks that "the prophetic word" refers to Old Testament prophecy as a whole, suggests that the light imagery refers to the eschatological age as a whole. Prophecy is no longer necessary because the redeemed live in divine light (cf. Rev. 21:23–24). Thus the expression reminds readers of another facet of the "precious and great promises" (1:4) that God has made to them.

Although 2 Peter has begun to speak of the charges against Christian teaching made by others, the focus of the entire first chapter remains the faith of those who believe. The small lamp that shines in murky darkness will eventually bring them to their own vision of the majesty and glory of the Lord. Second Peter has distinguished the divine revelation found in scripture, both the prophets and the gospel, from competing forms of religious and philosophical propaganda. As long as believers hold fast to the apostolic tradition, the gospel, and the prophets, they can anticipate a vision of divine glory that carries with it participation in God. Who would want to turn aside from such a promise? With the exception of the explicit denial of Jesus' return at the Parousia, the other opposing arguments in 2 Peter belong to the more general topoi of antireligious polemic. If so-called Christian teachers were using them against the Parousia or divine judgment, then antireligious elements from the larger intellectual culture have corrupted Christian faith. This example poses a challenge for Christians today. Second Peter uses language and argumentation characteristic of educated people in his time. Christians are not asked to be intellectual dimwits, but they are challenged to evaluate how cultural assumptions enter into the formulation of faith. They are asked to make a conscientious effort to understand what the scriptures and apostolic tradition present as the truth from God. New forms of theology, spirituality, or ethics should preserve the light, not shut it out.

False Prophets Will Be Condemned

2 PETER 2:1–22

Second Peter turns from true prophecy to false prophets. The testament genre required the dying patriarch to foresee the future of his offspring. He has described the eschatological glory of those who remain faithful to the apostolic witness. Now the Old Testament examples of false prophets among the people lead to a warning that false teachers will also appear among Christians (2:1–2). Their appearance can even be treated as a sign that the last days are at hand (3:3). The tone and imagery shifts from philosophical topoi to apocalyptic prophecy. Much of the content for that prophecy in 2 Peter 2:1—3:3 is closely linked to Jude 4–18. The order of material and verbal echoes indicate that 2 Peter has borrowed from Jude rather than the other way around. However, since extended verbal parallels such as one finds in the Synoptic tradition are not evident in the Jude/2 Peter relationship, 2 Peter may not have been copying directly from the text of Jude. The assumption that 2 Peter modified material from Jude maintains the integrity of the rhetorical argument advanced in both letters (see Watson, 160–87).

Table 4 highlights the parallels between 2 Peter and Jude. The first major addition to the material adapted from Jude (2:7–9) confirms the positive relationship between the author and his audience established in the opening chapter of the letter. The story of Lot confirms the Lord's power to rescue the righteous who are appalled by what they see going on around them. Rhetorically, 2 Peter presents the apostle's guiding presence as a success. The "many" who are led astray by the false teachers are carefully distinguished from the audience even though some readers may be taken in by the opponents initially (2:3). Where Jude spoke of the wicked contaminating the fellowship meals of the community (Jude 12), 2 Peter only refers to their feasting with the addressees (v. 13). Those most at risk of being misled are new converts who have barely left their past way of life (v. 18). Second Peter 2:19–22 adds a direct attack on false teachers to the material from Jude. They prove the depths of their irrationality by turning away from holiness to eat vomit.

Table 4
2 Peter's Use of Jude

2 Peter	***Jude***
False prophets also arose among the people, . . . *denying* the *Master* who bought them . . . , (2:1) and many will follow their *licentiousness.* (2:2)	Certain persons sneaked in; . . . impious, they put aside the grace of our God for *licentiousness* and *deny* our only *Master* and Lord, Jesus Christ. (v. 4)
God did not spare *the angels* who sinned, but cast them into Tartarus *in chains of darkness,* keeping them until *judgment.* (2:4)	*Angels* who did not keep their own rank . . . *he keeps* for the *judgment of the great Day* with eternal *chains in darkness.* (v. 6)
God condemned and reduced to ashes the *cities* of *Sodom and Gomorrah,* setting an *example* for those who would be impious, (2:6)	*Sodom and Gomorrah* and the *cities* around them, which committed fornication . . . , are set forth as an *example,* suffering a punishment of eternal fire. (v. 7)
especially those who follow the *flesh* in passion for *corruption* and *despise authority.* Bold and arrogant, they are not afraid to *blaspheme the glorious ones,* (2:10)	Yet these dreamers *corrupt the flesh* and *set aside authority and blaspheme the glorious ones.* (v. 8)
whereas *angels* greater in strength and power *do not bring a blasphemous judgment* against them from the *Lord.* (2:11)	Michael the *archangel,* when he argued with the devil, . . . *did not* dare *bring a judgment of blasphemy,* but said, "The *Lord* will rebuke you." (v. 9)
These people, like *irrational creatures,* born *physical beings* for capture and *destruction, blaspheme what they do not know,* and in their destruction *they will be destroyed.* (2:12)	*These* people, *what they do not know, they blaspheme;* what they understand *physically,* like *irrational creatures,* in those things *they are destroyed.* (v. 10)
They are *stains* and blemishes, reveling in their deceitful pursuits, while *feasting with you.* (2:13)	These people are *stains* on your fellowship meals; *feasting* fearlessly, they shepherd themselves. (v. 12)

2 Peter	*Jude*
Leaving the straight path *they are deceived,* following the way of *Balaam* son of Bosor, who loved the *wages* of wickedness. (2:15)	Woe to those who follow the way of Cain and abandon themselves to *the deceit of Balaam for wages.* (v. 11)
These people are *waterless springs* and mists driven by storms, for whom the *gloom of darkness is kept.* (2:17)	These are . . . *waterless* clouds carried about by wind, fruitless trees . . . , wild waves of the sea, . . . for whom the *gloom of darkness is kept forever.* (vv. 12–13)
Uttering foolish *boasts,* they deceive with the licentious *passions* of the flesh those who recently fled from people who live in error. (2:18)	They are murmuring grumblers who follow their *passions,* and their mouth speaks *boasts.* (v. 16)
Beloved, I am now writing . . . (3:1)	But you, *beloved,* (v. 17)
that you should *remember* the *words spoken before* by the holy prophets and the command of your *Lord* and Savior through the *apostles.* (3:2)	*remember the words spoken before by the apostles* of our *Lord* Jesus Christ. (v. 17)
In the last days scoffers will come, scoffing, *following* their own *passions.* (3:3)	They told you that *in the last time* there will be *scoffers following the passions* of their impiety. (v. 18)

2 Peter 2:1–3
False Teachers Will Arise

The word "ruin" or "destruction" *(apōleia)* echoes through this section. On the one hand, false teaching provides the occasion for bad morals and destroys true piety. On the other, destruction is waiting for the false teachers and their followers. Whatever they may think about the future, divine judgment has already been passed against them (v. 3). These teachers are the ones who fabricate doctrines in order to lead people astray. The accusation of greed as the basis for such fabricated doctrine was a typical charge in philosophical polemic. The term *hairesis* (RSV: "heresy"; NRSV: "opinion") was used in a neutral sense for the doctrines characteristic of a particular school. Second Peter gives it a negative sense by specifying the result of following such doctrine as destruction. He also describes the activity of introducing such teaching as underhanded or surreptitious. Ordinarily, a philosophical school or a school of medicine would only claim a single doctrine. Second Peter attributes destructive "doctrines" in the plural to his adversaries. That modification contributes to the negative depiction of these teachers. Philosophers often accused opposing schools of generating a myriad of irreconcilable teachings. Like the passions that govern their conduct (v. 2), the false teachers do not have a real doctrine, only "fabricated arguments" (v. 3). That expression is equivalent to the "sophistic myths" that they had alleged constituted the apostle's teaching (1:16).

Neyrey's attention to the social codes of honor and dishonor highlights another aspect of the treatment of the opponents in this passage. Their activities show ingratitude and disrespect for God. The Master who purchased the slaves in the household should be treated with obedience and respect. This argument echoes a traditional formula that depicted the death of Jesus as the ransom price for slaves (1 Cor. 6:20; 7:23; Rev. 5:9; 14:3–4; Neyrey 1993). The claim that false teachers "blaspheme" things of God is introduced in verse 2 with an allusion to Isa. 52:5. The behavior of an unfaithful people blasphemes the Lord among the nations. Second Peter replaces "the name" with "the way of truth" (cf. 1:12). Their teaching and behavior dishonors God and the Christian way of life. However, God does not remain aloof or neutral toward such persons. Judgment is already prepared for them.

Most of this section contains established polemical topoi. The assumption that false teaching was motivated by greed and the desire to indulge perverse sexual appetites is a staple element in disputes over true and false teaching. One cannot draw conclusions about specific issues at stake in a dispute from such rhetorical conventions. Many modern readers find this polemical attack distasteful. Yet sexual immorality and greed or fiscal mismanagement remain the two favorite weapons in the arsenal of negative campaigning. We have probably replaced the charge of leading others into immorality with the charge that someone is "soft on crime" or "lets crooks roam the streets." Our passion for name calling and slander may have shifted from the religious to the political sphere, but it remains alive and well nonetheless.

Polemical topoi aside, 2 Peter raises another question for Christians today. Are we too unconcerned about the truth of religious claims? Many people have accommodated the pluralism of our culture and even their own families by holding religious beliefs to be private and individual, not public. Parents whose young adult children no longer practice any identifiable form of Christianity often say to me, "Well, he (or she) really is a good kid, so it's okay with me." Of course, it's not quite "okay" or the person would not have volunteered that piece of information. College students make the same accommodation that their parents do when faced with behavior on the part of a friend or roommate that makes them uncomfortable. "I don't really like his (or her) drinking (casual attitude toward sex; treatment of others; occasional drug use) or whatever, but otherwise . . ." In other words, a general moral or behavioral test substitutes for belief, convictions, and in some cases even for a morally coherent way of life. Cultural attitudes like that are more effective and surreptitious false teachers than any group of persons within the church.

2 Peter 2:4–10a
God's Judgment in the Past

The warning about judgment that caps the opening attack on false teachers provides the introduction to a series of examples aimed at demonstrating the certainty and seriousness of God's judgment. Thoughout the demonstration of judgment taken from Jude, 2 Peter never forgets that God also rescues the righteous. After reminding readers that even the fallen angels suffer terrible punishments, 2 Peter 2:5 adds a reference to Noah's preservation (2:5a); after Sodom and Gomorrah, a reference to Lot's deliverance (2:7–9a). Since these two counterexamples are found in other discussions of the same topic (Wisd. Sol. 10; Philo, *Life of Moses* 2.53–65), some scholars think that

2 Peter has employed a variant tradition (Bauckham). However, the counterexamples serve to adapt the material from Jude to our author's rhetorical identification with the audience and could have easily come from his own knowledge of the Old Testament.

Second Peter deals with the issue of judgment delayed by speaking of the earlier figures as kept in chains or subjected to punishment until the judgment (vv. 4b; 9b). Second Peter's allusion to the story of the fallen angels continues the pattern of introducing common Greco-Roman formulations into Jewish material. The place where the angels are kept is identified as Tartarus (v. 4). By balancing punishment, eventual public condemnation, and God's care for the righteous who have suffered the presence of the wicked around them, 2 Peter demonstrates the justice of divine judgment. Second Peter 2:8 uses the figure of Lot to awaken in the audience the pain that living among the wicked should cause. They might use the Lord's Prayer to ask that God will rescue them from the temptation (*peirasmos;* NSRV: "trial") that they face (v. 9; for the possibility of an allusion to Matt. 6:13, see Bauckman). The stories of Noah and Lot demonstrate God's ability to deliver the righteous from even more extreme circumstances than those faced by the addressees (also see Sir. 33:1).

By incorporating the deliverance of the righteous into the judgment material from Jude, 2 Peter reminds readers that judgment is an aspect of salvation. God did not establish commandments, send the prophets, and ransom humanity through the death of Jesus in order to maximize the population in hell. Quite the contrary. God and the Lord Jesus are generous benefactors. They have extended both present and future salvation to us. But as long as we live in this world, we human beings are faced with the choice between following our own desires or looking to God. Contrary to the charges voiced by some philosophers that stories of divine punishment are mere fantasies to keep people in line, the false teachers and their followers are not deterred in the least by warnings of such judgment. But those who have not followed the crowd may find their faith confirmed. They are to remember the salvation that God promises the righteous and to recognize the offense to God's glory that false teaching and sin entail.

2 Peter 2:10b–16
False Teachers Are Irrational Beasts

The next set of examples highlights the sheer irrationality of the behavior that false teaching engenders. Second Peter shifts the order of the list from Jude, so that it concludes with the story of Balaam, and frames a new conclusion for it in order to fit the tale into the argument against false teaching. An ass is given human speech in order to restrain the insanity of the prophet (v. 16). Second Peter also adds a description of the vices of his opponents in verse 14. Their insatiable appetite for sin makes them "cursed children." False teaching, with its associated immorality, has not only deprived the opponents of their human nature, it has made them worse than animals.

The first example of irrationality (vv. 10b–11) involves blasphemy against "the glorious ones," angelic beings. Second Peter's version omits the legend of Michael's contending for the body of Moses found in Jude. The parade example of blasphemy against angelic beings occurs in Dan. 7:19–27 in which the fourth beast, speaking blasphemy against God, wages war against the "holy ones of the Most High" and attempts to change "the sacred seasons and the law" (v. 25; for a discussion of "holy ones" as angels in Daniel, see Collins, 313–18). For Daniel, blasphemy involved dislocation of the cultic calendar.

The debate over divine providence that underlies the polemic in 2 Peter suggests an allusion to the angels as astral powers. Like the Epicureans who denied the influence of the stars on human affairs, the opponents deny the angels any role in ordering God's creation. Second Peter has dropped the legend of Michael and Satan because it is not relevant to the argument of the letter. Verse 11 alludes to another common function of angelic beings, to oversee human activities and report in the heavenly court (cf. Job 1:6–12). By rights, the angels ought to bring such blasphemous judgments against the wicked into the heavenly court, but they do not do so. (Commentators like Bauckham, who think the angels in question are the fallen angels of verse 4 have missed the metaphorical and polemic setting of this passage.)

The second example (vv. 12–14) highlights the animal character of the opponents' behavior. They follow physical desires and lack all understanding. Their nature makes them suitable for hunting and destruction. Second Peter takes the initial comparison from Jude and underlines the certainty of destruction. Verse 13a reminds readers that "destruction" of the wicked is not simply killing a wild, dangerous animal. It is a matter of divine justice. They will reap the reward of the injustice they have done. If the conclusion to verse 12 is read as a reference to destruction of others as the cause of the false teacher's destruction, then verse 13a focuses on the justice of retribution for what they have done to others (Neyrey 1993). Verses 13–14 provide further examples of the dissolute behavior of the opponents. Second Peter has expanded the initial image from Jude to highlight their perversity. Carousing in midday (v. 13b) was considered particularly reprehensible in antiquity (Isa. 5:11; Juvenal, *Satires* 1:103; Cicero, *Discourses* 2.41, 104; hence Peter's reference to the hour in Acts 2:15). Because of their behavior such persons even defile feasts they attend with other Christians (v. 13c). Second Peter has recast Jude to remove any suspicions that these banquets are formal celebrations of the Christian fellowship. His point is to warn readers against any association with these persons. Even their respectable feasts cannot help being contaminated if such persons are present. The additions in verse 14 provide further evidence of the danger caused by the presence of such persons. They are always on the lookout for some evil and will draw others into their sin.

The final example uses the Balaam story as the climax of this section. The phrase "wages of injustice" (v. 13a) returns in connection with Balaam's actions (v. 15). The story, as 2 Peter develops it, reflects Jewish traditions about Balaam that are found outside the Old Testament (see Neyrey 1980). The content of the donkey's censure was expanded in later tradition to include deception of the people and misuse of prophetic power. Legend also treated Balaam as an example of greed. The Targums to Num. 22:30 have the ass charge Balaam with lack of understanding and vanity in thinking he had power to curse Israel. Balaam was also said to have died in his madness (Philo, *Change of Names* 203; Bauckham, 269). Second Peter apparently created the unusual word *paraphronia* for "madness" rather than the usual *paraphronēsis* because of its poetic similarity to the word for transgression at the beginning of verse

16, *paranomia* (Bauckham). Readers could take a jingle away from the summary of Balaam's story. *Paranomia* leads to *paraphronia*, lawlessness leads to madness. In comparison with Balaam, the "irrational animals" (v. 12) prove to be reasoning creatures; at least they are capable of recognizing God's order.

These examples have been crafted to demonstrate the utter absurdity of the wicked. The particular examples seem far removed from many people's experience. Angelic guardians of the cosmic order and Balaam's talking ass are not part of our everyday conversation or even of many Sunday sermons. However, 2 Peter presents two challenges. First, to consider ways in which we as a culture mask the real absurdity and even dehumanizing effect of all sorts of behavior. People easily point to the big news items: random violence, permissive and irresponsible sexual behavior, and drug use. All are "glamorized" when people suppress the real human costs of such behavior. A conversation with two high school teachers in the parish brought up a simpler case. Their school has taken a hard line against students using bad language and demeaning opposing teams or referees during basketball games. They also hope to address the problem of violence during hockey games. Any student who violates the code of behavior is removed from the stands. Training the parents will be next! But one teacher noted that the students actually like the new limits, even though they would not say so directly. Everyone enjoys the games more when people compete but treat one another with respect.

The second challenge 2 Peter presents concerns the question of whether there are some forms of behavior that should lead us to disassociate ourselves from those who engage in them. This disassociation does not mean that we would refuse to help individuals change their behavior. It does mean that we will not "go along" with everything. It sometimes seems odd that while many Americans will demand that smokers several tables away in a restaurant put out their cigarettes, they will tolerate other forms of abusive behavior or speech at parties without a whimper. I always told the teenagers that anytime they found themselves in an uncomfortable or unpleasant situation, they could get out with an excuse that blamed their departure on me. Cab fare or a pickup was available, no questions asked. Just tell me what I was alleged to be demanding. Second Peter speaks of his opponents looking around at feasts to trap the unstable. My safety valve was rarely used. Just knowing that it existed made it easier for teenagers to set their own limits. Recently, a mother told me that her son was so scared of being a teenager that he refused to tell his age for six months after his thirteenth birthday! Second Peter is right. Human beings are not irrational animals. We need order and limits.

2 Peter 2:17–22
False Teachers Are Full of Corruption

The final section develops from an image in Jude to a full scale condemnation of the corruption that has overtaken the false teachers. What appears to be a promise of freedom becomes the worst form of slavery to the passions (vv. 18–19). Verse 17 changes the metaphors taken from Jude. Instead of natural phenomena that might promise benefits from a distance but are either dead or destructive, 2 Peter selects examples that have no reality to them at all: a spring with no water; storm-driven mist. Several proverbial sayings are used to expand the treatment of the false teachers (vv. 19b, 20b, 22). Verse 21 is also cast in a conventional form: it would be better . . . than . . . (cf. Prov. 15:17; Matt. 5:30b; Bauckham). The content has been reformulated to refer specifically to Christians who have defiled their calling to know God by adopting the false teaching of the opponents. They would have been better off never having converted. Second Peter may presume that there is no repentance for those who defile their baptismal calling to holiness (cf. Heb. 6:4–8). "The last state has become worse . . . than the first" (v. 20b) appears in the Gospels attached to the parable of the seven devils (Matt. 12:45; Luke 11:26). Verse 19b was already a common proverb, "a person becomes the slave of whoever overpowers him" (Bauckham). The impact of these proverbial sayings is to show that common wisdom does not support the freedom that the false teachers claim to provide.

Second Peter saves its most dramatic proverb for the end (v. 22). It reminds readers once again that the opponents are no better than irrational animals. The sayings about dogs returning to their vomit and swine rolling in the mud were familiar (Prov. 26:11 [dogs]; *Ahikar* 8:15 [swine]). Ancient dogs were not our well-tended domestic pets but the half-wild creatures still seen today in third-world countries or where numbers of working dogs are kept. "Dog" was generally a term of insult. Hence, dogs and swine were more closely associated in feeling and tone than they are today. Jewish tradition had especially negative associations with pigs as "unclean animals." However, even our domestic dogs will go back, sniff around a digestive disruption and sometimes try to lick it up. The expressions of disgust this behavior evokes from the younger children would make an excellent, audible illustration of the reaction that 2 Peter hopes to inspire. The children usually leave the room taking the dog with them while the unlucky adult gets to clean up the mess. Sometimes the dog is banished to the backyard or the garage. Disassociation and disgust are exactly the point in 2 Peter. There does not seem to be a possibility of "cleaning up," that is, restoring the false teachers to true Christianity. Therefore, the only course of action open to the readers of the letter is to keep them away from the community (Neyrey 1993).

Trust God's Word of Promise

2 PETER 3:1–18

Second Peter returns to the figure of the apostle as author and authority behind the teaching of the letter. In addition, he invokes an earlier letter (presumably 1 Peter) known to the community. Both letters are invoked as reminders of true apostolic tradition. By telling the audience to remember the tradition of "your apostles" (v. 2), the author steps beyond the fictive moment of Peter's final testament to the postapostolic age. Having reestablished personal contact with the readers, 2 Peter provides further refutations of the opposing arguments. The end of the letter will establish Peter's authority as interpreter of another collection of apostolic letters, those of Paul (vv. 16–17). Misinterpretation of those letters constitutes the final danger to the faith of the recipients. A doxology brings the epistle to a close (v. 18b).

2 Peter 3:1–7
The Power of God's Word

The denunciations of chapter 2 encouraged readers to respond to the false teachers with loathing. Second Peter shifts away from the tone of sharp denunciation to that of philosophical argument. Before proceeding, he reestablishes the authority behind the teaching that the letter presents: the prophets, the command of the Lord, and apostolic tradition (v. 2; 1:16–21). Though 2 Peter has taken over from Jude the reminder that scoffers will appear in the last days, he does not attribute the prediction of their appearance to the apostles. Instead, following the conventions of the testament genre, Peter makes the prediction directly and goes on to cite their argument (v. 4). They invoke the evident sameness of the world as evidence against the claim that it is to end. Epicurean philosophers argued for the eternity of the atoms and the void against Stoic doctrines of cosmic cycles of destruction. If the Stoic view were correct, everything would have passed out of existence and nothing could have brought it back (Lucretius, *On the Nature of Things* 1.225–37). Though 2 Peter's opponents are familiar with Epicurean arguments, this objection challenges God's promise directly. They note that nothing has changed in the world since the death of the "fathers." Usually, "fathers" refers to the patriarchs and other Old Testament figures (John 7:22; Rom. 9:5; Heb. 1:1). Since 2 Peter is presented as a testament—apparently of the last member of the apostolic generation—some interpreters think that "fathers" must be a reference to the apostolic generation. If Christ has not come even though that generation has died, he will not do so at all (Bauckham).

The opponents are described as referring to the "beginning of creation," not as philosophers who believe in the eternity of the world. If they accept the fact of the creation, then the opponents should remember the agency of God's word in creation itself. God's word was powerful enough to create all things and to bring earth out of destructive waters a second time after the flood. God's word continues to sustain all things in existence. However, this existence is not one of eternal sameness as the opposition claims. Rather, God is keeping all things until the day of judgment (vv. 5–7). Jewish tradition often described the flood and the destruction of Sodom and Gomorrah as examples of the destruction at the judgment.

2 Peter 3:8–10
Delay Is a Sign of God's Mercy

Second Peter has used the creation and flood stories to argue for the power of God's word. If God has the power to control all things, then 2 Peter must explain the delay in God's use of that power. The first part of his argument contrasts human and divine perceptions of time. Psalm 90:4 provides evidence that a thousand years are like a day in God's sight (v. 8). Coupled with an allusion to Hab. 2:3 LXX that phrase from the psalm indicates that even the suspicion of delay is false. The end time will certainly come. But there is a more important reason for God's apparent delay: It provides all with the opportunity for repentance. This interpretation of God's forbearance was also a commonplace (Joel 2:12–13; Jonah 4:2; *1 Enoch* 60:5; *2 Bar.* 11:13; 12:4; 21:20–21; 2 Esd. 3:30; 7:33, 74; 9:21). Similar arguments appear in pagan authors. Epicureans used lack of any evident judgment against the wicked as evidence that the gods are not involved in human affairs. Second Peter's reply will incorporate Stoic images of the conflagration of all things into the Jewish perspective. Therefore, readers familiar with Greek thought will be able to formulate an argument in their own terms.

However, the delay will not be eternal. Second Peter reminds readers of the well-established tradition that the end will comc like a thief (v. 10; cf. Luke 12:29–40; 1 Thess. 5:2; Rev. 3:3; 16:15). The roar that accompanies the passing of heaven and earth (cf. 1QH 3:32–36) belongs to the genre of a divine theophany (Ps. 18:13–15; Amos 1:2; Joel 4:16). Therefore the roar is more than the noise of fire at the judgment. It signals God's appearance as judge. The parallels between this Jewish apocalyptic imagery and the Stoic vision of cosmic conflagration is taken up in the next phrase. All the elements *(stoicheia)* will be dissolved. For the Stoic, all things returned to the original spirit from which they came. Second Peter is really interested in the Parousia as divine judgment against the wicked, not as a cosmological theory.

2 Peter 3:11–13
All Things Will Be Dissolved

Biblical eschatology cannot be turned into ancient Stoic or even modern cosmology because the fate of the universe expresses divine judgment. Second Peter reminds readers that the same dissolution of the elements that meant condemnation for the wicked signals salvation for the righteous. It is the precondition for the new heaven and new earth (v. 13; cf. Rev. 21:1—22:5; 2 Esd. 7:30–44). Second Peter encourages readers to anticipate the coming day of the Lord. As long as they live in holiness, they will be part of the new creation. In contrast to the skepticism of the false teachers, 2 Peter speaks of his readers "waiting for and hastening the coming [*Parousia*] of the day of God" (v. 12). The expression is unusual: "Parousia" ordinarily has a person as its subject (as in 1:16; 3:4), and "day of the Lord" is the usual expression for the day of judgment (3:10; 1 Thess. 5:2). Second Peter may have modified the familiar phrases to fit the Stoic imagery of all elements being dissolved in fire that he uses in this passage (Neyrey 1993). In any case, readers should not be concerned with the details of how this creation ends. Their lives should reflect the righteousness that belongs to the new creation.

Christian belief in the coming of a new creation, not fear of divine judgment, forms the basis for holiness as a way of life. Most parents know that when we tell children not to do something or they will be punished, that is not the end of the story. On the one hand, the apparent rewards of the moment frequently drive out any thought of punishment. On the other, we really expect our children to grow into the kind of people who do what is right because it is good for themselves and others. Once they have developed the ability to govern their own behavior, we no longer have to lay down the rules. Or when we do make a rule, it can be framed as a request that honors some greater good. Second Peter knows that the false teachers can lead new converts and unstable persons astray. Its readers are not depicted as members of that group. They have enough maturity to agree with his description of the absurdity of what the false teachers are proposing. They should also have the maturity to live as people who will inherit the new creation.

2 Peter 3:14–18a
Await Salvation in Holiness

Ancient letters usually concluded with a series of instructions or exhortations to be carried out in the author's absence. This section of 2 Peter includes references to topics already discussed in the letter. Continue to wait for the end time in holiness (v. 14). Do not be disturbed by the delay of the Parousia. It is an opportunity for repentance and evidence of God's mercy (v. 15a). Continue to grow in grace and in knowledge of Jesus Christ (v. 18a). Their "spotless" and "unblemished" community will show that they were not contaminated by the evils that false teachers sought to introduce (2:13–22). If they are at peace, then they have not been stirred up by the arguments against the apostolic faith introduced by the opposition (2:17).

However, this conclusion contains a new piece of information. False teachers are apparently distorting passages from Paul's letters to make their case (vv. 15b–17). Earlier readers were told that the opposition rejected God's prophetic word as mere human interpretation (1:20). Second Peter insists that Paul's letters agree with the apostolic tradition preserved in this letter. Certainly it is easy to find Paul exhorting his churches to live in holiness while they await the coming of the Lord (e.g., 1 Thessalonians 5). Pauline letters generally include exhortations to holiness and reference to the future coming of salvation. Yet we know that some people came into Pauline churches arguing that the resurrection had already happened (2 Tim. 2:18). Second century Gnostic authors also used Pauline texts to support their claim that salvation came through knowledge of the heavenly revealer and the soul's return to the divine world. Older commentators often thought that 2 Peter was written to oppose such views. These examples show that it was possible to use Paul's letters as evidence against traditional Christian teaching about the end time. Second Peter does not indicate how Paul was being misinterpreted. The comment that opponents distort Paul "as the other scriptures" (v. 16) shows that a collection of Paul's letters enjoyed canonical authority. Second Peter does not deny that Paul spoke with a wisdom given by God. However, the teaching in the letters is sometimes difficult. Therefore, 2 Peter tells its readers to compare any claims made about Paul with the apostolic testimony in his own letters. Then they will not be confused or swept away by the errors of false teachers (v. 17).

We can understand the principle that 2 Peter suggests for interpreting Paul as an example of what we call "canon criticism" today. Theologians began speaking of "canon criticism" as a way of understanding the significance of Scripture for theology. The tools of historical criticism make it possible to speak about diverse traditions within the Bible. They explain the particular situation and theological context to which particular parts of the Bible spoke. But that approach made it appear that the Scripture contained a random and somewhat incoherent collection of religious ideas and convictions, something like a child's toy box when he or she has been told to pick up in a hurry. Canon criticism insists that to discover the message of Scripture we have to read its individual parts in light of the whole. The Bible provides the larger horizon within which the individual pieces make sense. Most children know how to sort out the jumble in their toy box because they know what the original set looked like. Second Peter tells readers to use the apostolic tradition as a guide to what the Christian truth is. The confusing parts have to be interpreted so that they are coherent with the revelation as a whole. Second Peter's refutation of the opponents' arguments and its defense of divine judgment show that the claims made by false teachers do not fit the whole picture. As long as readers remember the general picture of God's promises and Christian life described in the epistle, they will not be misled by those who twist the meaning of individual passages.

2 Peter 3:18b
Concluding Doxology

Second Peter follows the convention of a final blessing, though it lacks greetings to any particular group or persons. Evidently, 2 Peter was not envisaged as an actual letter to specific churches but as a testament in letter form. Even here the author has introduced some modifications to reinforce points made earlier in the letter. The "glory" that we attribute to Christ is the same "glory" given by God at the transfiguration (1:17). Instead of ending with "forever" *(eis tous aiōnas),* 2 Peter says "to the day of eternity." That expression reminds readers that the creation that is ushered in by the judgment will last forever just as they have been promised entry into the "eternal kingdom" (1:11). Every time we praise God by speaking of the glory of Christ, we are also thanking God for the certain promise of our salvation.

BIBLIOGRAPHY

General

Ancient Writers

Aristeas, Letter of. Translated by R.J.H. Shutt in *The Old Testament Pseudepigrapha.* Vol. 2. Edited by J. H. Charlesworth. Garden City, N.Y.: Doubleday & Co., 1985.

Clement of Rome. *The Apostolic Fathers.* Vol. 1, 8–121. Translated by Kirsopp Lake. Loeb Classical Library. Cambridge, Mass.: Harvard University Press, 1912.

Dead Sea Scrolls. In Geza Vermes, *The Dead Sea Scrolls in English.* 3d edition. Harmondsworth, Middlesex: Penguin Books, 1987.

Eusebius. *The History of the Church.* Translated by G. A. Williamson. Baltimore: Penguin Books, 1965.

Fourth Ezra [=2 Esdras], in Michael Stone, *Fourth Ezra.* Minneapolis: Fortress Press, 1990.

Malherbe, Abraham J. *Moral Exhortation: A Greco-Roman Sourcebook.* Philadelphia: Westminster Press, 1986.

Philo, *Life of Moses. Philo, vol. 6.* Translated by F. H. Colson. Loeb Classical Library. Cambridge, Mass.: Harvard University Press, 1935.

———. *On Husbandry. Philo, vol. 3.* Translated by F. H. Colson and G. H. Whitaker. Loeb Classical Library. Cambridge, Mass.: Harvard University Press, 1930.

———. *Sacrifices of Abel and Cain. Philo, vol. 2.* Translated by F. H. Colson. Loeb Classical Library. Cambridge, Mass.: Harvard University Press, 1929.

Pliny. *The Letters of the Younger Pliny.* Baltimore: Penguin Books, 1963.

Testaments of the Twelve Patriarchs. Translated by H. C. Kee. In *The Old Testament Pseudepigrapha,* edited by J. H. Charlesworth. Vol. 1, *Apocalyptic Literature and Testaments,* 782–828. Garden City, N.Y.: Doubleday & Co., 1983.

Other works

Brown, Raymond E., and Raymond F. Collins. "Canonicity: The Canon of the New Testament." In *The New Jerome Biblical Commentary,* edited by R. E. Brown, J. A. Fitzmyer, and R. E. Murphy, sec. 66:70–86. Englewood Cliffs, N.J.: Prentice-Hall, 1990.

Brown, Raymond E. and John P. Meier. *Antioch and Rome.* Ramsey, N.J.: Paulist Press, 1983.

Collins, John J. *Daniel.* Minneapolis: Fortress Press, 1993.

Conzelmann, Hans. *Gentiles, Jews, Christians: Polemics and Apologetics in the Greco-Roman Era.* Translated by M. E. Boring. Minneapolis: Fortress Press, 1992.

Feldman, Louis H. *Jew and Gentile in the Ancient World.* Princeton, N.J.: Princeton University Press, 1993.

Kraemer, Ross Shepard. *Her Share of the Blessings: Women's Religions among Pagans, Jews, and Christians in the Greco-Roman World.* New York: Oxford University Press, 1992.

Malherbe, Abraham J. *Paul and the Thessalonians: The Philosophic Tradition of Pastoral Care.* Philadelphia: Fortress Press, 1987.

Martin, Dale B. *Slavery as Salvation: The Metaphor of Slavery in Pauline Christianity.* New Haven, Conn.: Yale University Press, 1990.

Perkins, Pheme. *Peter: Apostle for the Whole Church.* Columbia, S.C.: University of South Carolina Press, 1994.

Pesch, Rudolf. *Simon-Petrus: Geschichte und geschichtliche Bedeutung des ersten Jüngers Jesu Christi.* Päpste and Papsttum, 15. Stuttgart: Anton Hiersemann, 1980.

Smith, T. V. *Petrine Controversies in Early Christianity: Attitudes toward Peter in Christian Writings of the First Two Centuries.* Wissenschaftliche Untersuchungen zum Neuen Testament, 2/5. Tübingen: J.C.B. Mohr (Paul Siebeck), 1985.

White, John L. *Light from Ancient Letters.* Philadelphia: Fortress Press, 1986.

1 Peter

Commentaries

Brox, Norbert. *Der Erste Petrusbrief.* Evangelisch-Katholischer Kommentar, vol. XXI. Zurich: Benziger; Neukirchen-Vluyn: Neukirchener Verlag, 1979.

Dalton, William J. "The First Epistle of Peter." In *The New Jerome Biblical Commentary,* edited by R. E. Brown, J. A. Fitzmyer, and R. E. Murphy, sec. 57:1–28. Englewood Cliffs, N.J.: Prentice-Hall, 1990.

Goppelt, Leonhard. *A Commentary on First Peter.* Translated by J. E. Alsup. Grand Rapids: Wm. B. Eerdmans Publishing Co., 1993.

Michaels, J. Ramsey. *1 Peter.* Word Biblical Commentary, 49. Waco, Tex.: Word Books, 1988.

Spicq, Ceslaus. *Les épîtres de Saint Pierre.* Sources Bibliques. Paris: J. Gabalda, 1966.

Other Works

Achtemeier, Paul J. "Suffering Servant and Suffering Christ in 1 Peter." In *The Future of Christology: Essays in Honor of Leander E. Keck,* edited by A. J. Malherbe and W. A. Meeks, 176–88. Minneapolis: Fortress Press, 1993.

Balch, David L. *Let Wives Be Submissive: The Domestic Code in 1 Peter.* SBL Monograph Series. Chico, Calif.: Scholars Press, 1981.

———. "Hellenization/Acculturation in 1 Peter." In *Perspectives on First Peter,* edited by C. H. Talbert, 79–101. Macon, Ga.: Mercer University Press, 1986.

Elliott, John H. "Peter, Silvanus and Mark in 1 Peter and Acts. Socio-exegetical Perspectives on a Petrine Group in Rome." In *Wort in der Zeit: Neutestamentliche Studien; K. H. Rengstorf Festschrift,* edited by W. Hanbeck and M. Bachmann, 250–67. Leiden: E. J. Brill, 1980.

———. *Home for the Homeless: A Sociological Exegesis of 1 Peter, Its Structure and Strategy.* Philadelphia: Fortress Press, 1981.

———. "1 Peter, Its Situation and Strategy: A Discussion with David Balch." In *Perspectives on First Peter,* edited by

C. H. Talbert, 61–78. Macon, Ga.: Mercer University Press, 1986.

Martin, Troy. *Metaphor and Composition in 1 Peter.* SBL Dissertation Series, 131. Atlanta: Scholars Press, 1992.

James

Commentaries

Dibelius, Martin, and Heinrich Greeven. *James.* Translated by M. A. Williams. Philadelphia: Fortress Press, 1976.

Laws, Sophie. *The Epistle of James.* New York: Harper & Row, 1980.

Martin, Ralph P. *James.* Word Biblical Commentary, 48. Waco, Tex.: Word Books, 1988.

Mussner, Franz. *Der Jakobusbrief.* Herders theologischer Kommentar zum Neuen Testament, vol. XIII. Freiburg: Herder, 1967.

Other Works

Cargal, Timothy B. *Restoring the Diaspora: Discursive Structure and Purpose in the Epistle of James.* SBL Dissertation Series, 144. Atlanta: Scholars Press, 1993.

Maynard-Reid, P. U. *Poverty and Wealth in James.* Maryknoll, N.Y.: Orbis Books, 1987.

Perdue, Leo G. "Paraenesis and the Epistle of James." *Zeitschrift für die Neutestamentliche Wissenschaft* 72 (1981): 241–56.

Ward, Roy B. "Partiality in the Assembly: James 2:2–4." *Harvard Theological Review* 62 (1969): 87–97.

Jude and 2 Peter

Commentaries

Bauckham, Richard J. *Jude, 2 Peter.* Word Biblical Commentary, 50. Waco, Tex.: Word Books, 1983.

Fuchs, Eric, and Pierre Reymond. *La deuxième épître de Saint Pierre, L'épître de Saint Jude.* Commentaire du Nouveau Testament, Deuxième série, XIIIb. Neuchâtel: Delachaux & Niestlé, 1980.

Neyrey, Jerome. *2 Peter, Jude.* Anchor Bible, 37C. New York: Doubleday & Co.: 1993.

Other Works

Charles, J. Daryl. "Literary Artifice in the Epistle of Jude." *Zeitschrift für die Neutestamentliche Wissenschaft* 82 (1991): 106–24.

Danker, Frederick. "2 Peter 1: A Solemn Decree." *Catholic Biblical Quarterly* 40 (1978): 64–82.

Dupont-Roc, Roselyn. "Le motif de la création selon 2 Pierre 3." *Revue Biblique* 101 (1994): 95–114.

Neyrey, Jerome. "The Form and Background of the Polemic in 2 Peter." *Journal of Biblical Literature* 99 (1980): 407–31.

Watson, Duane F. *Invention, Arrangement, and Style: Rhetorical Criticism of Jude and 2 Peter.* SBL Dissertation Series, 104. Atlanta: Scholars Press, 1988.

REFERENCE LIST

Achtemeier, Paul J. 1993. "Suffering Servant and Suffering Christ in 1 Peter." In *The Future of Christology: Essays in Honor of Leander E. Keck,* edited by A. J. Malherbe and W. A. Meeks, 176–88. Minneapolis: Fortress Press.

Aristeas, Letter of. 1985. Translated by R.J.H. Shutt in *The Old Testament Pseudepigrapha.* Vol. 2. Edited by J. H. Charlesworth. Garden City, N.Y.: Doubleday & Co.

Balch, David L. 1981. *Let Wives Be Submissive: The Domestic Code in 1 Peter.* SBL Monograph Series. Chico, Calif.: Scholars Press.

———. 1986. "Hellenization/Acculturation in 1 Peter." In *Perspectives on First Peter,* edited by C. H. Talbert, 79–101. Macon, Ga.: Mercer University Press.

Bauckham, Richard J. 1983. *Jude, 2 Peter.* Word Biblical Commentary, 50. Waco, Tex.: Word Books.

Brown, Raymond E., and Raymond F. Collins. 1990. "Canonicity: The Canon of the New Testament." In *The New Jerome Biblical Commentary,* edited by R. E. Brown, J. A. Fitzmyer, and R. E. Murphy, sec. 66:70–86. Englewood Cliffs, N.J.: Prentice-Hall.

Brown, Raymond E., and John P. Meier. 1983. *Antioch and Rome.* Ramsey, N.J.: Paulist Press.

Brox, Norbert. 1979. *Der Erste Petrusbrief.* Evangelisch-Katholischer Kommentar, vol. XXI. Zurich: Benziger; Neukirchen-Vluyn: Neukirchener Verlag.

Cargal, Timothy B. 1993. *Restoring the Diaspora: Discursive Structure and Purpose in the Epistle of James.* SBL Dissertation Series, 144. Atlanta: Scholars Press.

Charles, J. Daryl. 1991. "Literary Artifice in the Epistle of Jude." *Zeitschrift für die Neutestamentliche Wissenschaft* 82:106–24.

Clement of Rome. 1912. *The Apostolic Fathers.* Vol. 1, 8–121. Translated by Kirsopp Lake. Loeb Classical Library. Cambridge, Mass.: Harvard University Press.

Collins, John J. 1993. *Daniel.* Minneapolis: Fortress Press.

Conzelmann, Hans. 1992. *Gentiles, Jews, Christians: Polemics and Apologetics in the Greco-Roman Era.* Translated by M. E. Boring. Minneapolis: Fortress Press.

Dalton, William J. 1990. "The First Epistle of Peter." In *The New Jerome Biblical Commentary,* edited by R. E. Brown, J. A. Fitzmyer, and R. E. Murphy, sec. 57:1–28. Englewood Cliffs, N.J.: Prentice-Hall.

Danker, Frederick. 1978. "2 Peter 1: A Solemn Decree." *Catholic Biblical Quarterly* 40:64–82.

Dibelius, Martin, and Heinrich Greeven. 1976. *James.* Translated by M. A. Williams. Philadelphia: Fortress Press.

Dupont-Roc, Roselyn. 1994. "Le motif de la création selon 2 Pierre 3." *Revue Biblique* 101:95–114.

Elliott, John H. 1980. "Peter, Silvanus and Mark in 1 Peter and Acts. Socio-exegetical Perspectives on a Petrine Group in Rome." In *Wort in der Zeit: Neutestamentliche Studien; K. H. Rengstorf Festschrift,* edited by W. Hanbeck and M. Bachmann, 250–67. Leiden: E. J. Brill.

———. 1981. *Home for the Homeless: A Sociological Exegesis of 1 Peter, Its Structure and Strategy.* Philadelphia: Fortress Press.

———. 1986. "1 Peter, Its Situation and Strategy: A Discussion with David Balch." In *Perspectives on First Peter,* edited by C. H. Talbert, 61–78. Macon, Ga.: Mercer University Press.

Eusebius. 1965. *The History of the Church.* Translated by G. A. Williamson. Baltimore: Penguin Books.

Feldman, Louis H. 1993. *Jew and Gentile in the Ancient World.* Princeton, N.J.: Princeton University Press.

Fuchs, Eric, and Pierre Reymond. 1980. *La deuxième épître de Saint Pierre, L'épître de Saint Jude.* Commentaire du Nouveau Testament, Deuxième série, XIIIb. Neuchâtel: Delachaux & Niestlé.

Goppelt, Leonhard. 1993. *A Commentary on First Peter.* Translated by J. E. Alsup. Grand Rapids: Wm. B. Eerdmans Publishing Co.

Kraemer, Ross Shepard. 1992. *Her Share of the Blessings: Women's Religions among Pagans, Jews, and Christians in the Greco-Roman World.* New York: Oxford University Press.

Laws, Sophie. 1980. *The Epistle of James.* New York: Harper & Row.

Malherbe, Abraham J. 1986. *Moral Exhortation: A Greco-Roman Sourcebook.* Philadelphia: Westminster Press.

———. 1987. *Paul and the Thessalonians: The Philosophic Tradition of Pastoral Care.* Philadelphia: Fortress Press.

Martin, Dale B. 1990. *Slavery as Salvation: The Metaphor of Slavery in Pauline Christianity.* New Haven, Conn.: Yale University Press.

Martin, Ralph P. 1988. *James.* Word Biblical Commentary, 48. Waco, Tex.: Word Books.

Martin, Troy. 1992. *Metaphor and Composition in 1 Peter.* SBL Dissertation Series, 131. Atlanta: Scholars Press.

Maynard-Reid, P. U. 1987. *Poverty and Wealth in James.* Maryknoll, N.Y.: Orbis Books.

Michaels, J. Ramsey. 1988. *1 Peter.* Word Biblical Commentary, 49. Waco, Tex.: Word Books.

Mussner, Franz. 1967. *Der Jakobusbrief.* Herders theologischer Kommentar zum Neuen Testament, vol. XIII. Freiburg: Herder.

Neyrey, Jerome. 1980. "The Form and Background of the Polemic in 2 Peter." *Journal of Biblical Literature* 99:407–31.

———. *2 Peter, Jude.* 1993. Anchor Bible, 37C. New York: Doubleday & Co.

Perdue, Leo G. 1981. "Paraenesis and the Epistle of James." *Zeitschrift für die Neutestamentliche Wissenschaft* 72: 241–56.

Perkins, Pheme. 1994. *Peter: Apostle for the Whole Church.* Columbia, S.C.: University of South Carolina Press.

Pesch, Rudolf. 1980. *Simon-Petrus: Geschichte und geschichtliche Bedeutung des ersten Jüngers Jesu Christi.* Päpste und Papsttum, 15. Stuttgart: Anton Hiersemann.

Philo. 1929. *Sacrifices of Abel and Cain. Philo,* vol. 2. Translated by F. H. Colson. Loeb Classical Library. Cambridge, Mass.: Harvard University Press.

———. 1930. *On Husbandry. Philo,* vol. 3. Translated by F. H. Colson and G. H. Whitaker. Loeb Classical Library. Cambridge, Mass.: Harvard University Press.

———. 1935. *Life of Moses. Philo,* vol. 6. Translated by F. H. Colson. Loeb Classical Library. Cambridge, Mass.: Harvard University Press.

Pliny. 1963. *The Letters of the Younger Pliny.* Baltimore: Penguin Books.

Smith, T. V. 1985. *Petrine Controversies in Early Christianity: Attitudes toward Peter in Christian Writings of the First*

Two Centuries. Wissenschaftliche Untersuchungen zum Neuen Testament, 2/5. Tübingen: J.C.B. Mohr (Paul Siebeck).

Spicq, Ceslas. 1966. *Les épîtres de Saint Pierre.* Sources Bibliques. Paris: J. Gabalda.

Stone, Michael. 1990. *Fourth Ezra* [= 2 Esdras]. Minneapolis: Fortress Press.

Testaments of the Twelve Patriarchs. 1983. Translated by H. C. Kee. In *The Old Testament Pseudepigrapha,* edited by J. H. Charlesworth. Vol. 1: *Apocalyptic Literature and Testaments,* 782–828. Garden City, N.Y.: Doubleday & Co.

Vermes, Geza. 1987. *The Dead Sea Scrolls in English.* 3d edition. Harmondsworth, Middlesex: Penguin Books.

Ward, Roy B. 1969. "Partiality in the Assembly: James 2:2–4." *Harvard Theological Review* 62:87–97.

Watson, Duane F. 1988. *Invention, Arrangement, and Style: Rhetorical Criticism of Jude and 2 Peter.* SBL Dissertation Series, 104. Atlanta: Scholars Press.

White, John L. 1986. *Light from Ancient Letters.* Philadelphia: Fortress Press.